# The Aesthetics of Contemporary Planting Design

*Essays by:*

Thorbjörn Andersson

Cristina Castel-Branco

Alexandre Chemetoff

Andrea Cochran

Kate Cullity

Erik Dhont

Richard L. Hindle

Laurie Olin

Tim Richardson

Mario Schjetnan

Christine Ten Eyck

Marc Treib

Peter Walker

# The Aesthetics of Contemporary Planting Design

Edited by Marc Treib

ORO EDITIONS / NOVATO, CALIFORNIA

Book Design: Marc Treib
ORO Project Coordinator: Jake Anderson
Proofreader: Alejandro Guzman-Avila

International Distribution:
www.oroeditions.com/distribution

10 9 8 7 6 5 4 3 2 1 First Edition
Library of Congress data available upon request.
World Rights: Available

ISBN: 978-1-954081-15-4
Color Separations and Printing: ORO Group Ltd.
Printed in China

Publication of this book was supported by grants from the Hubbard Education Trust; the Richard and Rhoda Goldman Distinguished Professorship, University of California, Berkeley; and the Graham Foundation for Advanced Studies in the Fine Arts.

For Alyssa Schwann

## Contents

# Preface

Planting design is, rather obviously, a complex topic, spanning as it does art, science, social need, and morality—especially during these days of increasing planetary environmental threat. Although certainly not denying the importance of scientifically appropriate practices, the symposium "The Aesthetics of [Contemporary] Planting Design" addressed planting design today, proposing a renewed concern for the cultural and aesthetic aspects of the landscapes that result. This book, which has been developed from the original presentations at the symposium, presents the thoughts of a select international group of landscape architects and historians who discuss the subject of planting design through the lens of their own work as well as the work of others, both contemporary and historical. They suggest that, as in real estate, the most important factor in selecting plants is "location, location, location." Certainly the Californian situation is far more forgiving than the aridity and other restrictive environmental conditions endemic to the Sonoran desert, or the frost and short growing seasons of Nordic lands that direct Scandinavian landscape architects to rely on native birches, pines, rowan, and moss. Most of us would agree that there are plants sensible for each climatic zone. Addressing environmental conditions is but the first step in the equation, however. There are also the issues of combination and composition.

Although a number of sub-themes and issues, such as the role of altitude as well as latitude, the critical role of maintenance, and the directives of clients, surfaced over the two days of the original program, the impetus for organizing the event, and its predominant theme, was simple: Is there still a place for an art of planting design in an age dominated by environmental and social demands and the need for resilient practices? Certainly, this was never intended to be a question of either/or: either beauty or responsibility. Or should not be. Instead, the pursuit of beauty—in its many guises and open to many readings—assumes that design with plants embodies art, science, and ethics, and does so with skill and knowledge.

All but three of the talks at the symposium were presented without written texts, which made producing this book a considerable challenge. In almost all instances then, after the video recordings were transcribed, I substantially rewrote the presentations, for some merely editing and clarifying the speaker's text, for others writing or rewriting, providing missing information and transitions where required, and perhaps even including some coercion to solicit the contributor's response. The speakers/authors then reviewed my reworkings and interpretations of their talks, correcting and commenting where needed, until we reached a version that we both agreed represented the final product. We now have a book with thirteen views on planting design, its role in our culture(s) as well as science, and its relation to people as well as the greater community of the natural world in which those people dwell. The particular point of view, and the balance among these discussions of the broader factors and ideas that bear on the authors' own work is personal and varies in each of the chapters—there was no attempt to impose a standard template on each contribution.

Despite the differences in discourse and terminology, each of the authors has attempted to position an aesthetic regard for landscape design within a greater social and environmental context. I would offer that most of these projects presented in each of the chapters are ecologically grounded, socially aware—and many are truly beautiful, thus supporting the spirit as well as the fate of the planet.

Marc Treib
Berkeley, October 2020

## Acknowledgments

When I first proposed "The Aesthetics of [Contemporary] Planting Design" as the subject for a symposium on the campus of the University of California, Berkeley, Louise Mozingo—chair of the Department of Landscape Architecture and Environmental Planning—immediately agreed. Her input and support, with the participation of staff and students was critical for the successful mounting of the symposium and for the making of this book, which follows two years later. In addition to facilitating the department's sponsorship of the event, Louise was instrumental in formulating the content of the program and the selection of the speakers, for which I offer profuse thanks. And now, her Richard and Rhoda Goldman Distinguished Professorship has also provided financial support for the publication of this book. Departmental staff Jessica Ambriz and Sue Retta played crucial roles in handling travel arrangements, logistics, and financial matters, and could not have been more effective and pleasant to work with. I thank them all.

Of course, I need also thank all the speakers, now authors, some of whom traveled to Berkeley across thousands of miles of land and sea, and for their efforts in providing or reviewing texts, and the excellent photographs as the visual material to illustrate their ideas and works.

Bonnie Lovell, with whom I have worked on several books, again provided excellent services as copyeditor for texts written by those coming from many different landscapes and who write in many different languages. And lastly, I must thank, once again, ORO Editions publisher Gordon Goff for his support of our work and Jake Anderson for his management of the production process.

I am grateful for financial support for the publication of this book provided by the Hubbard Educational Trust; the Richard and Rhoda Goldman Distinguished Professorship, University of California, Berkeley; and the Graham Foundation for Advanced Studies in the Fine Arts.

All involved sincerely hope that the substantial time and effort spent in its writing and production have resulted in a book readers will find informative—and perhaps even inspiring.

MT

# THE AESTHETICS OF CONTEMPORARY PLANTING DESIGN

Marc Treib

1.

**1-1**

Dieter Kienast. Krummenacher garden. Zurich, Switzerland, 1995. [Marc Treib]

During the last four decades, discussions of sustainable practice, environmental resilience, and social justice have dominated the discourse of landscape architecture. In contrast, the regard for planting design in respect to emotional impact, fragrance, and *as an art* has to a large degree languished. Among other factors, innovative planting design has been hampered by local ordinances that restrict the acceptable species of street trees, a paucity of plant varieties available in nurseries, and unimaginative planting design education in university curricula. A focus on planting design, it seems, has just not been a priority for the profession. While garden designers—especially those working in Great Britain and the Netherlands—continue to enthusiastically explore the innovative use of plants for harmonious or striking aesthetic effects, this has been less true in the broader practice of landscape architecture, where surface areas are far greater than the garden, and constituencies are larger than the single client or family. Without question, notable exceptions to this rather broad generalization have existed and do exist, and there are certainly landscape architects who have designed with plants in an environmentally responsible *and* creative way, using plant form, color, and growth patterns to produce attractive and engaging landscapes [1-1]. Among them are the contributors to this book.

Although always linked to the conditions of the greater environment, whether in urban or more natural settings, the selection and composition of plants is necessarily local. Whether endemic, indigenous, or exotic, the selected species must acknowledge the conditions of the particular site. As an intervention, each new landscape constitutes a disturbance to existing conditions; this intervention can be responsible or without due regard; the consequences can be positive or negative. Although in formulating their presentations for the original symposium, and in preparing their contributions to this book thereafter, the authors were requested to focus on the aesthetic intentions driving their design with plants, it was assumed that these were rooted in ecologically responsible practice—a fact especially evident in more extreme environments like those of the American Southwest, Mexico, Australia, and Scandinavia. Hopefully, even on projects beyond the scale of the garden, or those with problematic climates and soils, we can achieve planting designs that surpass functional requirements such as remediating polluted soil or providing nutrients necessary for the survival of bees. It should not be a question of either/or, but of *both/and*. It is not a question of environmental responsibility or aesthetics, ecology or beauty, but how by addressing the first do we produce the second. Selecting species appropriate to the particular conditions of the site

**1-2**

Piet Oudolf, planting design; James Corner Field Operations, landscape architects; Diller Scofidio+ Renfro, architects. High Line. New York, New York, 2009; 2014+. [Marc Treib]

**1-3**

Eucalyptus Grove. University of California, Berkeley. [Marc Treib]

and the needs of the society constitutes only the base level of design. How those trees, shrubs, and flowers are used—in what combination and in what configuration—are the acts that raise mundane designs to a level of beauty that garners greater appreciation by those who use the landscape.

Over time, newly introduced species have augmented the designer's palette, while familiar species can be used through innovative ways. Tastes change over time—another consideration in the selection and composition of plants. Grasses, for example, once scorned as too common, are now appreciated for composing a guise more closely approximating nature, at least in the minds of some. Vegetal design schemes by the Dutch plantsman Piet Oudolf, who has designed notable landscapes in the Netherlands, Sweden, and England, have increased professional and public awareness of and appreciation for grasses and perennials; American landscape architects like James van Sweden and Wolfgang Oehme, sharing those interests, brought them to American shores, where their influence has been widespread [1-2].[1]

To be used in their designs, however, plant species must be available to the landscape architect. Those varieties offered for sale by nurseries are usually guided by the economics of the market, taking into account what is both easily propagated, and what is hardy, popular, and easily sold. Today, the choices are greater than ever. The internet has provided designers with access to the extensive holdings of nurseries across the country—and in Europe, across the continent—greatly broadening the availability of exotic species. Abundance and availability do not necessarily provide wisdom, however, and knowledge, skill, and taste are still required for creating resilient and beautiful landscapes as the product of outstanding planting design.

## Native or Non-Native?

In California, as in many other parts of the world, discussion has centered on the demand for the use of native plants, in some ways seeking to turn back the clock to those halcyon days before human habitation, when nature was imagined to have been innate and pure. Settlement, lumbering, and agricultural propagation changed all that, as did human dietary and aesthetic preferences that sought the novel in place of the habitual. The eucalyptus was imported to California from Australia in the nineteenth century for use as windbreaks and for railroad ties (which, as it happens, did not work out as hoped), and in less than a century eucalyptus became a major—if not dominant—tree species throughout the state, especially in its southern regions [1-3].[2] In many quarters its ubiquity is reviled. Ongoing demands by "native-only" groups have today called for eradicating the eucalyptus —in reality, a hopeless task—thereby ridding the California landscape of the species' pernicious presence. Yet, the eucalyptus remains ever-present, as does the popularity of most non-native flowers and shrubs.

In botanical quarters and landscape architectural practice, the call for native plants has been moral as well as botanical, a call that at its extreme might fairly be termed "species cleansing." The argument is premised on the idea that the use of natives makes sense; if the plant is truly of the place it will thrive; it will not invade the territory of other species and at the same time it will produce a presence that resonates with the indigenous landscape. To a large degree, this is a sensible position. In the United States and many other countries worldwide, municipalities today require the use of native trees with little consideration that they grow in the *native* conditions of the forest or plain and *not* in the conditions of the urban street or plaza, as the Belgian landscape architect Bas Smets once pointed out to me.[3] Poignant examples of this reality are found in the Hyllie Plaza in Malmö, Sweden, designed by Thorbjörn Andersson and realized in 2011 and discussed in chapter 9 [1-4]. Andersson selected the native beech *(Fagus sylvatica)* based on its ubiquity in the southern Swedish landscape, and developed a design that both celebrated the tree and used it to structure the plaza's spaces. However, sustaining the beech in the urban conditions of the plaza required a special soil mix that fostered aeration and nutrition as well as continued care. The trees have done well, but it has required effort and resources, proving that native species may not be the best choice for sites with inhospitable conditions. In New York City the selection, preparation, and care required for the survival of Peter Walker Partners' 9/11 Memorial depends upon a complex subterranean network of tubes for feeding and irrigation (see chapter 13). As in Malmö, their selected species (*Quercus bicolor*, swamp white oak) was acclimatized, but conditions within the metropolis are demanding and the trees require continued technological support [see 13-21]. As these two examples demonstrate, the selection of native species is not always the most sensible one. Although the plant selection may begin with a design concept, it is ultimately the botanical properties of the plant that will determine whether it can be used. Once the species are approved, the design derives from number and configuration; the arrangement of the trunks; the height of the canopies; the understory, as well as the ground plane. True planting design is more than the display of trees, shrubs, and flowers—it is a spatial practice and it is ultimately an art.

Whether the context is urban, suburban, or rural, plant selection should embody an aesthetic idea based to some degree on the desires of the client and environmental constraints and benefactions—soil, wind, water, and climate among them. Must plants always be native? I think not. At the Fazenda Vargem Grande (1976–1991) in Areias, Brazil, Roberto Burle Marx did rely to large degree on native plants such as bromeliads and palms to construct a new landscape for the former coffee plantation [1-5]. However, Burle Marx *also* imported trees from as far away as Madagascar—at considerable expense, one might add [1–6]. Yet despite any troubling issues of adaptation, these botanical immigrants successfully acclimated to the garden without any major problems. In areas of his designs Burle Marx consistently relied on single species to yield a low shape, or shaped, volume to transform the ground plane into a vegetal relief. In and around the pool on the garden's upper level the plants comprising the vegetal blocks were chosen for their color, texture, and the height to which they naturally grew. As they matured they formed a low sculpture of varied greens [1-7]. In this way, without the need for undue pruning and maintenance, Burle Marx reinvigorated the traditional French *parterre de broderie* which, as the French term indicates, were conceived as panels of embroidery enacted in low vegetation.

Burle Marx, an expert botanist and plantsman as well as artist and landscape architect, understood Brazilian plants and carefully selected individual species for their formal characteristics and aesthetic impact. From his friend, the botanist Henrique Lahmeyer de Mello Barreto, Burle Marx learned what he termed "the social relationships of plants," and with this understanding selected his plants and designed his landscapes.[4] On the one hand, the landscape architect held that "To build a garden means to act ethically and aesthetically."[5] But his intention was not to replicate nature, but instead to design the garden to reveal "the realities of nature by abstracting and accentuating certain aspects, which might be described as conveying the essence of nature rather than its image."[6] One vehicle for achieving this goal was the use of "local flora, to facilitate the social and pedagogical function of the garden, including helping people to discover the natural wealth in which they live."[7] Despite favoring native species, Burle Marx fully embraced exotic flora, and was quite open to the use of alien species, assuming they could thrive in Brazilian soils and its climate—and were not invasive or otherwise detrimental to the native environment. "Even for me, in Brazil," he confessed, "where I have a choice of five thousand trees and shrubs, there are limitations. With the richest national flora in the world, I

**1-4**

Thorbjörn Andersson / Sweco Architects. Hyllie Plaza. Malmö, Sweden, 2009. [Marc Treib]

**1-5**

Roberto Burle Marx. Fazenda Vargem Grande, Areias, Brazil, 1979–1991. Water lilies and vegetation on the pool level. [Marc Treib]

**1-6**

Roberto Burle Marx. Fazenda Vargem Grande. Entrance to the courtyard and house. [Marc Treib]

have to borrow to find plants that will give flowers in flower beds."[8] In the end, of course, it is not only the plants Burle Marx used, but how he used them, that is more critical. On that score he was indeed a master.

We might also question how the word or term "native" is commonly defined. One can apply to become a naturalized American citizen after seven years of residence, but how long is required for a plant to be regarded as native? The scientist Stephen Jay Gould questioned the very definition of "native" by noting that "the great majority of successful species are highly stable in form and behavior over long periods of geological time—not because they are optimal, but because they are locally prevalent."[9] After dismissing both evolutionary and geographic determinants as explanations, Gould summarized by stating: "'Natives,' in short, are the species that happened to find their way (or evolve *in situ*), not the best conceivable for a spot"; native does not "imply superiority," as the successful influx of species such as eucalyptus and kudzu demonstrates.[10] Will a strong invasive species become "native" in time?

**1-7**

Roberto Burle Marx. Fazenda Vargem Grande, Areias, Brazil, 1979–1991. Using the natural heights of plants to create a vegatal relief. [Marc Treib]

**1-8**

Christopher Tunnard. Rooftop foliage. [*Gardens in the Modern Landscape*, 1948]

## In the Twentieth Century

For many modernist landscape architects, the ornamental or olfactory properties of plants appear to have been of less concern than their ability to define space or their sculptural form. Theorists such as Christopher Tunnard called for a "structural" use of plants, asserting that the shape and mass of the plant were its consequential attributes, and *not* the prettiness of its flowers or its botanical rarity—although he wrote at length about color, texture, and mass.[11] In his writings Tunnard decried, at least to some degree, the proliferation of species and colors characteristic of the Edwardian garden so beautifully represented by Gertrude Jekyll's mixed borders. Behind his thinking was the modernist notion of intensification through reduction, an idea he shared with many modernist architects [1-8]. Being a work of art, wrote Tunnard, the garden is "only natural in terms of its materials.... It follows that trees, flowers and stones in the garden are in a sense artificial objects, and are valuable only in relation to their surroundings or to the feelings they arouse in the beholder."[12] Like our words, the effects and meaning of landscapes are collective, acquired through juxtaposition and composition over time. For Tunnard, modern art provided inspiration and the source of a vocabulary for the modern garden.

At almost the same moment that Tunnard's *Gardens in the Modern Landscape* appeared, the Japanese architect

**1-9**

Sakai Hoitsu.
*Flowering Plants of Summer and Autumn.*
Screen painting, eighteenth century.
[Tokyo National Museum, Wikimedia Commons]

**1-10**

Sutemi Horiguchi.
Okada garden.
Tokyo, Japan, 1934.
[Sutemi Horiguchi
Archives,
Meiji University,
Tokyo, Japan]

Sutemi Horiguchi turned for his inspiration to the painted screens of the eighteenth-century Rimpa school, in particular their setting of individual plants against a simple background of gold or silver leaf [1-9]. "What would happen," he asked rhetorically, "if a plain gold screen was placed in the back of the autumn grasses? ... This is the idea that motivated me to design a garden of autumn grasses."[13] Horiguchi's 1934 Okada garden in Tokyo translated a two-dimensional screen painting into three dimensions, treating individual plants as if the elements of a flower arrangement. While the concept was aesthetic and somewhat abstract, Horiguchi was quite specific in his selection of plants based on their growth patterns and seasonal change. Through analogy, he referenced the screen's figures, although in his design he transformed their painted images into "lines and dots from *susuki* [Japanese pampas grass], *hagi* [bush clover] and *nadeshiko* [Japanese fringed pink] ... [C]lumps of Japanese pampas grass have individualized shapes, and moreover, the beauty as a whole is well composed [1-10]."[14]

Planting palettes of the modern landscape were often sparse, even in California where the relatively mild, if dry, climate supports a plethora of species—albeit with some aid from irrigation. The planting plans for Thomas Church's gardens, often only a single sheet, usually include a note saying simply "planting" or "color"—leaving the choice of species and hues to those in the field, the local nursery staff, or even the client him- or herself. Church, of course, understood the value of the site's vegetation and relied on trees as the armature for his designs. This is evident in his celebrated 1947 Donnell garden in Sonoma County, where a clever appropriation of the existing California coastal live oaks (*Quercus agrifolia*) provided an instant armature and framework for the garden's pool and small buildings [1-11]. Garrett Eckbo shared Tunnard's supposition, noting in an modern architectonic way that the primary value of plants and trees was their ability to define space; properties such as color and fragrance, though certainly factors in landscape design, were secondary. Planting, he stressed, "must be worked out in terms of *selection*, *arrangement*, and *maintenance*. ... These are all mutually interdependent and retroactive" (italics in the original) [1-12]. Trees provide the primary structure. Herbaceous material, on the other hand, must be considered as "enriching —rather than surfacing, enclosing, or sheltering."[15]

An alternate attitude toward plant selection begins with a certain flower or leaf that the landscape architect finds particularly interesting or beautiful, or hardy, or colorful, and ponders how it might be used in a suitable project. Or

**1-11**

Thomas Church. Donnell garden. Sonoma, California, 1947. The existing California coastal live oaks provided the garden's primary spatial structure. To the right is the *Quercus virginiana* (Southern live oak) that replaced the deceased *Quercus agrifolia*. [Marc Treib]

**1-12**

Garrett Eckbo.
Alcoa Forecast
Garden.
Los Angeles,
California, 1960.
[Garrett Eckbo]

**1-13**

Pietro Porcinai.
Villa Bonomi (Ratti).
Como, Italy, 1958.
[Marc Treib]

perhaps the brief requires the incorporation of the plant, as in the design of a botanical garden. Botanical determinants also guide the choice of the best species within a genus, or even a variety or cultivar. Elms are dying, but is there a new disease-resistant cultivar? Or should one instead use a tree sharing a similar shape, color, or other formal characteristic? The entry allée to Dan Kiley's celebrated 1957 Miller garden in Columbus, Indiana, was replanted several years ago with *Aesculus glabra*, the Ohio buckeye, replacing the original horse chestnut trees (*Aesculus hippocastanum*) that suffered from some pathological issues. In attempting to maintain the character of Thomas Church's Donnell garden, the family and their gardener chose to plant the Southern live oak, *Quercus virginiana*, rather than replace the original California coastal live oak, *Quercus agrifolia*, as the latter did not do well on irrigated land with heavy clay content [see 1-11]. Availability of species is another issue that directs plant use. The Italian landscape architect Pietro Porcinai faced this problem in the 1960s when trying to use species so common to the native landscape that Italian nurseries found no reason to propagate them. In response, for several of his projects, Porcinai's gardeners actually dug up the needed materials from nearby woods and transplanted them within the garden. On the other hand, like Burle Marx, Porcinai could also call for a substantial number of species in his garden designs. Both native and imported plants were used, with selection and application prompted by the nature of Porcinai's vision and what conditions allowed [1–13]. At times his plant lists numbered in the hundreds, and their procurement came from several countries throughout Europe, Germany, and the Netherlands in particular. In all, it was the artistic idea, tempered by the conditions of botanical reality, that guided plant selection in his gardens—parameters which, in the end, direct the selection of plants by most landscape architects.

This reduction of species, which characterized the work of some modernists, had confronted head-on the practice of planting in abundance that had perhaps reached its apogee in the gardens of Gertrude Jekyll. In a way quite different way from that of the modernists, Jekyll based her selections and arrangements on the life forces and growth patterns of her plants, and profited from their combination rather than employing them in isolation. Although celebrated as an artist for her herbaceous borders filled with bouquets of subtly gradated chroma, shapes, and textures, Jekyll was equally the scientist in selecting species [1-14]. She knew plants as a painter knows oils or watercolors. Science stood behind her art, and both artist and scientist were necessary for creating a vibrant and enduring border. What colors

**1-14**

Gertrude Jekyll. Hestercombe. Taunton, Somerset, England. Planting under the pergola. [Marc Treib]

would bloom together and interact, and for how long? How much care would be needed and how often would the border need to be replanted? (Three times a year, as it happens.) Jekyll was not above inserting plants in pots into her borders when needed, adjusting their heights with rocks or other props hidden in the foliage. Art, with the help of science, trumped Nature operating alone. Relying solely on native plants was not an issue. To create gardens that will engage and endure requires knowledge about how to make them thrive, how to maximize their duration until their eventual decay. That "Jekyllian" tradition continues in modified form in English, Dutch, and German garden design—termed the New Perennial movement—although it is but one approach among many in those countries (see chapter 3).

Maintenance requirements also inform the selection of colors, shapes, and species of trees and shrubs. What resources will be available to feed, water, weed, and prune the plants? The question of limits—whether the limits imposed by upkeep, climate, geography, budget, or availability—guides the choice of species. Certainly, we must begin by addressing the constraints imposed by the environment and the social and economic factors that influence the design of the site and its vegetation. The question then becomes: What level of beauty and appeal can we achieve within these constraints—or does some way exist to completely *surpass* them? That is to say, how does a consideration of aesthetics, and even art, inform the process of planting design? Great landscapes must offer more than massed shrubs and grasses that consume neither tons of fertilizer nor drastic amounts of acre-feet of water. Beauty is a worthy goal; why lack the aspiration to pass beyond sustainability or resilience alone? Science is only one half of the equation; art is the other.

Over a decade ago, several formerly hard-curbed streets in Seattle were converted to streets flanked on either side by green bioswales. Given the city's annual precipitation, this was without question an intelligent strategy for reducing the reliance on storm sewers, using percolation to retain more of the rainfall on-site. In two test projects, the streets were wiggled to retard the flow of water, as were, somewhat curiously, the sidewalks adjacent to them. Encountering one of these streets today, some ten years after construction, we find vegetation that appears as spontaneous growth, whose presence and disposition display neither rhyme nor reason [1-15]. The effect is, without question, an improvement, pleasant, and far more attractive than the untreated streets in the surrounding neighborhood. But I would ask for even more. Instead of the undifferentiated masses of leaves and shrubs, the planting might have graced the block with an

**1-15**

Street edge alternative planting. Seattle, Washington, ca. 2006. [Marc Treib, 2017]

orderly rhythm, or used differences in heights, volume, and texture to create a sense of syncopation along its path. Either design approach for the planting—and of course there are others—could have provided some degree of unity and interest to a rather heterogeneous streetscape. Can we do more than merely absorb water and let things grow? Other landscapes have achieved more.

The site for what is today the Gulbenkian Park in Lisbon, Portugal, was once a fairground occupied mostly by lawn with limited vegetation. When the buildings for the Calouste Gulbenkian Foundation offices and museum were constructed in the mid-1960s, it was determined that the parking would be set underground and that much of the site would be devoted to a public park. The landscape architects Gonçalo Ribeiro Telles and António Vianna Barreto employed principles of ecology and plant succession to guide their design and vegetation.[17] The center of the park was shaped as a pond to retain rainwater and serve as a visual resource. The planting—a carefully composed mix of grasses, shrubs, and trees—was configured in a manner that allowed their growth and resulting change to enrich the design as the plants moved toward their mature forms [1-16]. Over time, the masses of the trees and shrubs have become sufficiently dense to completely screen out the urban hubbub that surrounds the park. The stepped paths through the wood and meadows produce a sense of interest and intrigue as the elements of the design are revealed through movement. The designers' understanding of plant growth has produced a park that in its 70 years of existence is always under constant change, but change within the patterns established from the start of the design.[18]

**1-16**

Gonçalo Ribeiro Telles and António Viana Barreto. Gulbenkian Park. Lisbon, Portugal, 1964. [Marc Treib, 2011]

### Selection and Arrangement

Regarded broadly, plants as artistic material offer a limited number of design opportunities. We can choose *natives* or *appropriate exotics*; we can let them grow *naturally*, or *shape* them with saw and shears. We can arrange them in an *orderly fashion* as an allée or a bosk, or we can plant them in *irregular* clumps as did Lancelot "Capability" Brown, who likened planting to writing, with clumps of trees serving as punctuation marks.[19] Each manner, formal or informal, has its benefits, each its appropriate application. The rigid grid of trees in the Patio of the Oranges in Seville may seem out of place in a neighborhood park starved for greenery by minimal municipal support—well, then again, maybe not [1-17]. Feigned naturalism may not be suitable to urban settings without sufficient area to allow the development of a convincing design—well, then again, maybe not. Perhaps

**1-17**

Patio of the Oranges (Patio de los Naranjos).
Seville, Spain, twelfth century+; 1930s.
[Marc Treib]

**1-18**

Richard Haag.
Bloedel Reserve.
Bainbridge Island, Seattle, Washington, 1986+.
The retention pond set within the forest.
[Marc Treib]

how the plants are configured is more critical than which plants are used.

Any new landscape design necessarily disturbs the existing conditions. The question is whether the disturbance creates positive or negative results. As in the treatment of individual plants, the range of possible design actions is limited. We can *insert* new vegetation into an existing landscape, as Rich Haag (aided by Laurie Olin) did at the Bloedel Reserve outside Seattle [1-18]. We can *appropriate* and *add*, as Gunnar Asplund and Sigurd Lewerentz did to the pine forest at the Woodland Cemetery outside Stockholm. A bosk of native birches screens the parking area and echoes the spacing of the columns of the main chapel's portico, and stands in contrast to the dark pines that form its background [1-19] We can *eliminate* as well, turning vegetated land into pastures and meadows—or even gravel—like the dry garden at Ryoan-ji in Kyoto. Sharing a similar religious purpose, the garden at Shoden-ji proposes azaleas in place of rocks [1-20]. And lastly we can *displace* or *replace*, as Henry Hoare removed an existing village on the grounds of Stourhead, or convert a river to an ornamental canal, as André Le Nôtre did at Chantilly. These approaches may be used individually or in combination, of course.

## Selection and Composition

In the practice of *ikebana* ("living flowers"), the Japanese art of flower arrangement, the artist composes a restricted number of vegetal elements to reveal their individual forms and life forces, to create a new collective aesthetic effect. [20] Through selection, isolation, and reconfiguration, another entity emerges, an integrated figure possessing an aesthetic presence greater than the sum of its individual constituents. Rules govern the creation of these arrangements, at least at the initiation of the work [1-21]. Historically, these rules have been strict, often using the aesthetic idea of mixed formalities (*shin-gyo-so*) to guide the structuring of the composition. Yet despite these seemingly restrictive constraints, *ikebana* fosters a creativity guided by the season and the artist's sensitivity to the flowers and branches he or she chooses [1-22]. The appreciation of natural and floral form does not prohibit seemingly contradictory practices such as contorting flowers into strained relationships or maintaining, with wire, the shapes of stems or branches purposefully broken to shape new lines. The Sôgetsu school, founded by Sôfu Teshigahara in 1927, went even further, incorporating into their works materials foreign to traditional *ikebana*, materials such as plastics and massive tree trunks. The lesson of *ikebana*, then, is not to directly emulate the natural environment as one's model, but instead to suggest a deeper investigation into botanical forms and their interrelationships to instigate innovative ideas for the presentation of flowers, leaves, branches, and stems. Might the lessons provided by the practice of *ikebana* inform planting design at a larger scale? Or is a transformation of approach required when working with vegetation very much alive, always growing, hopefully thriving, but ever tending to die?

In closing, let me restate that I in no way deride the quest for biological balance or reductions to our constructed infrastructure. Without question, they are needed. But I do question the narrow ambition of designers who address function alone, and who assume that good morals automatically yield good landscapes. One must know the craft. As the French poet Charles Baudelaire wrote: "We write poems with words, not ideas." Ideas propel design. Analysis can support creation, but it cannot substitute for it. The goal of this book is to examine what landscape and planting design can offer beyond the address of functional and botanical issues, and how they provide a foundation for a rich and rewarding aesthetic experience, whether spatial, chromatic, olfactory, or luminous.

**1-19**

Gunnar Asplund and Sigurd Lewerentz. Woodland Cemetery. Enskede, Sweden, 1915–1940. The birch bosk in winter. [Thorbjörn Andersson]

**1-20**

Kobori Enshu. Shôden-ji. Kyoto, Japan, seventeenth century. [Marc Treib]

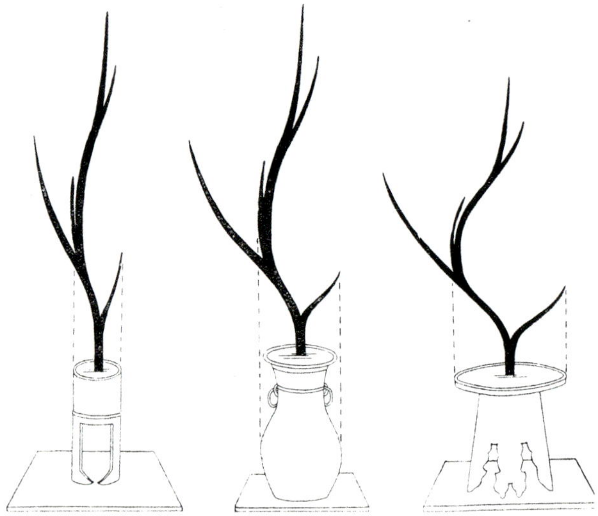

**1-21**

Alfred Koehn. "Fig. 78. The tip of tai-shin and the curve of the shin must never exceed the greatest width of the receptacle." [*The Way of Japanese Flower Arrangement*, 1935]

**1-22**

Ikenobu school. Ikebana exhibition. Takashimaya Department Store, Kyoto, Japan, 2013. [Marc Treib]

## Notes

**1** Wolfgang Oehme and James van Sweden, with Susan Rademacher Fry, *Bold Romantic Gardens: The New World Landscapes of Oehme and van Sweden*, Reston, VA: Acropolis, 1990; James van Sweden with Tom Christopher, *The Artful Garden: Creative Inspiration for Landscape Design*, New York: Random House, 2011; Piet Oudolf and Henk Gerritsen, *Dream Plants for the Natural Garden*, London: Frances Lincoln, 2013; and Piet Oudolf and Rick Darke, *Gardens of the High Line: Elevating the Nature of Modern Landscapes*, Portland, OR: Timber Press, 2017.

**2** By the early 1800s, there were 16 non-native plant species, but this jumped to about 134 species by 1860. The number has been increasing ever since; today, there are over 1,000 non-native plant species living in California (and nearly 5,000 native species). https://www.independent.com/news/2011/jan/15/how-eucalyptus-came-california/.

**3** In conversation, Brussels, Belgium, July 2015.

**4** Gareth Doherty, "On Burle Marx and His Lectures," in *Roberto Burle Marx Lectures: Landscape as Art and Urbanism*, Zurich: Lars Müller, 2018, p. 67.

**5** Roberto Burle Marx, "Concepts in Landscape Composition," 1970, in Doherty, *Burle Marx Lectures*, p. 89.

**6** Roberto Burle Marx, "Landscape Projects for Large Areas," in Doherty, *Burle Marx Lectures*, p. 217.

**7** Burle Marx, "Concepts in Landscape Composition," p. 97.

**8** Roberto Burle Marx, "The Garden as a Form of Art," 1962, 1991, in Doherty, *Burle Marx Lectures*, p. 117. Doherty notes that "Less than half the plants in the Parque del Este [in Caracas] were native to Venezuela," p. 67.

**9** Stephen Jay Gould, "An Evolutionary Perspective," in *Nature and Ideology: Natural Garden Design in the Twentieth Century*, ed. Joachim Wolschke-Buhlmann, Washington, DC: Dumbarton Oaks, 1997, p. 15.

**10** Ibid., p. 17.

**11** Christopher Tunnard, *Gardens in the Modern Landscape*, London: Architectural Press, 1948.

**12** Ibid., p. 116.

**13** Sutemi Horiguchi, "Akikusa no niwa" (Garden of Autumn Grasses), 1934. [Melanie Hong, trans.]

**14** Ibid.

**15** Garrett Eckbo, *Landscape for Living*, New York: Duell, Sloan and Pearce, 1955, p. 96.

**16** Ibid., p. 102.

**17** Francisco Caldeira Cabral and Gonçalo Ribeiro Telles, *A Árvore em Portugal* (The Tree in Portugal), Lisbon: Assíro & Alvim, 1969, includes diagrams showing the progression of plant growth toward the "climax forest," pp. 47–49.

**18** While this is an idealized portrait, additional structures have been inserted into the park, and there are places that could be fairly regarded as overgrown and in need of pruning and thinning.

**19** In conversation with Brown at Hampton Court, Hannah Moore recorded the landscape designer's comments on his method: "'Now there,' said he, pointing his finger, 'I make a comma, and there,' pointing to another spot, 'where a more decided turn is proper, I make a colon; at another part, where an interruption is desirable to break the view, a parenthesis; now a full stop, and then I begin another subject.'" Quoted in Peter Willis, "Capability Brown in Northumberland," *Garden History*, Autumn 1981, p. 158.

**20** Alfred Koehn, *The Way of Japanese Flower Arrangement*, Tokyo: Kyo Bun Kwan, 1937; Shôzo Satô, *The Art of Arranging Flowers*, New York: Harry Abrams, 1965; and Teshigahara Sôfu, *Kadensho: The Book of Flowers*, Tokyo: Sôgetsu Bunkajigyo, 1979; 2011.

# NATURE AND AESTHETICS IN PLANTING DESIGN

Laurie Olin

2.

Laurie Olin.
Abigail House.
New Albany, Ohio,
1988+.
[Laurie Olin]

Near the beginning of the last century Gertrude Jekyll wrote in reminiscence: "of all [the] kinds of planting for pleasure, wild gardening needs the greatest caution and most restraint." Regarding her own efforts at Munstead Wood, she reflected that "Now, after forty years, it has all grown into a state of satisfactory maturity" [2-1].[1] Planting is one thing; surviving to maturity is another. In addition, restraint is often a virtue. "In these days," Jekyll continued,

> *when gardening possibilities are so vast and the designer may be tempted to run wild... he should restrain himself and strive to regain the older simplicity and charm, remembering that the first purpose of a garden is to be a place of quiet beauty such as will give delight to the eye and repose and refreshment to the mind.*[2]

While one may justifiably question whether her garden at Hestercombe meets today's ideas of simplicity and restraint, these quotes from perhaps the greatest garden innovator and polemicist of the past century introduce several key subjects when considering aesthetics in landscape design: nature and naturalism, time and the dynamics of change in the natural world, and the omnipresence of fashion and style in human culture [2-2, 2-3].

First, consider aesthetics. Prior to the twentieth century, a sizable portion of the discourse on the topic of aesthetics focused on art, nature, and the human subject. Is beauty subjective or objective? Does the phenomenon reside within the beholder or with the thing beheld? Could feeling or perception be universal or are both culturally determined? Are they the products of nature or nurture? Writings debating those questions have been violently contested in journals and institutions over many years. There is evidence for support on both sides.

Despite its recurring cycles of seasons, for as long as recorded thought humans have held nature to be wild and chaotic, violent and unpredictable. Especially in Western societies, wild nature has long been considered ugly and unknowable. The American continent and its vast natural landscape seemed as terrifying and malevolent to the first Europeans who arrived here as it was promising for physical and spiritual rewards. As people became more familiar with the landscapes of the New World, artists like Frederic Edwin Church began to see nature and its beauty as an expression of divinity, complementing physical experience with the spiritual realm [2-4]. Today, however, most members of advanced societies consider nature neither unknowable nor chaotic due to the new forms of mathematics, and scientific discoveries that have appeared in physics and chemistry.

**2-1**

Gertrude Jekyll. Woodland garden, Munstead Wood. Godalming, Surrey, England, 1896–1932. [Marc Treib]

**2-2**

Gertrude Jekyll.
Dutch Garden,
Hestercombe.
Taunton, England,
1904.
[Marc Treib]

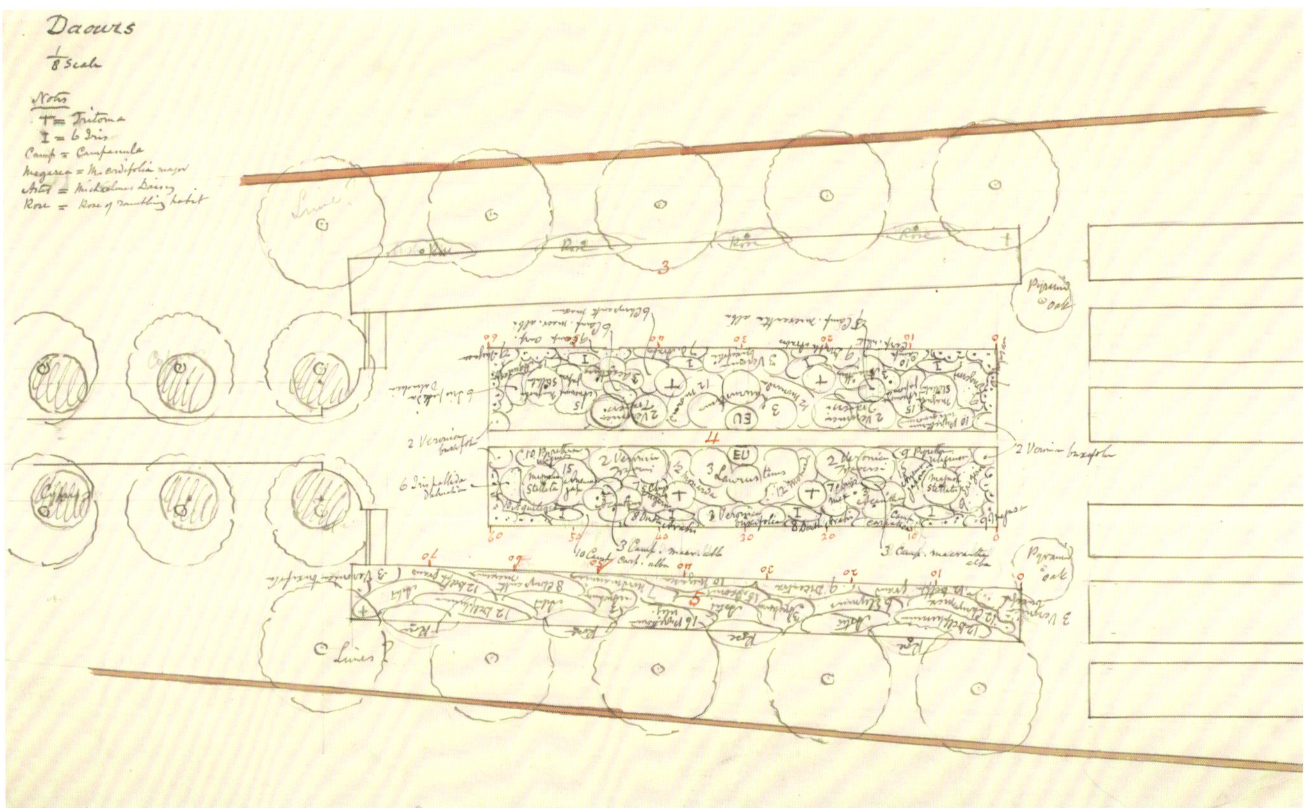


**2-3**

Gertrude Jekyll.
Military cemetery.
Daours, France,
1917.
Planting plan.
[Environmental
Design Archives,
University of
California,
Berkeley]

**2-4**

Frederic Edwin Church. *El Rio de Luz* (The River of Light), 1877. [National Gallery of Art, Washington, DC, Wikimedia Commons]

Yet even today the majority of the population still views nature and wilderness as foreign and confusing. The problem stems from a lack of intimate familiarity with nature, and the inability to see and understand its processes, especially for those who spend their childhoods in cities. In recent times ecology and geology have provided the analytic tools for understanding nature's complex forms and interactions. With the aid of computer science, we can understand and describe all manners of natural events and phenomena at varying scales, from subatomic particles and mitochondrial DNA to cyclonic storms. Nevertheless, a major earthquake or hurricane is still described as a "natural disaster," when in truth, the resulting destruction is usually a "human disaster." In actuality, nature is only releasing energy in a particular event, whether as a storm or a tremor. The damage inflicted is measured against buildings and infrastructure—both the products of human actions.

A number of contemporary writers have declared the "end of nature" in much the same manner as some nineteenth-century authors declared the "death of God." Discussions of an "Anthropocene" are useful in acknowledging that through their activity humans have altered the geo-biophysical and chemical nature of the Earth. Thanks to the laws of thermodynamics and a few other mechanisms, however, nature and natural processes are still very much at work everywhere. We are all creatures of nature. If we are to talk about planting and planting design, we are necessarily plunged into considerations of nature, as plants are among the most ubiquitous and familiar aspects of nature on earth. They are also a major part of the palette of landscape architecture, a factor that distinguishes the profession from other practical or fine arts. Plants are not only interesting, complex structures, but are also alive, changing in size and shape, only to eventually die. They blow and wiggle in the wind, produce a surfeit of twigs, seeds, leaves, and generally make for a rich but messy place. They also instigate our thinking about what is "beautiful." Beauty is phenomenal. It is an attribute or result, an effect of events, things, and ideas that generate feeling. It is a property like yellow or B-flat. It's not a thing, but truly in the eye, ear, or mind of the beholder; it occurs within an individual's sensibility, influenced by a synthesis of animal sensations and cultural background. A slippery diversity and difference in categories of things considered beautiful has troubled many, especially considering that the experience of beauty seems tied to pleasure and the stimulus of the senses or intellectual delight.

Our ideas of what is beautiful—or merely attractive, acceptable, dull, vulgar, or ugly—are framed in part by our acquired ideas regarding nature and what we think is "natural." In the most effervescent years of the Enlightenment, theories of planetary movements, vision, and metaphysics supported the strict use of Euclidean geometry in design and planning. With other mathematicians and philosophers, René Descartes contributed to the conception of the cosmos and the natural world for figures like André Le Nôtre, who used grids, lines, and planes to organize and plant vast territories considered beautiful from his day to our own [2-5]. More recently, landscape architects such as Daniel Urban Kiley and Peter Walker have employed related geometries to design landscapes also perceived to be attractive and on occasion truly beautiful—although not subscribing to the theology, cosmology, or politics of the seventeenth century [2-6].

Changes in sensibility, politics, and philosophy in eighteenth-century England produced a remarkably different rhetoric about nature and the perception of what is beautiful in gardens. The so-called informal planting of noble estates along with undulating landforms, water bodies, and curving paths, comprised schemes as vast as those of Le Nôtre, and similarly screened their contexts with a different functional order and geometry. The differences between the way masses of trees were used in these two bodies of work is their most obvious distinguishing feature. Le Nôtre's ranks of trees often lead off into the distance with the implication of endless extension, and by implication the possession and control of the territory beyond. In contrast, Lancelot "Capability" Brown and his contemporaries habitually encircled estates with thick shelter belts and forest plantations that limited their ultimate territory while masking what lay beyond [2-7].

William Kent's and Capability Brown's landscapes were equally as laborious and expensive to create from the chalk and clay terrain of southern Britain as Le Nôtre's had been in France. Although employing vast quantities of nursery-grown plants, they were nonetheless referred to as "natural" by contemporaries. These landscapes began as artistic contrivances, but over time they evolved into habitats for diverse communities of plants and animals, and today play an important role in the ecology of their regions. Some at the time considered them beautiful, while others found them too simple, empty, and socially destructive to the villagers displaced by their construction. Nevertheless, what they share with wild nature that leads people to consider them beautiful is of interest, especially because it is intimately connected to their planting. Scale, generosity of diverse foliage, ample meadows, and their accompanying surfaces reflect and refract light, and engage the broad sky in a manner similar to that of natural situations.

**2-5**

André Le Nôtre.
Parc de Sceaux.
Sceaux, France,
ca. 1680.
[Marc Treib]

**2-6**

Peter Walker.
Kempinski Hotel
garden.
Munich, Germany,
2000.
Geometric
patterning of
hedges and
paving.
[Marc Treib]

**2-7**

Lancelot
"Capability"
Brown.
Chatsworth.
Derbyshire,
England, ca. 1765.
[Marc Treib]

Until relatively recently, many historians believed that eighteenth-century English parks were monochromatic symphonies of green; in fact, they were enriched with a wealth of showy flowering plants.[3] Brown and his assistants planted masses of flowering shrubs, fruit trees, and perennials within their broad parklands. By the eighteenth century both England and France had profited from the importation of interesting and useful plants shipped from their colonies around the globe. Nearly all this colorful planting was located within close proximity of the villas and along favorite walks and drives of these estates. Most examples have disappeared in subsequent centuries, although in gardens such as Stourhead and Longleat, remnants or re-creations of the cornucopia of colorful herbaceous and flowering shrubs remain from the time of Brown and Humphry Repton [2-8].

Traces of this fashion for imported plants can be found throughout the parks of Europe and Britain. A stunning allée of American bald cypress, brought as seedlings to France from the bayous of Louisiana, was planted by Auguste Famin in 1809 at the chateau of Rambouillet. Equally unknown is a superb allée of giant sequoias lining the entry drive to Dunmore Park at Airth in Scotland, built for John Murray, the former governor of colonial Virginia and the British West Indies. Given the role of Scottish botanists and plant hunters in America and Asia, it is no surprise that one can find fine examples of these once fashionable trees on a number of estates in England and Scotland. Pine, larch, ash, oak, and cypress, paired with masses of rhododendrons, azaleas, and a wealth of other flowering trees from Asia and America, were planted widely.

Frederick Law Olmsted's plantings are also mistakenly believed to have been limited to pastoral efforts that relied almost solely on acres of greensward, trees in massed plantings, a handful of heroic specimens, and background drifts of monotonous shrubs. In fact, Olmsted senior was quite knowledgeable about plants installed in his parks and gardens, many of which had completely disappeared by the 1950s. It is undeniable that he adapted aspects of the pastoral English park to American use, and that he decried excessive horticultural display, arguing against imported plants he felt inappropriate in American landscape design. On numerous occasions instead, he suggested humble natives were adequate and more desirable, species such as "Nannyberry, hazel, shadbush, dogwood, even elder, or if an evergreen (conifer) will benefit the place, a stout, short, shock-headed mountain-pine, with two or three savins and a prostrate juniper at their feet" [2-9, 2-10].[4] He bristled at what he saw as inappropriate uses—"Planting without a system or design is a waste of money"—and asserted that naturalism was not really natural:[5]

> *There are those who will question the propriety of regarding the production of the poetic beauty of natural landscape as the end of landscape gardening, on the grounds that the very term "natural beauty" means beauty not by man's design, and that the best results of man's labor will be but a poor counterfeit, in which it is vain to look for the poetry of nature.*[6]

In his 1878 essay "Landscape Gardening" (for a time the name he preferred to landscape architecture), Olmsted described a proposed design for a front yard; and in lieu of an ordinary straight hedge he suggested that

> *its bushes shall not all be of one sort, and in good time they shall be bushes in earnest, leaping up with loose feathery tops, six, eight, and sometimes ten feet high. And they shall leap out also toward us. Yet from the house half their height shall be lost behind an under and out-growth of brake and bindweed, dog-rose and golden-rod, asters, gentians, buttercups, poppies, and irises.... There will be coves and capes and islands of chickweed, catnip, cinquefoil, wild strawberry, hepatica, forget-me-not, and lilies-of-the-valley, and, still farther out, shoals under the turf, where crocuses and daffodils are waiting to gladden the children and welcome the bluebird in spring* [2-11].[7]

Olmsted had his ideas about nature, and we have ours, which depending upon one's age, region, and education may vary considerably. These certainly will influence one's view of what is beautiful in terms of planting.

A generation later, Jens Jensen summed up many of his thoughts on the use of native vegetation in landscape design in an essay for an international garden congress held in Berlin in 1938. Jensen, whose work openly derived from an appreciation of the native plants of the American Midwest, clarified that he was not sympathetic to the ideas of his German contemporary Willy Lange or the National Socialists then in power—both strong advocates for indigenous planting. But like them, Jensen found the natural plant associations—in this case, the Midwest prairie—beautiful and was deeply interested in developing an American landscape as a true cultural expression [see 3-7]. While aware that a garden isn't a prairie, he wrote: "A garden of variety and novelty, flowers packed in like sardines in a box, discarded when they are done blooming, has no spiritual worth."[8]

The major shifts in theoretical concepts of nature, the world, and its order from the late eighteenth through the nineteenth centuries affected Western society's sense of aesthetics and

**2-8**

Henry Hoare II.
Stourhead.
Wiltshire, England,
1740s+.
View from the
Temple of Apollo.
[Marc Treib]

**2-9**

Olmsted and Vaux.
Prospect Park.
Brooklyn, New York,
1871+.
[Marc Treib]

**2-10**

Olmsted and Vaux.
Central Park.
New York, New York,
1858+.
[Marc Treib]

**2-11**

Frederick Law
Olmsted.
Biltmore Estate.
Asheville, North
Carolina, 1895.
Cutting garden.
[Marc Treib]

beauty in art—and in turn planting design.[9] A number of revolutions, wars, and the discrediting of rationalism, the rise of modern physics, and the world wars of the twentieth century—all exerted their influence. Landscape design wasn't immune to trends sweeping through art and architecture, although until very recently not much had been said since Christopher Tunnard voiced his thoughts about planting design in 1938 [2-12]. Shapes of planted areas and masses of color, paired with a tendency to position lone or groups of specimen trees in striking asymmetrical situations, echoed the compositional strategies of earlier practitioners such as Olmsted, or Asian prints and brush drawings. This tendency is especially evident in the work of the leading landscape designers of their times such as Hideo Sasaki, Dan Kiley, and even Garrett Eckbo, who embraced a modernist pastoral combined with a dash of De Stijl or Mondrian in his disposition of plants [2-13].

In the first half of the last century most landscape architects learned horticulture as undergraduates in colleges founded as agricultural schools and knew their plants well. After the Korean War, however, the leading landscape programs migrated to graduate schools and downplayed plants and biology, while emphasizing spatial composition, social use, and materials. Knowledge about trees continued, however, simply because trees could be used in architectural ways to shape space and produce sculptural effects. Leading designers such as Sasaki, Eckbo, Kiley, and Lawrence Halprin, who had learned their plants in an earlier era, nevertheless eschewed diverse herbaceous and understory plants in their work, instead favoring more "architectural" schemes that emphasized spatial arrangements and contemporary materials such as concrete.

Following the Vietnam War, a significant intellectual and ideological paradigm shift had a distinct impact upon plant use in landscape architecture. The environmental movement that followed on the heels of efforts for civil rights and against war, coincided with a distrust of authority, governance, industry, and planning control. Just as modernist architects and landscape architects had rejected neoclassical and beaux arts aesthetic traditions, so too had many in the field of landscape architecture now turned from modernist pastoral or more architectural compositions, toward planting schemes based upon ecological ideas, often employing what were considered native plants. Among other beliefs, this profound shift in sensibility expressed a disdain for gardens and plants used in orderly geometric compositions, whether as a stately row of a single species of tree or as bold and colorful planting arrangements.

Wild nature was lauded as the "ideal," and "native plants" in various stages of succession and association were the means to achieve it. Traditional lawns that had graced village greens and residential neighborhoods throughout America—a sight that had calmed and delighted Americans for centuries—were now seen as aesthetically passé, and even aesthetically and morally corrupt. A "born free" attitude spread across the country and through the profession, advocating the removal of lawns and replacing them with wilder grasses, ground covers, and shrubs, purportedly to provide habitat for myriad creatures. Some states went so far as to pass laws that only "native species" could be planted on state property and in public parks.

Some landscape architects went whole hog and couldn't bring themselves to plant two or three trees of the same species, much less in a row. Perhaps the most dramatic result of this attitude was the replanting of Jacques Gréber's handsome allées along the Benjamin Franklin Parkway in Philadelphia with a mélange of species, the designers believing the practice was environmentally beneficial. In fact, the result was not appreciably beneficial, and was certainly less graceful and beautiful. Such ideas in the hands of skilled designers, however, when employed in other more appropriate settings did produce handsome results. Examples include the large park plantings by Andropogon, a prominent ecologically driven firm in Philadelphia, in its scheme for the rehabilitation of the Morris Arboretum in Philadelphia and the Crosby Arboretum in Mississippi [2-14].

To say that all art or landscape design comes from nature in some way is one thing, but to trace all its varieties from direct imitation to abstraction is another. So too is designing to evoke the memory of a place distant in time or space. Design employing "natural" processes may be the most difficult, for example, using fire to maintain a particular landscape character as it does in the wild. A variety of concepts in regard to the natural world often coexist at any one time. The professional concerns and daily activities of scientists today are noticeably different from those of landscape architects and artists, although the two groups appreciate and often believe and respect the ideas of the other. In the essay "The Imitation of Nature," cultural geographer J. B. Jackson wrote that to attempt to imitate nature is both a bad idea and impossible to achieve. Without question we need to bring nature into our cities and lives, particularly those aspects that stimulate our senses such as those qualities presented by vegetation: color, light, pattern, texture, variable and rich forms, sound, and movement. While I agree there is a need for adopting natural processes

**2-12**

Christopher Tunnard. Gordon Cullen, delineator. Conifers. [*Gardens in the Modern Landscape*, 1948]

**2-13**

Garrett Eckbo. Union Bank Plaza. Los Angeles, California, 1968. Coral trees (*Erythrina*) as primary species. [Marc Treib]

**2-14**

Andropogon, landscape architects. Euine Fay Jones, architect. Crosby Arboretum. Picayune, Mississippi, 1984+. [Marc Treib]

**2-15**

Isamu Noguchi.
*California Scenario.*
Costa Mesa, California,
1984.
Desertland.
[Marc Treib]

**2-16**

Isamu Noguchi.
*California Scenario.*
Mountain Meadow.
[Marc Treib]

into the making of our cultural environment, I am also interested in the potential for representation and purposeful meaning deriving from an artful expression. How can we do so?

Some of the more beautiful landscapes created in the last century have abstracted one or several properties found in natural situations and deployed them skillfully. At times this has been accomplished with a remarkably minimalist touch; at other times, in broader manner, it has taken form in a more sweeping and fulsome way. Among the most rarified abstract representations of natural landscapes is *California Scenario,* created by sculptor Isamu Noguchi in an office park set within the sprawl of Costa Mesa, California. There he produced what might almost be called "landscape dioramas" that recall the now-historic thematic displays of natural history museums a generation ago. In his design Noguchi abstracted several distinct landscape types from locations in California and reshaped them as sculpture: a circular mound peppered with desert plants evokes the sere landscape of gravel desert regions such as the Mojave Desert or Joshua Tree National Monument [2-15]. He also points the visitor to the coastal redwood groves that fill the valleys of the Pacific coast ranges; riparian plants that line the streams and arroyos of the foothills; and the wandering rivers and alluvial plains that underlie the vast agricultural enterprise of the Central Valley [2-16]. *California Scenario* is skillful, witty, and markedly modernist in its formal composition—a piazza-sized version of a tabletop still-life painting by Cezanne, Braque, or Morandi.

A more recent work by Michael Van Valkenburgh for the Isabella Stewart Gardner Museum in Boston, purposefully directs our thoughts and feelings toward the second-growth forests of New England by featuring a twisting stone path leading through thickets of thin-paper birches, paperbark maples (*Acer grisium*), shadbush (*Amelanchier*), ferns, and kinnikinnick (*Archtostaphylus*) [2-17]. With its regional plants and obvious references to the second-growth forests that once ranged from Pennsylvania to the Mississippi, this garden pits reference against verisimilitude: a work of art made from the very stuff, the actual material that it is representing, but which is neither a copy nor an imitation. While many visitors, whether lay or professional, may mistake the garden as "natural," it is neither a literal copy nor could it ever be so. One reason that it is not natural regards scope. Real prairies, old fields, and young (or old) forests are more extensive spatially, often vastly so. Also, old fields are dynamic; some evolve into woodland, some are transformed by fire or are beset by plagues and destroyed. In contrast, this is a garden arrested in time; through maintenance and weeding it will remain. It is a work of artifice not nature, even as it loses its youth and becomes in truth an older landscape.

The Monk's Garden at the Gardner Museum embodies a taste and aesthetic different from those of earlier eras that took pleasure in the beds of massed ornamentals that so pathetically filled municipal gardens, railroad stations, and Victorian estates at the end of the nineteenth century. It also departs from 1960s modernism, dependent as it was upon Christopher Tunnard's tepid orientalism and vague employment of elements drawn from surrealism. With the rare exception of Roberto Burle Marx in Brazil, who was a superb horticulturalist and plantsman, such ideas haven't had many skilled proponents until recently [2-18].

Two exemplary projects employing highly controlled abstractions of natural landscapes, while not natural in and of themselves are the Soros garden in Southampton, Long Island, completed in 1965, and the Lurie Garden in Millennium Park in Chicago, opened in 2004.[10] The Soros garden, designed by A. E. Bye, is an evocation of the regional Atlantic-coast seaside landscape of dunes, their forms, and their vegetation. Subtle grading of the land presents a set of undulating forms that welcome the daily and seasonal movement of light and shade. Bye's plant choices were consistently minimalist, schemes that disposed masses of shrubs in drifts that highlighted the landform. This approach to planting represents restraint in its palette with generosity in the quantum of plants used. Regrettably, the current owner has littered the original and unique graceful spaces with large modern sculptures, transforming a superb work of landscape art into an inert backcloth for more common objects.

At the very same time that Bye was creating his gardens, a countervailing aesthetic strategy could be seen in the work of Dan Kiley and later Peter Walker and myself. Inspired by André Le Nôtre's employment of trees, we have taken pleasure in the geometric order of ranks, allées, and bosks—sometimes in urban contexts, sometimes in rural ones. In projects like Novartis in Basel, Switzerland; the IBM Solana campus in Texas; and the 9/11 Memorial in Manhattan, Walker's return to geometric order is evident [see 13-20, 13-23A–D]. It is also evident in my design for the Wexner estate in Ohio, and portions of the J. Paul Getty Center in Los Angeles [2-19, 2-20]. At times reductive, these projects often represent an exercise in formal composition with little or no particular reference to nature, except for their use of natural elements. Rather than from variety, their pleasure

**2-17**

Michael Van Valkenburgh Associates. Monk's Garden, Isabella Stewart Gardner Museum. Boston, Massachusetts, 2013. [Laurie Olin]

**2-18**

Roberto Burle Marx.
Fazenda Vargem Grande.
Areias, Brazil,
1979–1990.
[Marc Treib]

derives from the texture, color, pattern, and spatial repetition that recall the minimalist music of the period by Philip Glass, Steve Reich, and Terry Riley.

The realization of the Lurie Garden in Chicago coincided with a renewed American interest in meadows [2-21]. Several sources fed this trend. The first was the strengthening of an ecological vision that saw turf lawns as polluting and un-ecological; the second regarded meadows as more beneficial in terms of landscape maintenance, stormwater treatment, and habitat for beneficial insects and small animals. A third factor was the resurrected interest in native plants once used by a handful of late-nineteenth-century designers and landscape architects in America and in northern Europe shortly thereafter, for example, Jens Jensen, the Olmsted Brothers, and Beatrix Farrand, who had collected, propagated, and employed native plants in her work. In the Netherlands, Scandinavia, and Germany prior to World War II, grasses, aquatics, shrubs, and alpine species had all become popular in gardens and parks. Meadows per se have been appreciated for centuries, whether described as flowery leas in poetry and song, or depicted in paintings and tapestries. Unbeknownst to most Americans who were besotted with lawns composed of cool climate northern European turf grasses, this love of meadows with their diversity of plants persisted abroad.

Few landscape architects in America shared this view when Wolfgang Oehme emigrated from Germany to the United States in 1957. With a deep horticultural knowledge, Oehme had worked in nurseries and gardens in Germany and England before his arrival in America. He was an admirer of Willy Lange and other prewar plantsmen who had advocated the use of native plants and grasses mixed with selected species of flowers and shrubs. By the 1970s, when his colleagues and the press took notice of the stunning gardens that he and his partner James van Sweden had been making in the mid-Atlantic region, others had also begun to experiment with meadows and so-called natural planting [2-22].

At almost the exact same time that Oehme, van Sweden's work was on the rise, in 1972 Peter Walker completed the Weyerhaeuser headquarters south of Tacoma, Washington, with its stunning wildflower meadow. Considerable differences distinguish Weyerhaeuser from Oehme, van Sweden work and the Lurie Garden, however. The Weyerhaeuser landscape was grounded in the mountain meadows of the West with their broad sweeps of lupines, grasses, and carexes. Although composed of only a few species, it, too, changes continuously like more natural meadows, that appear

**2-19**

Laurie Olin.
Getty Center.
Los Angeles,
California, 1998.
Terrace landscape.
[Marc Treib]

**2-20**

Laurie Olin.
Getty Center.
Los Angeles,
California, 1998.
Bougainvillea
planting.
[Marc Treib]

**2-21**

Kathryn Gustafson
and Piet Oudolf.
Lurie Garden,
Millennium Park.
Chicago, Illinois,
2004.
[Laurie Olin]

**2-27**

Laurie Olin, landscape architect. Peter Eisenman, architect. Wexner Center, The Ohio State University. Columbus, Ohio, ca. 1987. [Felice Frankel]

**2-28**

Laurie Olin, landscape architect. Wexner Center, The Ohio State University. Prairie grasses. [Felice Frankel]

**2-29**

Laurie Olin and Dennis McGlade. Getty Center. Los Angeles, California, 1993. Cactus garden. [Marc Treib]

**2-30**

Laurie Olin, Dennis McGlade. Getty Center. Cactus garden. [Marc Treib]

**2-31**

Laurie Olin, landscape architect. Robert Frasca, architect. Conference Center, Church of Jesus Christ of Latter-day Saints. Roof garden. Salt Lake City, Utah, 1996. [Susan Weiler]

**2-32**

Laurie Olin, landscape architect; Conference Center, Church of Jesus Christ of Latter-day Saints. Roof garden. [Zimmer Gunsel Frasca]

In contrast to this exercise at the Getty, I have experimented for a number of years with landscape designs that directly refer to the region in which they are located, using a select number of elements to represent particular aspects of that environment. These are not to be construed as pretending to recreate wild nature, however. The first is a conference center facility for the Church of Jesus Christ of Latter-day Saints in Salt Lake City, designed in collaboration with architect Robert Frasca and his firm, ZGF. In this case the landscape was draped over a giant building nearly ten acres in floor area, and a 22,000-seat auditorium. Treating the landscape/building as a mesa or mountain, we clad the blank sides of the auditoriums with the vegetation that grows in the canyons of Utah and on the steep slopes of the nearby Wasatch Mountains [2-32, 2-33]. The trees are mostly firs and maples, but they have been heavily planted to bring into the city an odd recollection of the nearby canyons. I will repeat that this was no attempt at any form of recreation. For example, Douglas firs (*Pseudotsuga menziesii*) are the most common conifer in the cool and shady mountain valleys; they would have been uncomfortable growing in urban conditions and quite likely end up too tall and leggy if planted on the rooftop. Instead slow-growing Serbian spruces (*Picea omorika*) were substituted for the Douglas firs. On a different portion of the rooftop, small bristlecone pines (*Pinus longaeva*)—a native of lands hundreds of miles farther south and to the west—were chosen for their dwarfish scale and to create a sense of distance and sweep when looking off toward the Great Salt Lake. The project was complete artifice; it was not nature.

In turn, the inspiration for a four-acre meadow on the central portion of the roof was that of the alpine meadows found along the length of the Rocky Mountains. To create this meadow, we contracted for tens of thousands of plants because no ordinary commercial nursery could provide such a diversity of native species in that quantity. Susan Weiler, one of my partners, directed over a hundred members of Salt Lake's Mormon Church community to carry up and plant the thousands of plugs, seedlings, and small pots over a long weekend. To our happy surprise, meadow mice, lemmings, and apparently some rabbits have found their way up the stairs and now live there—only to be hunted by hawks and owls, as they do in the wild. In addition to offering habitat, this scheme has resulted in utilitarian environmental benefits regarding heat, energy, water, and longevity for the building's roofing. But none of that was the instigating motive. I simply wanted to present an aspect of the local environment that I considered beautiful to people for their pleasure.

Elsewhere, a client for a private estate in France desired a pond. In the past I had designed a number of ponds and small lakes, in part inspired by summer experiences as a youth in the interior of Alaska. One such lake was about 30 miles south of Fairbanks, where I helped build a Boy Scout camp in the woods. The lake was filled with life: spatterdock, lilies, irises, and reeds with birches, willows, and spruce; with fish and beaver—all in all, a powerful source of reverie, form, and plant palette.

The French estate plan we developed combined existing elements of the site with the proposed interventions. Among these were a forest with paths, two small private walled gardens, a meadow, a buffer plantation around the perimeter—and a pond [2-34]. While working on this scheme in the valley of the Seine River north of Paris it was hard not to think of Monet's garden in nearby Giverny [2-35]. Copying was not the answer, but on the other hand, I felt that although it would be almost impossible not to echo in some way Monet's magnificent pond—the inspiration for many of his greatest paintings—there was no reason for not making another composition utilizing much of the same palette to achieve many of the same pleasurable effects.

Several years of studying and writing about the eighteenth-century landscape, parks, and gardens of southern England left me curious to explore directly a trope in disrepute at the time, despite a lip service respect for Olmsted: namely, the pastoral park. The creation of an extensive private estate in Ohio provided the opportunity to design in a more naturalistic manner. While it took over a decade to achieve fruition with its extensive meadows, ponds, bosks, and woodlands, the landscape at Abigail House in New Albany has been received warmly by owners and community alike [2–36, see also chapter opening]. Continuing to work there through last year my office has learned a great amount about the artifice required to produce something seen by most as "natural."

The meadow that resulted by transforming the banal horse paddock covered with a German fescue today features a mixture of American and European grasses and perennials. Fortunately, we have learned how to establish grasses in a shorter period of time, but even so, it takes a few years for them to settle down, and requires careful maintenance, mostly mowing, several times a year. The pond also needs fairly rigorous cutting and harvesting of the water plants to keep the water open. The trees nearby will take time to shed their adolescent character, but time is part of our medium and maturity occurs within a few years. This landscape is not natural, but it is made of natural organisms and materials.

It has already joined the local ecology of plants, animals, pests, and diseases as it operates under the laws of nature despite its origin in artifice. Its prime purpose is to provide pleasure through sensory pleasure as is offered by more famous antecedents both wild and domestic.

A recent experiment at another scale is the design for Apple Park in Cupertino, California, nearing completion at the time of writing. For me it has been a direct meditation upon the nearly vanished natural and cultural landscapes of the immediate region [2-37, 2-38]. This landscape, comprising some 150 acres, is a complete fabrication. There is nothing natural about it. It's all artifice, although its subject is nature and the cultural landscape. The buildings on-site measure over three million square feet of office and research and development space, and will be used daily by 12,000 people as the setting for their waking, working lives. In the design of the landscape I purposefully set out to recall the lost orchards of the Santa Clara Valley which had once covered the site, as well as the natural plant communities that the orchards had replaced, composed largely of oak forest, oak savanna, and chaparral. To me, orchards, like most of the agricultural and ranchland of the California coast, are quite beautiful, as are the hills and ravines and the combination of pasture and native vegetation. How to evoke the properties and qualities of this former landscape without copying or imitating any particular thing or place within it?

Landform and planting offered the two most effective devices for realizing such an aspiration. Therefore, we constructed a series of hills and small valleys on what was originally a totally flat site formerly composed of parking lots and two-story Hewlett Packard buildings. On these hills we've planted a wide selection of native plants along with a number of other American and Mediterranean species that, considering climate change, are appropriate to the slope and solar aspect. Over 8,000 trees have been planted, including over two dozen species of oaks, accompanied by a variety of conifers, manzanitas, sycamores, a wide variety of shrubs, perennials such as ceanothus, native salvias, and dozens and dozens of other species.

We've also planted over 800 fruit trees comprised of 13 varieties of heirloom stone fruits such as apricots, plums, nectarines, pluots, and cherries, and 11 varieties of apples. Like most people in our field, we are concerned about climate change and the vulnerability of a number of native species in this location to succumbing in the very near future. In response we introduced a number of trees, shrubs, herbaceous plants, and bulbs from other regions that we

**2-33**

*(opposite above)*

Laurie Olin.
Pond and meadow.
Private Estate.
Picardy, France, 2014.
[Laurie Olin]

**2-34**

*(opposite below)*

Claude Monet.
The painter's
water garden.
Giverny, France,
1893+.
[Marc Treib]

**2-35**

Laurie Olin.
Abigail House.
New Albany, Ohio,
1988+.
The bosk.
[Laurie Olin]

suspect will survive in the future in the altered climate of the Bay Area. To assist with solving this problem our client also built a pipeline to bring recycled water from a Santa Clara water treatment plant to ensure the plants' establishment and address extended droughts.

Given Apple Park's urban location and restrictions against air-polluting techniques, such as using fire to manage the meadow and grassland, we embarked on a research project with two grass and seed suppliers to experiment with various mixtures of native grasses and wildflowers. Learning that some of the grasses that give the characteristic golden look of the California hills were actually of European origin introduced by early settlers, we felt secure in exploring what combination might give us the effect we were after. We eventually settled upon a group of mixes for different places on the site chosen for the ability to thrive in different microclimates, with social use, and symbolic or artistic relevance.

Ultimately, to many people the trees, shrubs, grasses, and bulbs of Apple Park will look "natural." The plants will behave naturally, responding as they must to biophysical laws, because they are de facto natural organisms—adding to the conceptual confusion. As the meadow-covered south hills at Apple Park slope gently toward the main building, everyone arriving will notice that they are in fact supported on one side by a four-and-a-half-story structural wall that runs for nearly a quarter mile. The artifice could not be more blatant, although recently installed portions of the hills and a jogging trail are clearly intended to emulate the character of the nearby terrain. As with all planting, these areas are inevitably going to evolve and change over time. The central problem regarding nature and its representation in making landscapes with any aspiration beyond utility or safety lies in the fundamental difference between the nature of art and the nature of nature. Nature and the natural world are in constant flux: things move, live, die, grow, decline, deposit, erode, are reborn, metamorphose, shift about, are unstable. In all, nature is dynamic, nature is constant, nature is infinite —it starts anywhere and goes in all directions. It is cyclical, and yet time goes in only one direction: the phenomena of time and entropy. This energy and absence of human control is part of our perception of its power, its profligacy, its evanescence, and its beauty.

The arts, on the other hand—whether the so-called fine arts such as painting or sculpture, or the so-called practical arts such as architecture, landscape architecture, and gardening—have as their normal goal the creation of something that is largely fixed and intentionally stable in the hope of achieving some long-lasting value for an audience or public. Beauty as a phenomenon of nature is transient, impermanent, but ultimately evanescent. A garden or landscape takes time to create, time to mature, and from its initiation entropy begins to alter its condition. Knowing that time is part of their tools and limits, designers employ planting plans that rely upon landform, masonry structures, slower growing plants such as trees, and cyclically self-renewing plants such as bulbs and perennials to assist in stability and long-term reward. Ultimately one must accept that any landscape design will change through time, eventually disappearing or evolving into something else; or it will be necessary to renew, replant, and even rebuild the landscape. Also, landscape design is never totally free of earlier sources of form, particularly those of nature, and our sense of its elements and attributes contribute to its beauty.

I feel compelled to conclude with the belief that beauty is a serious matter; it is deep and has great value for humans. While beauty has many manifestations, one of the most accessible has been—and remains—to be found in plants in both natural and designed settings. A loss or diminution of our interest or comprehension of beauty regarding either would indeed be a great loss. As Sigmund Freud once remarked: "Beauty has no obvious use: nor is there any clear cultural necessity for it. Yet civilization could not do without it."[12]

**2-36**

Laurie Olin.
Apple Park.
Cupertino,
California, 2019.
[Laurie Olin]

## Notes

**1** Gertrude Jekyll, *A Gardner's Testament*, London, Country Life, 1937, reprinted Antique Collectors' Club, 1982, p. 14.

**2** Ibid., p. 58.

**3** See Georgina Masson's essay on flower collectors' gardens in Italy in the seventeenth century in the first Dumbarton Oaks Landscape Architecture Colloquium, *The Italian Garden*, David R. Coffin, ed., Washington, DC: Dumbarton Oaks, 1972, where she attacked the misconception that Italian gardens were solely evergreen compositions. See also Claudia Lazzaro, *The Italian Renaissance Garden*, New Haven, CT: Yale University Press, 1990; Mark Laird, *The Flowering of the English Landscape*, Philadelphia: University of Pennsylvania Press, 1999; David Brown and Tom Williamson, *Lancelot Brown and the Capability Men: Landscape Revolution in Eighteenth-century England*, London: Reaktion, 2016.

**4** Frederick Law Olmsted, "An Ideal View: Landscape Gardening" (1877), in *Frederick Law Olmsted: Writings on Landscape, Culture, and Society*, ed. Charles Beveridge, New York: Library of America, vol. 270, 2015, p. 552.

**5** Frederick Law Olmsted, *Essential Texts*, ed. Robert Twombly, New York: W. W. Norton, 2010, p. 159.

**6** Olmsted, "An Ideal View," p. 553.

**7** Ibid., p. 551.

**8** Jens Jensen, "Garden Design: Special Lecture," in *Jens Jensen: Writings Inspired by Nature*, ed., William H. Tishler, Madison: Wisconsin Historical Society Press, 2012, p. 106.

**9** There is by now a huge literature on this subject; useful references are Christopher Tunnard, *Gardens in the Modern Landscape* (1938, revised 1948), reprint, Philadelphia: University of Pennsylvania Press, 2018; Peter Walker and Melanie Simo, *Invisible Gardens: The Search for Modernism in American Gardens*, Cambridge, MA: MIT Press, 1996; Marc Treib, *Modern Landscape Architecture: A Critical Review*, Cambridge, MA: MIT Press, 1993; Kenneth Helphand, *Lawrence Halprin*, Athens: University of Georgia Press, 2017; Alison Hirsch, *City Choreographer: Lawrence Halprin in Urban America*, Minneapolis: University of Minnesota Press, 2014 ; Lawrence Halprin, *A Life Spent Changing Places*, Philadelphia: University of Pennsylvania Press, 2011; Marc Treib and Dorothée Imbert, *Garrett Eckbo: Modern Landscapes for Living*, Berkeley: University of California Press, 2005; Dan Kiley and Jane Amidon, *Dan Kiley: The Complete Works*, Boston: Bullfinch Press, 1999; William Saunders, ed., *Daniel Urban Kiley: The Early Gardens*, New York: Princeton Architectural Press, 1999.

**10** A. E. Bye, *Art into Landscape/Landscape into Art*, Philadelphia: PDA Publishers, 1999; Michael Van Valkenburgh, *Transforming the American Garden: 12 New Landscape Designs*, Cambridge, MA: Harvard University, Graduate School of Design, 1986.

**11** James Corner Field Operations, Elizabeth Diller, and Rick Scofidio, *The High Line*, New York: Phaidon Press, 2015; Piet Oudolf and Rick Dark, *Gardens of the High Line: Elevating the Nature of Modern Landscapes*, Portland, OR: Timber Press, 2017.

**12** Quoted by Hubert Damisch, *The Judgment of Paris*, Chicago: University of Chicago Press, 1996, p. 57, and by Jeremy Gilbert-Rolfe, *Beauty and the Contemporary Sublime*, New York: Allworth Press, 1999, p. 41.

**2-37**

Laurie Olin. Apple Park. Cupertino, California, 2019. [Laurie Olin]

# NATURALISM THROUGH THE "LONG" TWENTIETH CENTURY

Tim Richardson

3.

Piet Oudolf.
Walled Garden.
Scampston Hall.
Malton, North
Yorkshire, England,
1999.
[Tim Richardson]

to experiment with what were then called hardy, exotic perennials—that is, perennials from places other than Northern Europe. He held that it was fine to use any plant from anywhere in the world—from Australia or South America or wherever—as long as it looked happy in its situation, as if it could grow there naturally. This is really not a scientific approach at all. Many illustrations in *The Wild Garden* show exotic plants growing happily with natives [3-2]. These ideas had been brewing for some time before 1870, of course, most notably in the form of the cottage garden cult, but Robinson refined and popularized them.

Robinson's focus was entirely on the planting of the garden rather than its structure, but he was also very concerned with art as opposed to nature. So in *The English Flower Garden*, he writes: "Nature is a good colourist, and if we trust to her guidance, we never find wrong colour in wood, meadow, or on mountain."[6] This idea that nature can never be wrong is a key tenet as we go forward and remains dear even to today's naturalistic designers. Robinson lived at Gravetye Manor, in Sussex, which in its current incarnation is a swanky hotel. Tom Coward took over as head gardener there about five years ago, and has been reintroducing planting in Robinson's manner [3-3]. Robinson was against the height gradation of plants in borders, as well as other practices we associate with the Victorian J. C. Loudon style of gardening:

> *Plant in naturally disposed groups, never repeating the same plant along the border at intervals, as is so often done with favorites. Do not graduate the plants in height from the front to the back, as is generally done, but sometimes let a bold plant come to the edge; and, on the other hand, let a little carpet of a dwarf plants pass in here and there to the back, so as to give a varied instead of a monotonous surface. Have no patience with bare ground, and cover the border with dwarf plants; do not put them along the front of the border only.*[7]

The Sheffield-based historian Jan Woudstra has described Robinson's contribution in the following way: "There is no evidence of phytogeographical or ecological principles being used in Robinson's work, and the distribution of planting is based on pictorial or aesthetic criteria only."[8] For Woudstra, Robinson's planting is unscientific and therefore does not chime with thinking in the present era.

This is the seed of the dichotomy in thinking about naturalistic planting—a schism of sorts between the aesthetes and the scientists—because there appear to be two fundamental

**3-3**

William Robinson. Gravetye Manor garden, West Hoathly, Sussex, England, 1885; re-created 2010s. [Marc Treib]

ways of thinking about what constitutes "natural." The first might be called the *archetypal* approach, which is the Robinsonian approach that attempts to capture the essence of natural habitat types by means of creative planting. The second approach is what we might call the *botanical* or *ecological* approach, which is the supposedly accurate replication or intensification of plant communities as found in the wild. This approach tends to be attempted by people who call themselves ecologists.

A near contemporary of Robinson's in Germany was Willy Lange, professor of garden design at Berlin University. Lange was a key promoter of the ideal of natural habitat gardening, with values quite similar to Robinson's. He famously lived alone in a woodland for seven years to get the feeling of what it was like. Like Robinson, he was a hugely successful author. His book *Gartengestaltung der Neuzeit* (Garden Design for Modern Times) of 1909 quickly sold 22,000 copies.[9] In the book he describes the composition of plant communities in the garden according to nature "motifs," which is an alternative term for archetype. At that time, to have photographs in a book convey feeling and mood—in some ways similar to the paintings of Caspar David Friedrich—was quite remarkable.

Although perhaps there's not much to be learned about landscape design from his images, Lange's pursuit of mood—*Stimmung*—is evident. Lange's work also generated a nationalistic feeling and unfortunately became bound up with this *Völkisch* idea of Teutonic blood and soil. Lange himself became embroiled in the National Socialist movement; ideas associated with naturalistic landscape design at this time developed fervent patriotic and ultimately racist overtones. His influence was strong not only in Scandinavia but also in America where Frank A. Waugh, who had studied with Lange in Berlin, wrote an influential book on his teacher. Lange's own house on the Wannsee near Berlin was a stylized woodland with Robinsonian naturalistic bulb plantings. In other gardens Lange worked the landscape to recreate a mountain environment using woodland planting [3-4]. Lange had a major influence on the thinking of the German emigrant to the United States Wilhelm Miller, who championed the appropriate landscape style of the Midwest in his 1915 small book, *The Prairie Spirit of Landscape Gardening*—as did Frank A. Waugh in *The Natural Style in Landscape Gardening* (1917), and Jens Jensen in *Siftings*, published as late as 1939 [3-5].[10] Wilhelm Miller was a fierce advocate of the Robinsonian wild garden, and early in his career (1911) even wrote a book titled *What English Gardens Can Teach Us*.[11]

**3-4**

Willy Lange. "Garden in Wannsee, Germany." [*Gartengestaltung der Neuzeit*, Plate IX]

**3-5**

Wilhelm Miller. "Conservation." [*The Prairie Spirit in Landscape Gardening*]

Any discussion of naturalistic gardens requires a word on native plants. Most naturalistic planters who consider what they are doing resist the idea of using only native plants, partly because of the ideological underpinnings noted above. After all, if you start excluding foreign plants from your gardens on principle, there are obvious analogies and metaphors to be made. But there are also very good botanical reasons not to do so. As it happens, and quite incredibly, in Britain we have perhaps only two dozen native species of plants. So, if you want variety in your garden, using only native plants is not really an option, is it? Consider that there are 5,800 native species in Cape Province alone. The scientist Stephen Jay Gould has examined this concept and wrote that native planting oscillates between the extremes of what he kindly calls "romanticism" and dangerous *Völkisch* nationalism.[12] Wilhelm Miller's term "Prairie Spirit" is a slightly more benign version of this nationalism—or naturalism as nationalism. The prairie spirit was defined by Miller as "an American mode of design based upon the practical needs of the middle-western people and characterized by the preservation of typical Western scenery, by restoration of local color, and by repetition of the horizontal line of land or sky, which is the strongest feature of prairie scenery."[13] Like Frank Lloyd Wright, in defining the Prairie School in architecture, Miller believed that the horizontal line was the fundamental aspect of the Prairie Spirit in landscape design—just as the vertical line was endemic to the Gothic style.

Perhaps Jens Jensen had a more visionary attitude toward the prairie landscape and, crucially, it was not an attitude bound up only with plants. He did use native plants, of course—for example in later works like the Lincoln Memorial Park, where he used native plants in groupings—but he wasn't strict about restricting exotics. His landscape designs were in many ways homages to the natural landscape with features like gently purling cascades [3-6]. But in his designs, he also included features like council rings and players' greens where theatrical productions could be mounted in very dramatic circumstances, perhaps in a natural amphitheater with the sun setting behind the action [3-7]. For the audience, this could be an incredible, transcendent moment.

While this was happening in the USA and in Germany, in Britain we were still obsessed with picturesque cottages—the Cottage Cult, if you like—a craze for cottages and cottage gardens popularized through paintings and writings, like those of Gertrude Jekyll. A parallel obsession among architects and writers was the rediscovery of the atmosphere of old English country houses, which came to be called the Arts and Crafts movement, using the writings of William Morris as a sort of manifesto. The cottage style was supported by squads of watercolorists who performed a kind of reverse commute, traveling from London out into the Home Counties to create images that overflow with old-fashioned flowers. They were sometimes called "Shakespearean flowers" at this time—species such as phloxes, lupins, foxgloves, dog roses, zinnias, delphiniums, campanulas, and marigolds [3-8]. All of these were considered old-fashioned English flowers, supposedly all artlessly arranged by the humble but happy cottage dweller. In fact, the cottagers didn't really do gardens like that; they usually only had sufficient space to grow lines of vegetables in front of their dilapidated and unsanitary houses, and they simply didn't have the time to make artistic creations.

Helen Allingham is often dismissed as a kind of "chocolate box painter," but she's more interesting than that because unlike many of the other painters of her time she had a knowledge of plants and gardening. In her paintings, each individual plant can be identified, and as such, they function almost as a planting plan. Her painting of Haddon Hall in Derbyshire is suffused with the sort of dreamy atmosphere that attracted the Arts and Crafts designers—places like Montacute and other seventeenth-century houses. References were the writings of Francis Bacon and John Evelyn, and there was a fetish for architectural elements like small pavilions and sundials.

These became the elements of the vocabulary of Arts and Crafts gardens around the close of the nineteenth century. Probably our best guide to the reality of the plantings of the time was Eleanor Vere Boyle, who published under the initials EVB. She wrote a series of books that are intense and lyrical, and perhaps a little bit over the top. She was a great friend of Gertrude Jekyll and in fact wrote the preface to her first book, *Wood and Garden*, published in 1899. Boyle said this: "Colour effects, wherever they appear in our garden, are seldom planned... but it is quite an exquisite delight to find the most beautiful accidents of colour in unexpected places all about the garden."[14] Here we see garden-making viewed as a picture, a place with pictorial qualities that is also graced by serendipity and happenstance. For Boyle, it is really the emotional aspects of the garden that most interested her; in this she was quite different from Jekyll.

Jekyll did not believe in gardening by chance. She learned her trade at the South Kensington Schools, then attached to the Victoria and Albert Museum, and emphasized artistic control, color, technical expertise; the picture-making aspects

**3-6**

Jens Jensen.
Columbus Park.
Chicago, Illinois,
1916.
Chasm.
[Marc Treib]

**3-7**

Jens Jensen.
Lincoln Memorial.
Council ring.
Springfield, Illinois,
ca. 1934.
[Marc Treib]

in her gardening relied on technical knowledge. She made her own vegetable dyes from plants and flowers, and was immersed in theories of color. Her home at Munstead Wood was set in a woodland, and that setting was very important to her. She is best known for her planting and color theory in terms of the herbaceous border, but the woodland garden was arguably what first piqued her interest [see 2-1]. While in some ways she was a technocrat, she designed as an aesthete, and was really an avant-garde artist in the context of her time. Her teachers at the South Kensington Schools had included Christopher Dresser, famous primarily for designing tea sets and other domestic objects. But Dresser actually designed objects of every sort and fits squarely within the Aesthetic movement in that period when designers "did everything." They studied all the "applied arts," as they were called.

Dresser was also a botanist and published *A Popular Manual of Botany* in 1860 and *The Art of Decorative Design* two years afterward. In this book he posited that the world of living things might provide an artistic medium in its own right: "The formation of an intimacy with nature will be found most conducive as it inevitably leads to the cultivation of taste. The wood, the garden and the hedgerow will each form a suitable studio."[15] Here he's talking about an outdoor studio. John Ruskin was writing on this very subject at the same time. This is the world in which Jekyll was caught up.

Another of her tutors was Richard Redgrave, who in his 1853 *Manual of Colour* created a true catechism of color for aspiring designers.[16] In this he was obviously influenced by Michel-Eugène Chevreul of the Gobelins tapestry works outside Paris, who advanced ideas about primary, secondary, and complementary colors that later also influenced the Impressionists. Redgrave, his disciple, assigned each color a numerical value; Jekyll very much looked upon color theory in this same way, as a scientific endeavor. In the woodland garden at Munstead Wood, the effect may have appeared naturalistic but the planting was tautly controlled.

So there were two emergent strains in Arts and Crafts planting at this time. The first and dominant one was the cottage look, or embroidered approach, practiced by Boyle and most others. The second was founded in Jekyll's artistry and technical approach with regard to color theory. This was much more difficult to emulate.

In terms of color, this is what Jekyll wrote in 1904 about Levens Hall in *Some English Gardens*: "The play of light and variety of colour of the green surfaces of the clipped

**3-8**

Helen Allingham.
*A Herbaceous Border.*
Nineteenth century.
[Private Collection, Wikicommons]

**3-9**

Gertrude Jekyll
Hestercombe.
Taunton, Somerset, England, 1904.
[Marc Treib]

**3-10**

Gertrude Jekyll.
Phillips Memorial Cloister.
Godalming, Surrey, England, 1913.
Planting plan.
[Environmental Design Archives, University of California, Berkeley]

evergreens is a delight to the trained colour-eye."[17] In her book *Old West Surrey*, published that same year, she described things like gates and doorways and so on, but in the background in one photograph a huge euphorbia is evident and plays an important structural role.[18] The Grey Garden beds at Munstead Wood were planted with pink hollyhocks, gray-blue echinops (the spiky balls), and the silvery artemisia at the front. In the Michaelmas daisy border you can see how muscular the planting was, how in places Jekyll controlled the masses whereas in other sections she used spiky plants. The red border was planted with red geraniums, *Dahlia* 'Fire King,' and salvias backed by hollyhocks. Jeykll's single-color gardens were very influential. Although they appear naturalistic if not natural, they are carefully planned. Jekyll's planting plans looked a lot like the painting-by-numbers art kits of the 1950s, but in fact it is not easy to do [3-10]. No one really ever gardened like Jekyll because no one was as skilled as Jekyll.

A Jekyll contemporary was Norah Lindsay, a professional who also gardened at Sutton Courtenay in Buckinghamshire, where she made a completely different sort of garden. It was dominated by columnar Irish yews, and in the interstices between the garden became a burgeoning, bubbling mass of cottage flowers. In this she followed a typical Arts and Crafts prescription for a very strong topiary structure with exuberant planting in and around. These ideas were intensified and promulgated through publications like *The Secret Garden* (1911) by Frances Hodgson Burnett. This is the idea of a garden to be discovered by accident, a sort of Tennysonian or Pre-Raphaelite vision of the garden that Burnett described as "the sweetest, most mysterious place anyone could imagine."[19] This was a private space halfway between childhood and adulthood, innocence and sexuality, modernity and antiquity, civilization and chaos.

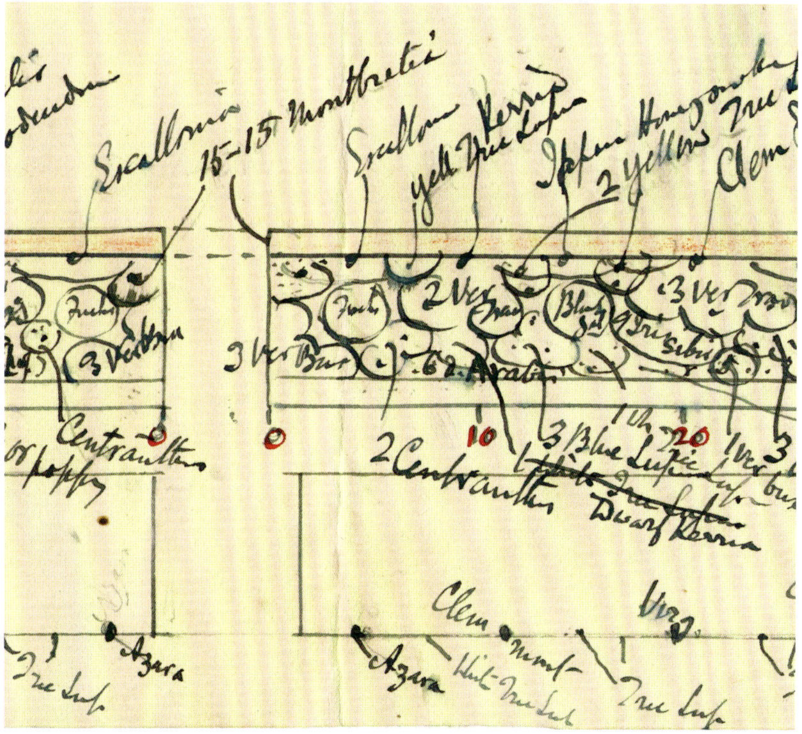

The Edwardian penchant for great swags of rambling roses on walls, pergolas, and on chains and gloriettes certainly owes something to *The Secret Garden*. Indeed, the book became a cult in its own right: Celia, Lady Scarbrough, made a "secret garden" at Sandbeck in Yorkshire immediately after reading it, and even nicknamed her son Dickon, a character in the book. The potent image of the secret garden has been remarkably resilient in the popular imagination and has also informed the romantic idea of "rescuing" a garden (something Dickon terms "'wakenin' up a garden"), which has been another key twentieth-century horticultural preoccupation, enhancing the emotional appeal of restored gardens.

**3-11**

Vita Sackville-West and Harold Nicolson. Sissinghurst Castle Garden. Cranbrook, Kent, England, 1930s+. [Marc Treib]

**3-12**

Karl Foerster.
Foerster garden.
Potsdam,
Germany,
1910s, 1930s.
[Marc Treib]

Sissinghurst is a seminal garden of its kind, developed by Vita Sackville-West and her husband, Harold Nicolson, with relaxed plantings of roses within a tightly controlled though spontaneously conceived structure. Sissinghurst is often described as a garden of rooms, but while it does contain discrete spaces, Harold Nicolson's design was quite loosely structured, and is deliberately illogical and unpredictable: his was not the dead hand of geometry and symmetry [3-11].

The prevailing tone was shabby chic—a kind of gardening version of the aristo-bohemianism of Bloomsbury—a super-relaxed rendition of Arts and Crafts planting in a loose formal structure, a structure that itself feels organically grown. Sackville-West reacted against the artful, pictorial compositions of Jekyll and in the process made a garden more in tune with Eleanor Vere Boyle's poetic romanticism. Nicolson affectionately described Sissinghurst as a "ram-shackle farm-tumble," which sums up its appeal for visitors in his time. As for his wife's gardening style, it was romantic yet practical, experimental but traditional, and in this her approach seemed to chime with that of thousands of others. Sissinghurst has been restored recently under Troy Scott Smith as the head gardener (from 2012 to 2019) and the authentically unbridled atmosphere of the Vita Sackville-West garden is returning.

As the century went on, these ideas were solidified in the writings of Marjorie Fish, a journalist who did a great deal to popularize the idea of cottage gardening. Her principal contribution to gardening was to promote pastel shades. *We Made a Garden*, published in 1956, was a great success. In it she wrote that "We all have our preferences, mine for the pastel shades, for with them it is possible to have a riot without disagreement. Pinks, lavenders, soft blues, and lilacs, with plenty of cream and white never clash."[20]

Fish did a great deal to popularize cranesbill geraniums as well as classic cottage plants such as delphiniums, lupins, nepeta, erigerons, achilleas, and penstemons. Conversely, she disliked oranges, yellows, and sealing-wax red, and helped pave the way for the move in ensuing decades toward a soft and muted color palette of pastels. The proscription of yellow continued in England through the 1970s and 1980s. East Lambrook Manor, her garden in Somerset, avoided any dependence on set pieces like a herbaceous border in that Jekyllian way. The Vita Sackville-West and Marjorie Fish cottage garden style was programmatic in that its intention was to create a transcendent dreamscape predicated on a particular romanticized vision of English rural life. It was not intended to be a simulacrum of nature, but a reprise and an enrichment of a vernacular tradition made by human beings. So, in that sense, it was not naturalistic in the way that term has come to be used.

The garden, instead, unfolded around you as a sort of tapestry, much like being encased within a cocoon. The edges were blurred to achieve a sense of a continuum, an idea that in Britain increased in importance as the century progressed, with attention turned again to mainland Europe—which brings us to the work of Karl Foerster in Germany. Foerster worked as a gardener's apprentice from 1880 to 1891, then spent 1892 to 1893 at the gardening academy at Bordighera on the Italian Riviera under the direction of the plant breeder Ludvik Winter. There, his passion for perennial plants began. He thereafter returned to Berlin and revived his parents' nursery, selling plants then known as "rustic," but which we know today as perennials.

At the time, these plants rarely appeared in nursery catalogs. Most plants then sold were exotic, annual plants with very colorful blooms that were often forced. Foerster's main interest, in fact, was breeding more than planting, and particularly in developing delphiniums. He transformed his own garden at Bornim, near Potsdam, into a sort of Mecca for this style of planting—an archetypal approach in the Robinsonian manner, with lots of plants jumbled up together [3-12]. The basic structure of his garden, however, was Arts and Crafts, an amalgam of Robinson and ideas promulgated through the works of Hermann Muthesius in Germany through the 1920s and 1930s.

Foerster aimed for a garden of interest through all seasons. As a breeder he concentrated on delphiniums, phloxes, and chrysanthemums, this last a species rarely associated with the naturalistic planting style. But the nursery was a commercial business as well as a laboratory, and it also bred and sold asters (Michaelmas daisies) and certain kinds of grasses. In fact, Foerster bred 370 new varieties of plants, tending to prefer those whose qualities he described as "pure" or "brilliant." His main ethos was to keep intact the basic character of the plant in the wild, but he bred plants to make what he considered better varieties for use in the garden. His collaborator Herta Hammerbacher once wrote that

> *Karl Foerster wanted to grasp, exaggerate and embellish the characteristics of a plant, but he didn't want to change the essence of its nature. He always kept the natural form in mind—the delphinium as the mountain forest perennial. It still had to have in it something of the mountain sphere, the elongated, intrinsically*

*graceful. It was the essence of his selections that they were still very close to nature.*[21]

His varieties of delphinium look as if they came from the natural world. A number of key plants, like *Calamagrostis* 'Karl Foerster', still occupy an important place in the vocabulary of planting designers working in this area. For example, his *Rudbeckia* 'Goldsturm' remains very significant, not least in the work of Oehme, van Sweden in the United States. Foerster was later associated with the public parks movement in postwar Germany. One of his pupils, Richard Hansen, was the founder of habitat planting, a quite literal version of perennial plant communities as found in the wild. "The overall aim," he wrote, "was to search for labor efficient plant associations, particularly for use in public green space."[22] One of the reasons the idea took hold was because naturalistic planting schemes were considered low maintenance. In the postwar British environment of public parks, this was, and remains, an important factor when opting for this sort of planting. Whether it is low maintenance or not is a moot point. Aesthetic quality was just one criterion for Foerster. He set up a design company with one of his colleagues, Hermann Mattern, and in their work you can find a sense of house and garden embedded in a natural landscape.

Leaping forward some decades, and from Europe to the United States, we encounter the work of Oehme, van Sweden (OvS), who were outliers working in the German tradition of naturalism. Wolfgang Oehme was German and very much embedded in the principles of Karl Foerster. He had studied with Richard Hansen and came to the United States, to Baltimore, in the 1950s, and worked in private practice as a designer. James van Sweden, though American, was very influenced by European models. He first studied architecture in Michigan and then moved to the Netherlands for post-graduate study under professors Jan Bijouwer and J. P. T. Sander. Van Sweden also came under the sway of Mien Ruys, the Dutch plantswoman and modern landscape designer. Oehme and van Sweden met in 1964, 20 years before what we now call the New Perennials (NP) movement began in Holland with Piet Oudolf and his colleagues.

In the USA, Oehme, van Sweden were really the isolated pioneers of the naturalistic approach to planting and the making of gardens. James van Sweden recalled the first time he experienced the garden of Wolfgang Oehme:

*I'll never forget the moment I walked through the back gate. There was no lawn, just a profusion of color and texture, the fluid movement of foliage and ornamental grasses. The planting was lush and dramatic, with colors ranging from dark green to soft blue-gray. In the summer light everything seemed to be in bloom, and the gentle afternoon breeze added to the enchantment. For the first time I saw how the movement of plants could integrate space and discovered the rich possibilities of great contrasts in scale, color, and foliage. Instantly, I was a believer.*[23]

There is a sense with the perennials and naturalistic garden movement that you are kind of converted to it, an evangelical feel. The Federal Reserve garden in Washington, DC, was the firm's first major public project. Its planting was quite shocking for its time, with many passersby interpreting its roughness as evidence of a lack of care and maintenance [3-13, see also 2-24]. The Oehme, van Sweden planting palette evolved very slowly over the years and they were always reliant on a tried and tested range of plants, a core repertoire of plants that can survive and thrive in the sometimes harsh climates in which they're working. Van Sweden once told me proudly that there were only 32 varieties of plants on the truck from the nursery." I asked, "So what happens if you want a 33rd?" "Well, we get rid of one"—a one in, one out, policy. They edited the plant palette to quite a narrow one. The jacket of Oehme and van Sweden's *Bold and Romantic Gardens* shows *Rudbeckia* 'Goldsturm' and *Echinacea*, species that over time became quite clichéd in NP planting, and which tend to work only in big swaths.

By the 1990s, the O,vS look had become an immediately recognizable "brand," with certain plants (notably *echinaceae* and *Rudbeckia*) familiar to the point of cliché. The designers claimed, however, that their planting style was not a formula but a concept, based on the simple idea of using single species of plants over large areas. Key O,vS plants include grasses such as *Pennisetum alopecuroides*, *Miscanthus sinensis* varieties, *Panicum virgatum* (switchgrass), and *Calamagrostis*. Among the favored perennials were *Perovskia* (Russian sage), *Liatris spicata*, *Eupatorium purpureum* (Joe Pye weed), *Sedum* 'Autumn Joy' and 'Ruby Glow,' *Salvia x superba* 'Mainacht', *hemerocallis* (daylilies), and *achillea* spp. The Evening Garden at the Chicago Botanic Garden uses many of Oehme, van Sweden's key species.

Shifting back to Europe and the precursors of the NP movement. The Thijsse Park by J. P. Thijsse, south of Amsterdam, is known as a *Heempark* or habitat park. These were neither dogmatically native nor scientific recreations [3-14]. Thijsse took native habitats such as woodlands, bogs, dunes, meadows, and heaths, and aimed to distill their character into archetypes while maximizing their aesthetic effect. This was a "pictorial" view that selected key "character species" and used them more intensively than in the wild (as per Robinson). The result was a patchwork of different habitats. Thijsse's approach was influential on the emergent New Perennial movement—disseminated first by C. P. Broerse and then by nurseryman Hein Koningen, who was a "father" of New Perennials, if Foerster was grandfather. One influential book was J. M. Houten's *Native Plants and Their Application in Our Gardens* (1935)—in it, he identified seven types of plant communities: arable, meadows, woodland, peat bogs, dunes, heaths, and moorland. He also listed nurseries supplying this material.[24] Less romantic in feel was the work of Mien Ruys, who in her own nursery in Dedemsvaart filled a modernist structure with naturalistic plantings that were tightly controlled [3-15]. She championed plants such as *Phlomis russeliana, Vitis coignetiae*, and various grasses, as well as many shrubs. There was again an emphasis on "good" or serviceable and reliable plants.

The New Perennial movement really began in the 1980s with Rob Leopold as its key early figure. In 1978 he had established the Cruydt-Hoeck Seed Company, producing a simple catalog consisting of a photocopied brochure on recycled gray paper. It contained a list of seeds of 276 indigenous plants and 73 nonindigenous species and herbs. The other key protagonist, Henk Gerritsen, provided the intellectual substance for the New Perennials movement. Together they mounted several conferences called "Perennial Perspectives," from 1980s through the 1990s, and several plant fairs at the nursery of Piet Oudolf, who over time became the putative leader of the movement. "For our first Open Days [at Hummelo] in 1984 we invited Rob Leopold," he reminisced. "We had heard about him and Cruydt-Hoeck from Henk Gerritsen, who was among our first customers. The Open Days were meant to generate attention and to bring in new customers."[25]

Oudolf talks of what was to become Cruydt-Hoeck's Big Seed list, which implied the creation of a kind of symbiosis between wild and cultivated plants.

> *Traditional gardening is going completely out of fashion; in ten years' time it will be gone, extinct. It is a theme we often discussed with Rob, traditional gardening consisting solely of dogmas, like the colour circle, deadheading, staking, making standard combinations, quickly replacing plants that do not fit the deal, using pots instead, that type of gardening. Actually these were only plant displays, sometimes combined into beautiful borders, but always with a degree of artificiality.... Our philosophy was: getting rid of the dogmas, of the dictatorship of traditional horticulture.*[26]

Revolutionary about Oudolf's approach was his claim to disregard color entirely when he plans his borders. At the Pensthorpe estate in Norfolk, his first big public commission in the UK, there was very little mingling in his style of planting [3-16]. This was an early work, however, and later on, and later in the season as well, the textures and colors really start blending together.

> *The form and structure of plants is more intrinsic to them than colour, and gardeners should be paying it more attention. Flower colour is with us for a relatively short season, compared with the shape of the plant—with perennials from spring until winter. If you want to create plantings that evoke nature and provide a long-lasting season of interest, then you should concentrate on learning about plant form, and think of colour only as an exciting extra.*[27]

For Oudolf, as for Robinson, there is no such thing as a "wrong" or "bad" taste color combination.

It is the shape of the plant that matters, so Oudolf creates repetition and rhythm by using a basic formula of three forms of plant—daisy forms (*Rudbeckias, Echinacea, Asters, Inulas*); flat-capped umbellifers (*Sedum, Angelica, Eupatorium, Achillea*); and spire plants (*Eremerus, Salvia, Kniphofia*)—all underpinned by plantings of grasses. This is the basic formula or ingredient list for the planting of the NP movement. Even if dead, the plants remain very important. Oudolf has said that a plant is only ever any good if it also looks good when it's dead.

Of course, there are critics of this style of planting. Writing in the *Financial Times*, Robin Lane Fox has called it the "waving Eurograsses." Some people in England find it a bit boring, turned away by the relatively limited plant palette. Instead, there was support for wildlife gardening from the 1960s through the 1980s, for example, in the work of Beth Chatto, with a belief in the right plant, right place notion. Chatto, in turn, influenced many designers, including Dan Pearson. At Highgrove, Prince Charles got in on the act with his friend Miriam Rothschild, making a series of wildflower meadows.

The decisive moment for the NP movement in Britain can be dated to 1994, when Piet Oudolf spoke at the "Perennial Perspectives'" conference held at the Royal Botanic Gardens, Kew, which turned out to be a historic moment in British horticulture. At the conference Piet Oudolf announced that he didn't consider color at all in choosing his plants. Of course, this was heretical in the context of the English tradition of color-themed borders. At that time in the early

**3-13**

Oehme, van Sweden. Federal Reserve garden. Washington, DC, 1976. [Marc Treib]

**3-14**

Jacobus Pieter Thijsse. Jac. P. Thijsse Park. Amstelveen, Netherlands, 1942. [Marc Treib]

**3-15**

Mien Ruys. Water Garden, Tuinen Mien Ruys. Dedamsvaart, Netherlands, 1954. [Marc Treib]

1990s there were probably half a dozen books published each year with titles like "Color Theme Your Borders," which have since almost disappeared. By the early 1990s, garden-making in Britain had reached the apotheosis of Arts and Crafts color-theming, its rococo moment in which herbaceous borders had become extremely rich and complex in terms of the variety of plant material involved and the intricacy, subtlety, and complexity of plant combinations selected for color, form, and texture—pumped up as if on steroids. In design terms, it was almost as if the herbaceous border had nowhere else to go.

There was probably no way of anticipating that this ideology—for that is what NP is—would surge across the North Sea from the Netherlands and Germany to influence British planting as the "Dutch Wave." English gardeners and designers who continued with shrubs, roses, and herbaceous borders soon sounded like so many King Canutes, vainly trying to hold back the tide. In retrospect, one can see that traditional English, color-themed border design had reached its apogee or end phase at places such as the walled garden at Hadspen in Somerset, an extraordinarily rich and complex example of connoisseurial plantsmanship, which I recall made me dizzy when I visited.

The narrative or episodic quality to traditional English garden design was to be jettisoned in favor of a garden structure in which there was no beginning, middle, or end, but a continuum of tone created by plantings that was moving toward an immersive as opposed to pictorial approach. More recently, the focus has fallen on the replication or selective quotation of "plant communities" experienced in the wild, and the treatment of gardens almost as labs for horticultural experimentation. The Sheffield School under James Hitchmough has led the way with this "scientific" attitude; another early name for this was "matrix planting" as NP proponents tend to dislike the term "naturalistic."

Oudolf's first project in England, Bury Court in Hampshire from 1996, was surprising in the way its plants had been arranged, which was more through juxtaposition than mingling [3-17]. The second of his large domestic projects in Britain was Scampston Hall, whose field of Molinia grasses greeted the visitor upon entry [3-18, 3-19; see also chapter opening]. The perennial meadow in its center is planted with masses of salvia and monardas. These were gardens not only interesting in the early summer months, but also in late summer and into the autumn—as if we now have a fifth season in gardens that extends from September, October, and into November when these gardens are at their height.

The Lurie Garden in Chicago, with Oudolf plantings, represents a more archetypal approach, with its mix of dark and light palettes, with certain conceptual resonances with the history of Chicago [3-20]. In late summer these plants, mostly but not exclusively native plantings, take on a new life. The planting itself is unmistakably Oudolf, with opulent grasses drifting across the space like chiffon-clad debutantes at a ball, and vivid color diffused by means of drift plantings and the diaphanous screening of feather-topped grasses and other fluffy-flowered subjects. The textural variety is huge. Repetition is a key technique, and for this design Oudolf has used small groups of *Hemerocallis* "Chicago Apache" and oriental poppy as a way of binding the plantings together earlier in the season, planting them not far from the edges of the deep planting panels.

There is an emphasis on native plantings throughout, for example, three species of native coneflowers (*Echinaceae purpurea*, *E. pallida*, and *E. tennesseensis*). As might be expected, native grasses feature strongly, including *Deschampsia cespitosa* (tufted hair grass), *Panicum virgatum* (red switchgrass), and *Sorghastrum nutans* (Indian grass). The spiky *Eryngium yuccifolium* (rattlesnake master) makes a great show in life, with its showy white flower heads—and then in death, from late summer, with its tall, black, skeletal stems. Among all this native material are some Oudolf signature plants from his European palette, such as the fluffy purple Russian sage *Perovskia* 'Little Spire', the ever-reliable cranesbill geraniums, sculptural *Sanguisorba canadensis*, thrusting spindles of yellow *Achillea* "Walther Funcke", astrantias, astilbes, and subtle things like epimediums.

The planting of the High Line in New York City is interesting because it was predicated on these four words or epithets: simple, wild, quiet, and slow. It certainly isn't slow, and it's not quiet (with all those visitors), and it's certainly not wild, given that it requires massive amounts of care supported by a budget many times that of the other parks in the city [3-21, 3-22]. And it's not simple—it's highly designed. In all, the High Line is an example of a sort of naturalistic fallacy.

In Britain today, various designers like Tom Stuart-Smith have taken on the influence of the New Perennial movement in their work. At Mount St. John, the contrast between Stuart-Smith's work and the other half of the garden, in a traditional English garden style, is striking [3-23]. Perhaps more than any other garden designer working today, Stuart-Smith's outlook represents an amalgam of these two major influences: traditional English Arts and Crafts planting and New Perennial. Stuart-Smith's response is the formulation

**3-16**

Piet Oudolf.
Millenium Garden,
Pensthorpe Natural
Park.
Pensthorpe,
Fakenham, Norfolk,
1999.
[Tim Richardson]

**3-17**

*(below)*

Piet Oudolf.
Courtyard Garden,
Bury Court Barn.
Bentley, Farnham,
Surrey, 1996.
[Tim Richardson]

**3-18**

Piet Oudolf.
Walled Garden,
Scampston Hall.
Malton, North
Yorkshire, England,
1999.
[Tim Richardson]

**3-19**

Piet Oudolf.
Walled Garden,
Scampston Hall.
[Tim Richardson]

**3-20**

*(opposite above)*

Piet Oudolf,
Kathryn Gustafson.
Lurie Garden,
Millennium Park.
Chicago, Illinois,
2004.
[Laurie Olin]

of an idea of a "continuum" in a garden that ebbs and flows with the seasons, without the use of specific highlights or designed episodes. This attitude stands in opposition to traditional color-theming, which is carefully organized so that the "mood" of the border or overall garden can be felt to change decisively as one moves through it [3-24].

Following the foundation laid by Oehme, van Sweden, a number of landscape architects in the United States have followed on the New Perennial path. In the United States, among them are Dan Hinkley in Seattle, Ron Lutsko in the San Francisco Bay Area, and Steve Martino in Arizona. Hinkley, who says he is "so over" the mixed border, claims he does not repeat plantings to create unity in the garden, but instead mimics the effect of certain combinations using a completely different palette of plant. As far as color goes, the aim is for "balance rather than harmony."

At one extreme, the naturalistic turn in planting has taken us to a place where "design" is almost a dirty word—it's all about establishing "plant communities" based on habitats found in the wild that are naturally "self-sustaining" and naturally beautiful, if far less diverse horticulturally than a traditional garden. A slew of recent books—such as *Planting in a Post-Wild World* by Thomas Rainer and Claudia West, and *Garden Revolution* by Larry Weaner and Thomas Christopher—promote a vision of gardening as a form of ecological management, while other authors such as Jonas Reif and Christian Kress in *Cultivating Chaos* have been extolling the virtues of self-seeding plants.[28]

At one time the greatest stars of the gardening firmament were garden designers. Now it is the "plant gurus" who hold center stage among the horticultural cognoscenti. People come from other countries—even other continents—to sit at the feet of these sages on open days or during weekly courses, hearing of their exploits in far-flung climes while mentally noting which of their plants might soon become the "choicest" of all—plants available to only a discerning (perhaps "deserving") few customers.

In the UK, the so-called Sheffield School has used technical study to determine seed mixes for plant habitats resembling communities in the wild. James Hitchmough and Nigel Dunnett are its lead proponents. They provide us with tables telling exactly how to create these habitats. It all began in the late 1990s with innocent-sounding articles by Hitchmough and Dunnett—often in collaboration with their colleagues at Sheffield University—with titles such as "New Public Planting: Research to Find Some Alternatives to Shrubs

(previous page)

**3-21** (middle)

Piet Oudolf, planting design; James Corner Field Operations, landscape architects; Diller Scofidio + Renfro, architect. High Line. New York, New York, 2009, 2014+. [Marc Treib]

**3-22** (bottom)

Piet Oudolf, James Corner Field Operations, High Line. [Marc Treib]

**3-23**

Tom Stuart-Smith. Mount St. John. Thirsk, North Yorkshire, England, ca. 2004. [Tim Richardson]

**3-24** (opposite)

Tom Stuart-Smith. The Barn, Serge Hill. Bedmond, Hertfordshire, England, 1990s+ [Tim Richardson]

for Public Planting Schemes" (1997) or "The Ecology of Exotic Herbaceous Perennials Grown in Managed Native Grassy Vegetation in Urban Landscapes" (1999).[29] This research supported the development of a planting philosophy based on the replication of plant communities seen in wild places around the world, parachuted to public spaces in Sheffield, Bristol, London, and elsewhere. Sheffield School adherents do not "design" gardens in the traditional way, with planting plans and color-themed borders, but instead instigate rather than create—sowing seed mixes and then allowing nature to do the rest, intervening only if one plant seems to be taking over. The aim is to create gardens that look as if they have arisen quite naturally, without human intervention: what Sheffield School followers term "enhanced nature." Hitchmough's travels have taken him to South Africa, the Russian steppes, and the Chilean semi-deserts, and he has used aspects of all these habitats in his work, for the idea is not simply to copy an existing habitat but to be inspired by it and then create something practical and appropriate to the British climate. They talk about going to create a meadow with everything they need (handfuls of seeds) stuffed in their pockets. One of their major works was the prairie meadow at the Queen Elizabeth Olympic Park in 2012 [3-25]. The seed mix used has produced incredibly rich meadow plantings with appearances that differ through the year. Although appearing natural and attractive to insects, these too require care—and unlike the traditional lawn, park visitors are not permitted to tread upon them.

We might summarize by saying that in recent years there are basically two schools of planting design: the habitat archetype/aesthetic romantic school with its long history, and the scientifically designed plant community. But is the scientific method truly as scientific as we are led to believe?

### *Issues with the "Scientific" Method*

1. Intensification of plantings—far richer than in the wild
2. Omission of key species as "troublesome"
3. "Random" use of non-native or non-appropriate species
4. Intensive maintenance regimes, including pruning, and on occasion, irrigation
5. Soil preparation, i.e., changing the nature of the soil
6. Not addressing the potential of "invasive habitats": entire plant communities that might behave like weeds
7. Placement of plant communities in "unnatural" (often urban) situations

**3-25**

James Hitchmough and Nigel Dunnett. Meadow, Queen Elizabeth Olympic Park.
London, England, 2012.
[Tim Richardson]

**3-26**

Piet Oudolf. Rivers of Grass, Trentham Estate. Stoke-on-Trent, Staffordshire, England, 2007.
[Tim Richardson]

*Issues with the "Scientific" Tone*

1. An evenness of tone across plantings quite unlike nature, which tends to be uneven and unpredictable
2. The human hand: Every naturalistic-plant ideologist, plant-community deviser, or habitat restorer has a distinctive approach, a signature style.
3. Habitat restorations often lack the tone of real, spontaneous flowerings on wastelands and brownfield sites. In that sense they can be understood immediately as inauthentic.
4. Seeded meadows, etc., are kept pristine, and wild nature is not pristine. It is polluted, compromised, attacked, ignored, unprivileged, poisoned.

*Issues with the "Scientific" Philosophy*

1. The assumption that the Humboldtian emphasis on climate—as opposed to geography—is inherently justifiable as the basis for habitat replication
2. The narrow view, inherited from Ian McHarg, that the only justifiable approach is the "scientific" one
3. The adoption of a high moral tone, allied with the fallacy that natural plantings will improve the populace's morality
4. Non-scientific definitions and vagueness with regard to the concepts of "naturalism" and "authenticity"
5. The cultural cringe with regard to the British horticultural tradition
6. An implausible denial of any deliberate aesthetic intentions

## Conclusion

Landscapes executed in the "scientific" manner can be spectacular and emotionally engaging, but in the finished work nature has been twisted and exaggerated to such an extent as to render the ecological research behind it all but meaningless. In my view, ultimately this method is no more scientifically rigorous than William Robinson's habitat archetypes. After all, the makers of these gardens are planting designers, not scientific researchers, creating landscapes with aspirations toward art rather than science. Distinguishing between the two schools is a slightly bogus endeavor because the scientific designers are really creating their own version of what William Robinson had proposed a century and a half ago. Perhaps these "fake meadows" are missing something: the human hand, the hand of the designer at work, as well as the idea that propelled it. Most people want a garden where the designer and the garden speak to them of something: human communication, a human relationship [3-26]. Of course, science is needed in order to construct our aesthetic ideas, but why should an impression of wild nature be the aim of a garden's design? That said, of course, some very good landscape designs have resulted from this approach, the High Line among them.

On a February visit to the landscape by Piet Oudolf that accompanies the premises of the art gallery Hauser & Wirth in Somerset, most of the plants on view were in fact dead above the ground [3-27]. I do not know how many people would find a garden such as this beautiful, but I certainly did. Perhaps, if well done, any approach to garden-making and planting is viable. But it must be done well.

**3-27**

Piet Oudolf.
*Oudolf Field.*
Hauser & Wirth.
Durslade Farm,
Bruton, Somerset,
England, 2014.
[Tim Richardson]

## Notes

**1** "Nature is perhaps the most complex word in the language." Raymond Williams, "Nature," in *Keywords*, New York: Oxford University Press, 1983.

**2** Tim Richardson, *Avant Gardeners*, London: Thames & Hudson, 2008.

**3** Mark Laird, *The Flowering of the Landscape Garden: English Pleasure Grounds, 1720–1800*, Philadelphia: University of Pennsylvania Press, 1999.

**4** The material in this paragraph, including the quotation from John Claudius Loudon, derives from Jan Woudstra, "The Changing Nature of Ecology: A History of Ecological Planting (1800–1980)," in *The Dynamic Landscape: Design, Ecology and Management of Naturalistic Urban Planting*, ed. Nigel Dunnett and James Hitchmough, London: Taylor & Francis, 2004, pp. 33–80.

**5** William Robinson, *The Wild Garden*, London: John Murray, 1870; and William Robinson, *The English Flower Garden*, 1883, reprint, London: Lawrence King, 1996.

**6** Robinson, *English Flower Garden*, p. 120

**7** Ibid., p. 38.

**8** Woudstra, "Changing Nature of Ecology," p. 29.

**9** Willy Lange and Otto Stahn, *Gartengestaltung der Neuzeit*, Leipzig: J. J. Weber, 1909.

**10** Wilhelm Miller, *The Prairie Spirit of Landscape Gardening*, 1915, reprint, Amherst: University of Massachusetts Press, 2002; Frank A. Waugh, *The Natural Style in Landscape Gardening*, Boston: Richard Badger, 1917; and Jens Jensen, *Siftings*, Chicago: Ralph Fletcher Seymour, 1939.

**11** Wilhelm Miller, *What English Gardens Can Teach Us*, Garden City, NY: Doubleday, Page, 1913.

**12** Stephen Jay Gould, "An Evolutionary Perspective on Strengths, Fallacies, and Confusions in the Concept of Native Plants," in *Nature and Ideology: Natural Garden Design in the Twentieth Century*, ed. Joachim Wolschke-Bulmahn, Washington, DC: Dumbarton Oaks, 1997, pp. 11–20.

**13** Wilhelm Miller, *The Prairie Spirit in Landscape Gardening*, 1915, quoted in Woudstra, "The Changing Nature of Ecology," p. 42.

**14** Eleanor Vere Boyle, *Days and Hours in a Garden*, London: Elliot Stock, 1884, p. 145.

**15** Christopher Dresser, *A Popular Manual of Botany*, Edinburgh: Adam & Charles Black, 1860; and Christopher Dresser, *The Art of Decorative Design*, London: Day & Son, 1862, p. 22.

**16** Richard Redgrave, *Manual of Colour*, London: Chapman & Hall, 1853.

**17** Gertrude Jekyll (and George S. Elgood), *Some English Gardens*, London: Longmans, Green, 1904, p. 63.

**18** Gertrude Jekyll, *Old West Surrey*, London: Longmans, Green, 1904.

**19** Frances Hodgson Burnett, *The Secret Garden*, London: Heinemann, 1911, p. 14.

**20** Marjorie Fish, *We Made a Garden*, London: W. H. & L. Collingridge, 1956, p. 170.

**21** Source not located.

**22** Richard Hansen, quoted in Woudstra, "The Changing Nature of Ecology," p. 34.

**23** Wolfgang Oehme and James van Sweden, with Susan Rademacher, *Bold Romantic Gardens*, Reston, VA: Akropolis Books, 1990, p. 36.

**24** J. M. van den Houten, *Native Plants and Their Application in Our Gardens*, Rotterdam: W. L. & J. Brusse, 1935.

**25** Piet Oudolf, "A Different Way of Looking," Rob Leopold Memorial, http://www.robleopoldmemorial.nl/piet_oudolf.htm, accessed 12 October 2019.

**26** Ibid.

**27** Piet Oudolf with Noel Kingsbury, *Designing with Plants*, London: Conran Octopus, 1999, pp. 16–17.

**28** Thomas Rainer and Claudia West, *Planting in a Post-Wild World*, Portland, OR: Timber Press, 2015; Larry Weaner and Thomas Christopher, *Garden Revolution: How Our Landscapes Can Be a Source of Environmental Change*, Portland, OR: Timber Press, 2016; and Jonas Reif and Christian Kress, *Cultivating Chaos: How to Enrich Landscapes with Self-Seeding Plants*, Portland, OR: Timber Press, 2015

**29** James Hitchmough and Nigel Dunnett, "New Public Planting: Research to Find Some Alternatives to Shrubs for Public Planting Schemes," *Landscape Design*, no. 264, 1997, pp. 49–52; James Hitchmough and Nigel Dunnett, "The Ecology of Exotic Herbaceous Perennials Grown in Managed Native Grassy Vegetation in Urban Landscapes," *Landscape and Urban Planning*, 2–3, 1999, pp. 107–121.

# PLANTING PORTUGAL: WATER, COLOR, TIME

Cristina Castel-Branco

4.

Cristina Castel-Branco (ACB). Amphitheater, Quinta das Lágrimas. Coimbra, 2008. [Photographer unknown]

The planting of gardens in Portugal today continues a tradition of garden-making that accompanied the arrival of the Romans in the second century. In selecting their site at the extreme end of the Iberian Peninsula for what is today Lisbon, the legions considered the quality of the soils and the promise of productive agriculture in a temperate climate—despite the meager annual rainfall and almost completely dry summers. At that time climate and topography, paired with limited natural resources, played a major role in the making of Portuguese gardens, and it still does today. That said, it has been the country's political history since the sixteenth century that has truly determined the importation and use of a diverse array of plants in the composition of these gardens [4-1]. Although graced by a mild climate—temperatures in Lisbon seldom dip below 5° Celsius (41° Fahrenheit)—but hampered by aridity, plant acclimatization has nevertheless tended to be successful and played a major role in the design of the country's landscapes.

During the sixteenth century, voyages transporting live plants from Portuguese colonies in the New World and Africa became so frequent that Frei José Mariano da Conceição Veloso wrote a guide describing how to successfully sustain the plants during their long months at sea. In the section of his *Instructions for the Transportation by Sea of Trees, Live Plants, Seeds and Other Natural Curiosities* dedicated to trees, Veloso tells that "they must be kept on the *tombadilho* [poop deck] and only during times of storms should they be stored inside for some hours.... They must be watered from time to time and if water is rare onboard, rain should be collected.... During times of strong winds and dry heat the plants must be covered with a hood or other form of protection." When successful, the result of these voyages was an abundance of exotic plants for pleasure gardens throughout the homeland.

The two centuries during which a diverse variety of plants and trees traveled the world between Brazil and India, China and Lisbon, and Africa and Brazil represent an important chapter in Portuguese history. Conde de Ficalho, a nineteenth-century botanist, studied this subject in depth and published *Memoir on the Influence of Portuguese Discoveries on Plant Knowledge*. In this treatise he states:

> *It is licit to assert that in no other moment in history were there added to the list of known plants, so many and varied new species. The completely new vegetation of Brazil, southern Africa, the rich flora of India, the Malaysian archipelago, and China... have enriched our knowledge of the world's plants in a unparalleled way, and in short period of time.*

These early investigations by naturalists were soon followed by more systematic scientific studies that in the eighteenth century led to the creation of major botanical gardens in both Lisbon and Coimbra [4-2]. To successfully transport and adopt these exotic species to Portuguese conditions required a sound knowledge of both botany and horticulture. During the following century, the collections of ornamental plants in Portugal increased exponentially: under scientifically rigorous control, plants from around the world were acclimated to reduce the demand for extensive care beyond the irrigation required during the five months of the dry season. Once acclimated, the plants were readily adopted for private gardens and farms. Like many aspects of material culture, however, the preferences for plant species both grew and changed with the times, and the initial excitement over subtropical exotics from Brazil and India was followed in the nineteenth century by a preference for Asian camellias, wisterias, azaleas, and the mixed borders that revealed origins in the British Isles. During the twentieth century—primarily after World War II—the landscapes of the modern movement set aside flowers, horticulture, and variety in ornamental planting, as it did in many of the countries that adopted a modernist perspective.

In Portugal, modernist landscape architecture grew from the same stem as modern architecture, whose spatial ideas and compositional principles were fully expressed by António Viana Barreto in his design for the 1953 Setúbal Park in Bom Fim and the Gulbenkian park in Lisbon, the latter designed and built in collaboration with Gonçalo Ribeiro Telles in 1964. There the two designers introduced an intricate composition of plants that defined spaces and voids, and created perspectives and contrasts in areas of light and shadow with planting designed on the ecological principle of plant succession [4-3].

From both Viana Barreto—and Edgar Fontes, who worked on the Gulbenkian park some years later—I learned to design using local flora; of course, I had already been interested in the lush, colorful, and exotic flora that can thrive in Lisbon. The tradition of rich plant collections used in historical Portuguese gardens that I studied while working on my master's degree attracted me because they were so adapted to our climate: the *Jacaranda*, *Tipuana*, and *Chorisia*, all of which have beautiful blooms [4-4]. These species had become such an integral element of the Portuguese palette of vegetal colors and materials that I considered them "native" and did not follow the demand for the other autochthonous species then in circulation.

**4-1**

Fronteira Palace and garden. Lisbon, ca. 1668. Built by the Marquês de Fronteira, the landscape displays four characteristics typical of the Portuguese garden: exotic plants, views, *azulejos*, and large reflecting pools. [Marc Treib]

**4-2**

Domenico Vandelli; Félix de Avelar Brotero. Botanic Garden, University of Coimbra. 1790s+. A 13-hectare garden in the heart of the city. [Marc Treib]

**4-3**

António Viana Barreto and Gonçalo Ribeiro Telles. Gulbenkian Park. Lisbon, 1964. [Marc Treib]

In 1989 I started teaching plants and planting design at the University of Lisbon, but from the beginning I wanted to avoid the traditional course structure that focused on species identification. The courses I devised were purposely named to distinguish the new approach from the old, and included titles "Plants for the Urban Landscape" and "Plants in the Rural Landscape." In a lecture at our university in 1990, Roberto Burle Marx described plants as artistic materials, much like watercolors for painting, or stone or clay from which to create a sculpture. In response, I created an assignment asking students to deconstruct the chroma of a painting using colored pencils for its later application to planting design. Each color was assigned a number, much in the manner of a paint-by-number hobbyist painting set then in vogue. These colors were then applied to a landscape design studio project, using plants to realize these colors as a landscape that profited fully from the character and chroma of the plant species selected.

While a graduate student at the University of Massachusetts, I became aware of the limits of plant diversity in the New England landscape—especially when compared to the exotic subtropical flora and vibrant blooms so prevalent in Portugal. That realization made me value and understand the potential for designing with a complete range of plants when I returned home. Accordingly, my thinking began to reflect a notion of the "cohabitation" of tropical, temperate Mediterranean and Atlantic plants, which in an intriguing homage to the past suggested that in some ways I was following in the footsteps of the Portuguese plant explorers from past centuries.

## Expo '98, Lisbon: Garcia de Orta Gardens

**4-4**

Jean Baptiste Bonnard. Public promenade, today the Garden of Estrela. Lisbon, 1860s. *Chorisia speciosa* blooming in November. [Antonio Sachetti, 2014]

The Expo '98 world exhibition held in Lisbon celebrated the "opening" of the oceans by the sixteenth-century Portuguese navigators after their arrival in India in 1498. In 1994, a year after being invited to head the exposition's landscape architecture authority, I submitted a proposal to its organizing board for a garden celebrating the exchanges and voyages of plants across the oceans. The administration welcomed the project: a landscape to be called the Garcia de Orta Gardens in honor of the celebrated Portuguese botanist, resident in India, who in 1563 published the first scientific treatise on the existence and use of subtropical plants for medicinal purposes. Working with experts in tropical horticulture from my university, we identified the regions to be represented in the gardens and determined the species to be requested from the governments of countries that ranged from India to Brazil, Mozambique to Macau.

These plants would need to thrive in the Lisbon environment without significant amounts of care.

We were fortunate in negotiating a waterfront location for the gardens and assembled an excellent planting-design team, with the Portuguese landscape architects João Gomes da Silva and Inês Norton called upon to develop the more architectural features [4-5]. Gomes da Silva's team was also responsible for identifying building materials that would allude to the landscapes from which the plants originated. While their design used traditional materials, the resulting gardens were nonetheless innovative and we introduced 80 new plant species to Lisbon. In the end, plants were donated by eight different Portuguese-speaking countries and the Atlantic Portuguese islands, arriving by boat and plane: from Macau in China, from Goa in India, from Timor in Indonesia, Mozambique and Angola in Africa, Brazil, and the Atlantic islands of São Tomé, Cape Verde, Madeira, and the Azores. With Maria João Cabral, a landscape architect and expert in exotic species, I designed a planting scheme for a linear garden (400 x 25 meters) divided into six plots, which was thankfully completed in time for the opening of the exposition on 21 May 1998.

Beginning in the 1990s, however, climate change scientists began to caution that global warming had already begun and was likely to only worsen over time. While the team put it at the bottom of our list of considerations, I nonetheless wanted to use species in the Garcia de Orta Gardens that could continue to thrive in an already seasonally hot climate. Accordingly, I met with the director of Kew Gardens in London and asked him, "Can we expect global warming to affect the growth of the plants selected for use in Lisbon in the years to come? And if so, should more subtropical species be used? How would climatic differences affect their periods of bloom?" His reply informed me that global warming, which was on its way, was a complex issue that had neither a simple cause (climatic warming) nor clear consequences (growth patterns). We were cautioned that the relationship between the two was not predicted to progress smoothly. Extremes were to be expected worldwide, but especially for cities along the oceans. Interestingly, however, a rise in average temperatures could actually permit a larger number of exotic plants to be incorporated into the landscape of Lisbon. So the decision was taken to extend the range of plants selected to include a more risky subtropical array of species.

Within the university consulting team, our selection of plants was guided by botanical experts to ensure the inclusion of species fully capable of thriving and blooming in Lisbon under hotter conditions. Some team members had a hard time accepting this decision, as scarcely anyone would fully accept that climate change was inevitable.

With the concern for global warming always in our minds, our final selection of plants considered three factors:

1. Scientific accuracy in representing the various geographical sites; agricultural crops such as rice, tea, and sugar were also to be included.
2. The aesthetic quality of the garden as a public place within Expo '98 that celebrated "The Oceans."
3. The expansion of the current plant palette for Lisbon gardens after the fair, renewing and augmenting the ancient array of plant species that has existed historically in the city's private gardens.

These were the goals. The challenges facing us included the precise selection of plants; transportation from their native habitats; the quarantine process required before entry into Portugal; and compliance with the requirements of CITES (Convention on International Trade in Endangered Species of Wild Fauna and Flora) agreements that govern the international transfer of endangered species and their propagation. In addition, we had to consider the maintenance necessary to sustain this significant number of novel species, many of which—it must be admitted—were unfamiliar to the design team. A good deal of education was needed to design intelligently; it was a challenge for the making of Expo '98 and a learning experience for the gardens' makers.

The design and selection of plants for each of the six zones addressed the vast differences in climate, soil, nutrients, and water requirements for plants whose origins ranged from the dry zones of Africa to the wet subtropics of Brazil [4-6]. In Lisbon, the African plants, for example, required exposure to 3,000 hours of sun each year; efficient drainage was required but no irrigation was needed. In contrast, plants from the subtropical Atlantic islands needed protection from the wind, an adequate amount of daylight, and a sufficient supply of water. Shade was essential for the plants hailing from Madeira and the Azores—including tea plants from Europe's only tea plantations; accordingly, shade structures were built [4-7]. A large, lofty shade structure was also constructed for plants from the tropical zone; it was equipped with misters to maintain an appropriate level of humidity [4-8]. Positioned in the center of the site, the tropical garden plot was sheltered from the winds by the other gardens, as well as a double allée of umbrella pines (*Pinus pinea*) [4-9]. In contrast, the flora native to Goa and Macau needed no

**4-5**

Chá da Gorreana. São Miguel Island, the Azores, Portugal. Two hundred tea plants from this unique tea plantation—the only one in Europe in 1996—were planted in the Garcia de Orta gardens in Lisbon in 1997. [Marc Treib]

**4-6**

João Gomes da Silva and Cristina Castel-Branco. Garcia de Orta Garden Expo '98. Lisbon, 1998. Basalt walls built of materials imported from the Azores. [Antonio Sachetti]

special protection; their plants thrived magnificently under the conditions of Lisbon and the riverside site.

Of the remaining gardens I will briefly discuss only a selection in greater detail. Representing an African desert in Lisbon presented a challenge to the team. At the northern entrance to the gardens we raised a stepped platform constructed of a warm-colored stone—a reference to the geology of the Bay of Tigers in the Moçâmedes Desert—and planted it with a characteristic ground-hugging *Gramineae*. Each plant, the majority of them from the *Cactaceae* family, was treated almost as an individual sculpture, illustrating the small number of regional species, which include beard grass (*Hyparrhenia*) and climbing aloe (*Aloe ciliaris*).

For the Cape Verde islands, the choice of planting fell on those from the "humanized landscape," from agriculture, using crops important to the island's life and economy. In contrast to the other gardens, which from the outset were intended to feature local flora, the Cape Verde garden featured the hyacinth bean, sugarcane, aloe, Barbados nut (*Jatropha curcas*), and indigo, a plant that once had possessed great economic importance. The dragon tree (*Dracaena draco*) had also been of economic importance at one time, for the extraction of the pigment "dragon's blood." Today it is a rare and protected species. The garden also contained the *Phoenix atlantica*, a palm tree endemic to the region.

Representing the subtropical rainforest, or *laurisilva*, were species such as Azores laurel (*Laurus azorica*), picconia (*Picconia azorica*), *Apollonias barbujana*, and Madeira laurel (*Ocotea foetens*). The traveler's tree (*Ravenala*) welcomes visitors to equatorial São Tomé with its vegetation of unfamiliar forms. In Lisbon, plants from a damp tropical climate cannot live outdoors without assistance. To address this problem, we provided the plants with shade, and irrigation in the form of mist. Native plants blended with introduced species such as the banana (*Musa paradisiaca*), taro (*Colocasia*), and the gourd (*Lagenaria*) that covers the ground with its wide leaves; in Lisbon, it fruits the year round. Shrubs and palm trees, such as the kittul palm (*Caryota urens*) in the Goa garden, mango, and hibiscus recall tropical climes. In other places, religious symbolism linked plants, such as the bo tree (*Ficus religiosa*) and the tree of sadness (*Nycthantes arbor-tristis*). The walk through the different gardens provides changing sensual experiences, passing from the hot desert through the tall grasses of the savanna to the humid tropical orchid forests of Brazil. In the lush garden of equatorial Saõ Tomé, a large fountain and pool accompanied plantations of banana, papaya, and mango trees [4-10]. A large bed of red peppers attracts visitors through the year, its leaves and bloom augmented by a mix of flowers, fruits, and exuberant ground cover.

Although each of the six garden zones could be read as distinct, they nonetheless cohered as a unified aesthetic experience. Both from planting and design, the Garcia de Orta Gardens delighted the eye as well as the other senses—including smell. But the project also constituted a scientific experiment, a laboratory, for testing the possible introduction of new plant varieties to Lisbon. There was little question that the planned cohabitation of subtropical and temperate plants had produced excellent results during the months that the doors to Expo '98 were open to the public. But would this garden and its plants endure as a park for the revived district of the city in which it was to be a part in the decades following the fair?

Twenty years later, in 2018, a carefully executed survey measured the success of the design and the survival of the imported plants. Naturally, the results varied among the regions represented, although the survival rate for the trees was our most surprising discovery. The trees of Indian origin had a survival rate of 93 percent; the African species fared far less well at 53 percent. Sixty-seven percent of the trees from the tropical Atlantic islands thrived; from Madeira and the Azores the rate was 76 percent. The Brazilian trees enjoyed a survival rate of 80 percent, due mostly to their having been acclimatized to the Portuguese situation long before Expo '98. In practical terms, the result of the project was an increase in the number of species that could be used in Lisbon's public spaces and private gardens. In 1981, only 37 species of urban trees had been planted in Lisbon. Eighty-one additional species were first introduced on the Expo '98 site, and today the number of tree species in Lisbon's public spaces stands at 112 [4-11].

Thus, we see that the Garcia de Orta Gardens served as a true experimental laboratory for plant adaptation and that the results were quite positive—not unlike those Lisbon gardens that had adopted exotic species during the eighteenth and nineteenth centuries. Despite the differences in climatic conditions from those of their native lands, 50 new species of trees have prospered. In all, the Garcia de Orta Garden stood in the avant-garde in addressing the effects of globalization on horticulture, and for its attempt to augment the number of appropriate species for use in Portugal during and after global warming. The majority of the plants and flowers used in this trial not only survived but have done well. The loss of the ground covers and the shrubs from

**4-7**

Cristina Castel-Branco and João Gomes da Silva.
Garcia de Orta Gardens, Expo '98. Lisbon, 1998.
Shaded plot with tropical plants from São Tomé and Brazil.
[Antonio Sachetti]

**4-8**

Cristina Castel-Branco.
Garcia de Orta Gardens, Expo '98.
Brazilian and São Tomé Garden planting.
Shade structures and misters supported the growth outdoors of tropical plants such as papaya, mango, and coffee.
[Cristina Castel-Branco]

**4-9**

João Gomes da Silva and Cristina Castel-Branco.
Garcia de Orta Gardens, Expo '98.
Two rows of Italian stone pines (*Pinus pinea*) shelter the water gardens from the winds.
[Cristina Castel-Branco]

**4-10**

João Gomes da Silva and Cristina Castel-Branco. Garcia de Orta Gardens, Expo '98. Goa Garden. Seen in 2018, Twenty years after their planting, the massive growth of *Ficus sp.*, *Erythrina crista-galli*, and *Thumbergia grandiflora* is evident. [Antonio Sachetti]

**4-11**

Chart showing the survival of the Atlantic islands trees after 20 years of growth in the Garcia de Orta Garden at the Expo '98 site. [Courtesy Sandra Mesquita, Francisca Pinto da Costa, João Cabral]

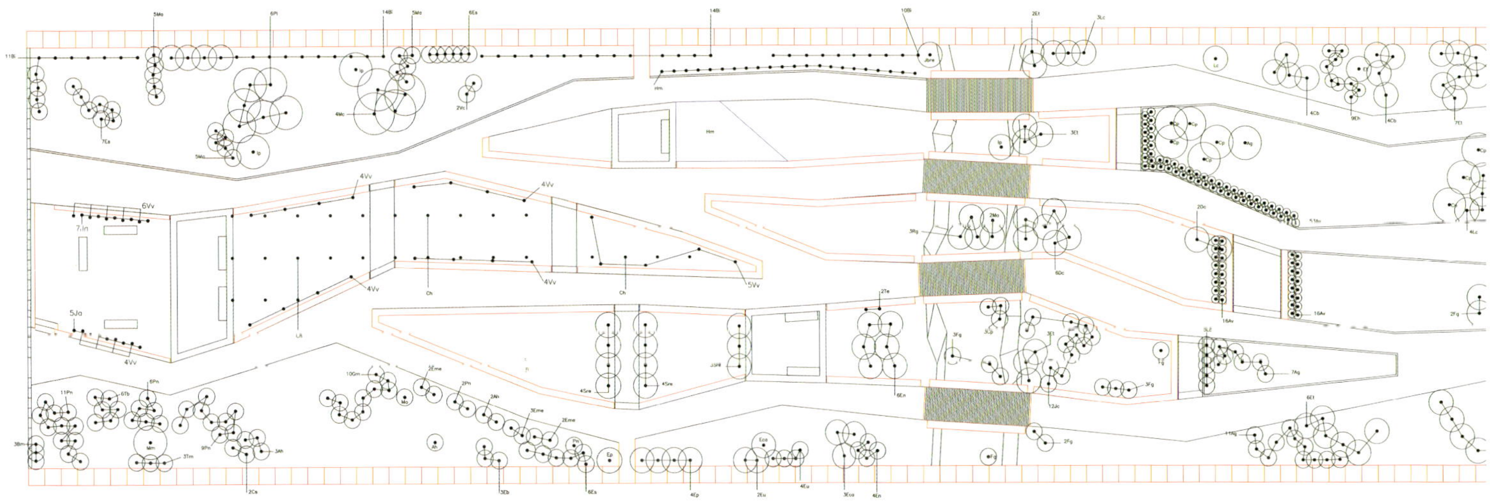

| | Number of species in the original plan | Number of species living in 2018 | Number of losses | % success |
|---|---|---|---|---|
| **MACARONESIA (Cape Verde)** | | | | |
| **Trees** | 8 | 4 | 4 | 67% |
| **Palm trees** | 2 | 2 | 0 | 100% |
| **Shrubs** | 10 | 2 | 8 | 33% |
| **Herbaceous** | 7 | 1 | 6 | 25% |
| **MACARONESIA (Madeira and Azores)** | | | | |
| **Trees** | 13 | 8 | 5 | 76% |
| **Palm trees** | 1 | 1 | 0 | 100% |
| **Shrubs** | 28 | 11 | 17 | 56% |
| **Climbers** | 3 | 2 | 1 | 80% |
| **Herbaceous** | 23 | 2 | 21 | 16% |

**4-12**

Cristina Castel-Branco (ACB).
81 Garden,
Quinta Patino.
Estoril, Portugal, 2005.
Plants, shade, and light.
[Marc Treib]

**4-13**

Cristina Castel-Branco (ACB).
81 Garden,
Quinta Patino.
The selection of plants followed a color palette drawn from the work of Sonia Delaunay.
[Antonio Sachetti]

2008 on was primarily due to lack of maintenance, but their capacity to survive in Lisbon and to be used for landscape design is now secure.

## Water, Color, and Time: Patino, Fronteira, and Lágrimas

Over the centuries, using water to reflect and enhance the presence of plants has been a continuing Portuguese tradition. In 2005 I had the opportunity to design a garden in which to display a private collection of contemporary sculpture at the Quinta Patino, a condominium in Estoril. I considered the garden as a site where art and natural elements would cross-fertilize and shape the space [4-12]. Water and vegetation provide the setting for large sculptural works, while walls of rusted Corten steel receive the shadows cast by the existing umbrella pine trees; the colors of Sonia Delaunay provided my inspiration and point of departure [4-13].

In the garden, shadows equal in importance the flat surfaces upon which they are cast and mark the interplay of steel and pines. During the day, sun and shadows are strong and marked by distinct edges. Light dances on the surface of the water; when the sun is low, the moving water reflects the sunset and lights the underside of the overhanging green roof almost as if dancing. The garden itself could be read as land art and a fitting setting and complement to the sculptures by Antony Gormley, Dan Graham, Thomas Schütte, Claes Oldenburg, and Coosje van Bruggen.

The grounds of the Palácio dos Marqueses de Fronteira in Lisbon includes one of the most important historical gardens in Portugal. Its design is marked by a sophisticated use of of the four key elements of Portuguese gardens: large surfaces of water; a wealth of *azulejos* (patterned ceramic tiles) that cover the surfaces of many walls and ceilings; a large array of exotic ornamental plants; and the manipulation of views both within and from the *quinta* (estate) [see 4-1]. In 2006, the former Marquis da Fronteira requested a new garden for an area set below the main terrace and not visible from within the historical seventeenth-century landscape. The design was required to be of Islamic inspiration, with water flowing in canals, tiled surfaces, and stands of orange trees and cypress used to shape the spaces and shade the seating [4-14]. Eduardo Nery, an artist specializing in *azulejos*, created the patterns and colors of the ceramic tiles that cover the five pools. Vegetation also played a major role. A set of fast-growing poplars (*Populus nigra*) interspersed with slow-growing Mexican white cedar (*Cupressus lusitanica*) screen the views of tall buildings in the distance. Mediterranean vegetation engaged in dialogue with the Islamic ambience: pomegranate and several species of citrus with orange fruits echoed the orange tints of the *azulejos*. An existing *Erythrina* confirmed the use of exotic blooming trees in historic gardens; three more of the same species were planted to complement the historic survivor.

The Quinta das Lágrimas in Coimbra includes a romantic garden dating from the nineteenth century that is dominated by a collection of exotic trees that have grown to substantial proportions: *Araucaria* sp., *Podocarpus* sp., camphor (*Cinnamomum camphora*), banyan (*Ficus macrophylla*), and sequoia [4-15]. In 2008, our office restored the water features and the vegetation that had become overgrown or had completely disappeared. A new place for performances and events was required as the nature of the property had changed from its eighteenth-century origins as a residential palace to its current function as a five-star hotel. In a formerly unused parcel of the garden, a grass-covered amphitheater for events and theater was constructed to accommodate an audience of up to 2,000 people. Trees were planted to augment those already present: exotic species like sequoia, tulip poplar (*liriodendron tulipifera*), and the jacaranda chosen for its beautiful pale violet blooms [4-16; see also chapter opening]. I have no issue with using exotic species in gardens after they have been acclimated and judged as benign to indigenous vegetation. Using only endemic and local vegetation would have provided a palette too restrictive for accurately renovating the landscape, especially considering the superb exotic species planted in the nineteenth century that required an authentic restoration.

In all these projects, I used water to reflect—and thus double—the presence of the vegetation, understanding the relation of reflection to viewpoint and that the angle of incidence equals the angle of reflection [4-17]. In some ways, the use of reflection has become one of my signature design features, and one part of a search for designs that heighten the aesthetic appreciation of plants. Roberto Burle Marx once noted that "Time completes our work." The sequoias that form the screen behind the stage of the amphitheater have already added more than twenty meters of height over the ten years since they were planted—and they have received no special care since their initial planting.

**4-14**

Cristina Castel-Branco. Orange Garden, Fronteira Palace and Gardens. Lisbon, 2010. Water, *azulejos*, and exotic plants designed with the Islamic air required by the client. [Cristina Castel-Branco]

**4-15**

Cristina Castel-Branco (ACB).
Amphitheater, Quinta das Lágrimas. Coimbra, 2008.
The selection of plants to be reflected in the water of the seventeenth-century pool was a strong design consideration.
[Photographer unknown]

**4-16**

Cristina Castel-Branco (ACB).
The Bamboo Pool, Quinta das Lágrimas.
Reflections are a hallmark of the planting design.
[Cristina Castel-Branco]

**4-17**

Cristina Castel-Branco (ACB).
Quinta das Lágrimas.
A lane of sequoias reflected in the surface of the round pool—a strategic aspect of the design.
[Cristina Castel-Branco]

## The Garden of Lost Exotic Ornamentals: Chantilly, Color, and Time

Exotic plants add new dimensions and richness to our gardens and provide an entire world of great horticultural aesthetic effects. To use them, however, requires knowledge and continued learning. Horticultural expositions can provide some of the means by which to acquire knowledge and expertise. The plant exhibitions on view in Chantilly, France, since 2015 followed in the steps of the earlier Journées des plantes in Courson that date to 1983. Held in May and October, the Journées feature the vegetal offerings of some 230 nurseries, which display and sell plants during the three-day event—an event that attracts an audience of about 25,000 people interested in buying and learning about plants and planting [4-18]. Prizes are granted to the most beautiful plants and their producers. The Journées des plantes are hardly the only events of this type, however. There are many others, among them the celebrated Chelsea Flower Show in London, whose juries always consist of experienced plantsmen and women. In Chantilly, the jury can include members from as many as seven nationalities: Dutch, German, Belgian, French, English, Portuguese, and Danish. Prizes are given in four categories. Unfortunately, few landscape architects attend these exhibitions, from which they could learn about the botanical materials crucial to our profession.

During the modernist decades, the loss of interest in plants, their propagation, and maintenance signaled the decline in their position in the making of parks and gardens in Europe and America. Although there have been some significant exceptions, the great landscape architects of the era gave priority to form and simplicity of design rather than stressing selection and composition. The exuberance of the plants found at Monet's nineteenth-century garden in Giverny, for example, stood in exact opposition to the principles that modernism defended: low maintenance, clean design, open spaces with lawns, and local—or even endemic—vegetation used as borders adapted to climate and soil. Of course, we can find exceptions in Europe, Britain, and in the Americas. In his work in Brazil and other subtropical American countries, Roberto Burle Marx achieved extraordinary effects using plants in masses and in low swaths of color [4-19]. In the prevailing pattern for the twentieth-century garden, in contrast, an accent on planting and the use of varieties has been missing, marked by a lack of the horticultural expertise that can be witnessed annually at Chantilly. There we find perpetuated the old nineteenth-century world of gardening as described by Laura Stoddart in *Up the Garden Path* and by Sir George Sitwell in *On The Making of Gardens*.

**4-18**

Journées des plantes. Chantilly, France, May 2017. An event centered on horticultural and botanical education as well as sales, and a biannual competition for the best vegetal materials. [Cristina Castel-Branco]

**4-19**

Roberto Burle Marx. Monteiro garden. Correias, Brazil, 1947. [Marc Treib

In Chantilly one learns about plants; I am quite aware that the aesthetics of plants differs considerably from the aesthetics of planting. However, I believe that a deep knowledge of plants and how to use them is required to compose fine gardens, in just the same way that composers must know musical notes to create a sonata. When Burle Marx was asked by a journalist, "What plant do you prefer to use?" he responded with his own question: "And you? With what letter do you prefer to write?" It is not a question of knowing about only notes or letters or words, but instead how they are used in sentences and stories. In a similar way, we must consider plants not only individually, but also as small groups and in the overall composition, whether a garden, a park, or landscape architecture in some other form.

Will the ideas presented in this book contribute to a renewed and vibrant aesthetics of planting design? Hopefully, yes. As in the past, the garden can serve as a laboratory for trial and adaptation; and if plants introduced to the landscape are not invasive or destructive in some other way, they may even help diversify habitat and stimulate the presence of autochthonous species in a new way, a new synthesis, and perhaps even a beautiful one.

# PLANTING TRADITION THROUGH ABSTRACTION

Erik Dhont

5.

**Unless otherwise noted, all landscapes illustrated in this chapter have been designed by Erik Dhont**

—

La Gara. Geneva, Switzerland, 2015. Yew topiary with cherry trees. [Georg Aerni]

My contribution to this book will be in three parts. First, I will introduce landscapes designed by our office by discussing the influences on my thinking and way of design— that is to say, the heritage that I share and the landscapes I have experienced. Next, I will present a selection of our projects, after which I will conclude with some reflections on the ideas behind our work in the past—and in all probability, in the future as well.

By way of introduction I should note that I was born and work in Belgium, one of the Low Countries of Europe. Over the years the immigration of people from other lands and regions has brought us an influx of materials, gardeners, and ideas, and these have considerably influenced our designs and shaped a good part of our garden experience. Antwerp, in particular, benefited from these additions to our culture and landscapes in the so-called golden age of the fifteenth century. Accompanying these new garden ideas was a particularly rich and rapid expansion of our horticultural practices. We find evidence of this imported knowledge in the recreated historical garden of the Rubens house in Antwerp where we see that the people of those times lived with plants and loved plants [5-1]. It was a way by which to see life. The ornate architecture of the baroque, with its characteristic stepped gables, occupies a major part of our architectural heritage and remains a signature style for our country today. The classical tradition that responded to the baroque was more restrained, with a greater stress on order. Even today we see the continuance of the classical tradition in Belgium in the work of Jacques Wirtz, who relied on a select variety of plants and used them more for the structural organization of the garden than for their inherent beauty [5-2]. While I accept the need to use plants to structure space, my designs rely on plants more to shape the lines of sight across the garden and landscape.

History offers sources from which we can learn. In Italy, for example, in the Boboli Gardens in Florence, the axis for movement—at times in the past used as an expression of power—is important; but for me the line of sight is more interesting than any political interpretation because it suggests places removed from circulation, perhaps more intimate spaces into which we may retreat from the grand promenade [5-3]. For me, the most representative garden in Italy is found at the Villa Medici in Rome. It is a garden structured and disciplined, at the same time displaying a profound knowledge of plants. Despite the seeming perfection of the garden's geometric order, when you look more closely you see what appear to be mistakes—something in the plants and their growth that just does not seem right [5-4]. These

**5-1**

Rubenshuis garden. Antwerp, Belgium, ca. 1600. Reconstruction, late twentieth century. Historic plant collection. [Photographer unknown]

**5-2**

Jacques Wirtz. Vandendriessche garden. Belem, Belgium, 1981, 2011. [Jean-Pierre Gabriel]

**5-3**

Boboli Gardens (La Cerchiata). Florence, Italy, ca. 1766. [Jean-Pierre Gabriel]

"mistakes" are very important to me. I wonder how we can learn from the natural processes that have affected the original design and from how the plants themselves have grown and evolved. These are my basics, and they constitute the foundation of my thinking about plants and aesthetics. Aesthetics are about experience, not about rigidity and abstract thought. Juxtaposition can provoke tension in space. On the other hand, when we consider the significance of heritage as a factor in our designs, it is always advisable to also evaluate what people have said and what people have written in the past. We learn from both experience and study.

Visiting historic places is critical to our learning and ultimately to practice. At Sanspareil in Bayreuth, Germany, the Chinese pagoda and massive rockwork are both indicative of the romantic age in which the garden was realized. The garden still exists and, seen on a visit, as we follow in the footsteps of history, the landscape is still impressive. Sadly, for security reasons, a fence screened by hedges has been added to the top of the rock [5-5]. On the one hand, this new feature is disturbing, if not totally absurd, but on the other hand it adds an architectural overlay and temporal dimension to the garden. It is this architecture with hedges, with neither alignment nor program, these aberrations, that I like very much. Its new form transgresses the historical line and moves beyond the program.

**5-4**

Villa Medici. Rome, Italy, 1544. Mixed laurel hedge. [Erik Dhont]

Of course, in many historic landscapes you still share the pleasure experienced there in the past, not only through vision but through all the senses. In Brussels there is a very fine residence, a house built for an immigrant but really a palace: the Palais Stoclet [5-6]. In 1900, Brussels offered the most favorable tax system in Europe, and this system of taxation attracted people to the city. This immigration fostered a rich mélange of discussions about culture and pleasure. It also stimulated a vastly increased importation of knowledge. Palais Stoclet remains in private hands and still serves the family that owns it. It is, of course, well known in Belgium, and when I was student, I too wanted to visit this famous garden. But how to get in? So I wrote a letter to the owners telling them that I would very much like to visit their garden. In the letter, I suggested that they might maintain their yews (*Taxus baccata*) in a better way and that I could consult with them about how this might best be done. No answer was ever received. That happens.

Regardless, with or without my consultation, the design of the Palais Stoclet displays its embrace of culture and architecture. It is more than a house: it is a total work of

**5-5**

Sanspareil. Bayreuth-Wonseees, Germany, ca. 1744. Engraving of historic rock formation. [Staatsbibliothek Bamberg]

**5-6**

Josef Hoffmann. Palais Stoclet. Brussels, Belgium, 1911. A total work of art. [Photographer unknown]

art, a demonstration of the total art of living—the total art of interior space, of exterior space. You live inside, you live outside; it is a work of pleasure, a work graced by proportion, logic, and balance. But other, more recent works, also appeal to me. During my school years I was more interested in the Bauhaus period than in the history of older times because its buildings appeared more modest than palaces. Its architecture concerned organization and rationalism. I visited Dessau to see the complex of modernist Bauhaus buildings there and was impressed [5-7]. The simple surfaces, the clear organization, the proportions, and the significance of small interventions and details—all have had a large influence on me over time.

On the Bauhaus grounds are houses for the professors, the Masters' Houses, beautiful modernist buildings set in a woodland that embody an architectural vision intended for a new democratic society. Here was a new idea for architecture and landscape, about how together they could create a new and better society for the future. Of course, everything ended abruptly with the outbreak of World War II; in the postwar period, traditions in architecture and landscape returned. But before the war, the Weissenhofsiedlung, a housing exposition held in Stuttgart, also offered a vision for dwelling in modern architecture. Visiting this project today—its design is the product of architects such as Le Corbusier, Mart Stam, and Mies van der Rohe—you feel a sense of history when you realize that at the same time, on an adjacent site, there was the Bundesgartenschau (Federal Garden Show), whose romantic naturalism stood in complete contrast to the ideas of modernism. Here was the confrontation between the future, as seen through modernism, and the conservative past, represented by the traditional National Socialist visions of architecture. Here was the great cultural clash of the twentieth century taking place on neighboring sites.

A client once asked me, "Erik, can you design a Japanese garden for me?" I replied, "Well, we'll try—but we are not Japanese, so we can't really design a true Japanese garden—we will have to translate those ideas into a garden for Belgium." And we did try. When I presented the first design to the client, I said that we should really go to Japan to determine if we had succeeded or not, and perhaps also to determine if any mistakes had been made. We went to Japan and among the many other gardens we visited was the garden of the landscape architect Mirei Shigemori. The garden, with a design begun in the 1940s, is today a historical site. Of course, the overall organization of the spaces is evident, but I found the garden more interesting

**5-7**

Walter Gropius. Klee-Kandinsky Master's House.. Dessau, Germany, 1926. Architecture in landscape. [Marc Treib]

as an exercise in scale [5-8]. The site is not large, but the design is so delicate that its intimate scale becomes very evident. In the garden you witness the taste of the period and the discipline of the landscape architect. But you also experience the poetics of the design, a poetics based on an idea of doing more with less. What can be done through abstraction or through the revelation of a philosophical theme? If we zoom in and focus on a single detail, or for the use of the garden as a vehicle for meditation, we can fly away—at least in our minds. These are the little pleasures of gardens that people often forget, among them the ability of the garden to provoke a more focused regard. It is not only the distinct separation of the mineral from the vegetal; it's more about how design can enhance the place as well as one's thoughts. Japanese-American Isamu Noguchi also achieved this quality in his landscapes.

**5-8**

Mirei Shigemori. Shigemori garden. Kyoto, Japan, 1970. [Marc Treib]

We opened our office 30 years ago. In our early years, a client commissioned us to design a garden for a house dating from about 1600. "How much time do you need for designing the garden?" he asked. I replied, "One year." "One year, just for thinking?" "Yes," I answered. "A historic site requires one year of thought." Fortunately, he gave us that year to think about the garden and its design. Responding to a historic place requires time; you need time to think and reflect to avoid making mistakes. You need time to research and to reflect. You cannot design a garden for a historic site in 14 days—that would be irresponsible. In addition, you also have to engage the client in a series of dialogues so that the result becomes 1+1=3. When a client knows about plants, you can discuss their color and other particular characteristics; you can discuss these considerations in greater detail than with somebody who knows little about plants. You are fortunate when you work with a client who knows about plants.

A garden near Antwerp was designed for people who love plants and know a lot about them. The core idea was simple: to create two "curtains" of hedges using yew (*Taxus baccata*) with a flower walk planted between them [5-9, 5-10]. The hedges also serve a second purpose: to conceal the houses around the site from view—in effect, providing visual protection. The task became a question of how to push away what was undesirable, and to turn a waste area into one with positive characteristics. Of course, hedges require considerable maintenance, but the use and care of hedges is a tradition in Belgium and is familiar to most gardeners. A love of sharing usually accompanies the love of plants. When the shrubs and flowers bloom, you invite friends to walk together between the hedges, sharing the pleasures of color and fragrance and the basic love of plants.

**5-9**

Ringenhof.
Lier, Belgium, 1997.
Topiary walk seen from above.
[Jean-Pierre Gabriel]

Most people believe that hedges should be straight, that hedges should be perfect, that hedges should be a kind of architectonic form. But to me the most beautiful architecture and gardens are not so perfect. Why should we not reduce the emphasis on perfection by using more organic forms? In our studies we design abstract landscape elements, for example, hedges that can create new perspectives within the garden [5-11]. Why can't we mix hedges with different varieties of plants to create an environment particular to the garden and personal to the owner? As studies, as formal research, we make models in plaster just to study and test plant forms and their potential uses—but with no reference to any specific project. If we later choose to use any of these formal studies, we scan the plaster maquettes and develop construction drawings using the computer. In some ways we use these models to reflect our search for limits, to determine how far can we go. In our designs we pursue the limits of what we can ask of the gardeners, and of course, the limits of the property owners. Despite this concern for form, we are also sensitive to location and local vegetation. In the gardens we also treat hedges as topiary, but the plants are always local and endemic to the site: in color and species the garden and hedgeforms share the same properties [5-12]. On the one hand, the garden requires some degree of maintenance, but it requires little water and is in fact a sustainable landscape.

**5-10**

Ringenhof.
Lier, Belgium, 1997.
Woodland walk.
[Jean-Pierre Gabriel]

The idea that generated a garden in Normandy was to create a paradisiacal island within the greater landscape, an island upon which to dream, to dream about life and nature [5-13]. In France, of course, the tradition of clipped hedges is longstanding—Versailles is only the best-known example. But when we design a garden, we always try to provoke ourselves, and perhaps the client, to go a little bit beyond what we are sure of, beyond our normal limits. In one garden we used a new form of topiary executed in yew to create a private terrace, a sort of paradise, a cocoon in an area in which agriculture prevails. In some ways it is a secret garden in the tradition of the Italian Renaissance *giardino segreto*.

Certain of our projects follow a different course and are rationally governed by their elements and our self-imposed restrictions on either the form of the units or their size. In one garden we decided to use only one type of blue stone of only a single size—1.5 meters by 1.5 meters [5-14]. All the terraces were made with that single module; in all, almost 1,000 units were used. A similar restraint guided the design for a garden on a historic property in Geneva, where the shrubs took the form of "diamonds" executed in topiary. These diamonds were intended as a kind of

**5-11**

Garden.
Provence, France,
2014.
Topiary model.
[Reiner Lautwein]

**5-12**

Garden.
Provence, France,
2014.
Gravel garden
with topiary.
[Jean-Pierre
Gabriel]

**5-13**

Garden.
Saint-Hymer,
Normandy, France,
2010.
Topiary model.
[Reiner Lautwein]

**5-14**

Garden.
Saint-Hymer,
Normandy, France,
2010.
Terrace garden
with topiary.
[Jean-Pierre
Gabriel]

**5-15**

La Gara.
Geneva,
Switzerland, 2015.
Yew topiary with
cherry trees.
[Georg Aerni]

**5-16**

La Gara.
Entrance court.
[Georg Aerni]

abstract intermediary between house and nature. As the garden was designed for a banker, we considered how businesspeople relax after business hours, hopefully by taking a walk in the landscape. The garden also serves as the setting for conferences and for making decisions, for example, to support board meetings. A table under the trees or among the hedgeforms provides venues for discussions outside the house, removed from the city, and within nature. Perhaps as a result the bankers will make good decisions about a beautiful future, reaching their conclusions within a natural setting. Complementing the yews are masses of ornamental cherry trees (*Prunus* × *yedoensis*) that in springtime flower a brilliant white [5-15; see also chapter opening]. Some trees are planted close to the terrace, others are planted farther away, and some even farther in the distance to extend the view into the distance. When the flowering trees are at their peak you feel to be among a world of blooms, a feeling determined by the placement of the trees.

Topiary is not always the solution, of course, but considering its shapes and the space it creates may support the consideration of one's limits and what can be accomplished within the limits set by the vegetation and its maintenance. Garden design also concerns light. How can plants and mineral surfaces catch the light? In California, of course, securing enough light is no problem, but at certain times of year in Belgium it can be an issue: light is quite important for us. And there is the social dimension as well. Hedges can be shaped to create spaces that encourage people to meet; smaller spaces might even help push people into conversations. Rather than being about form alone, or even just the spaces hedges define, topiary may be used to guide activity around a site and even provoke unplanned encounters.

The plaster models I cited above are primarily for my own formal investigation and are usually free of any connection to a particular commission. We may also model topographic propositions in plaster, perhaps a small hill or an amorphous form free of architecture. Thereafter, we may transplant this abstraction into the reality of a specific project. In a landscape for a factory, we inverted the direction suggested by the study: that is to say, we created negative rather than positive forms: small dimples in the land shaped to retain water and increase percolation thereafter [5-16]. Much of the thinking behind the design involved considerations of scale as well as form, and the size of each depression was carefully considered as the new landforms are fully visible from the offices of the factory. In times of rain, the terrain becomes a landscape of small pools that reflect the sky; in periods of dry weather, the landscape reads as sculptural terrain. In either state the visual impact is quite spectacular in both size and form.

The hillside site for a garden in Malibu, California, was already rich in vegetation, with the land covered by perennials, grasses, and California coastal live oaks (*Quercus agrifolia*). The owner, an art collector, saw the garden as a setting to display his collection of sculpture to advantage. As the existing vegetation was already beautiful, in response to the owner's request we proposed a garden made only by sculpting the terrain. Those unavoidable features that disturbed the existing situation were concealed—not with hedges, which is not the tradition in California—but by grading the site. The reshaped land was then hydroseeded and planted with the endemic oaks—a renaturalization of the southern California landscape [5-17]. By manipulating the topography, we could completely remove the neighboring houses from view, and through grading also make the mountains appear as part of the property. Some sculptures were installed near the stream, which provided a setting of greater intimacy. Rather than stress the richness of the collection by density, we tried to find the right position for each sculpture, joining together art and nature. In contrast to the naturalism of the greater garden landscape, the tennis court reflected rationality. We doubled the thickness of the wall surrounding courts to 1.2 meters (roughly four feet) so that the architecture became more quiet. Exaggerating the wall's dimensions produced a greater sense of calm while giving the new planting greater prominence.

About the same time we were making the garden in California, we were also designing a garden in the Azores on a piece of land almost in the middle of the Atlantic Ocean between America and Europe. There we purposely overscaled the thickness of the walls of lava stone, again to create a greater sense of intimacy [5-18]. The wind from the seas blows almost continuously in the Azores. The winters can be cold, their storms intense, and protection against the wind is a necessity. But we also considered the process of occupation and aging: What will the clients do when they are 85 years old? The garden should be enjoyed not only by those who live there now, but also by those who will live there for a long time. Perhaps they will no longer jump from the bench into the pool; perhaps they will enter the water slowly, from the shore. We continued the use of a local material, lava stone, which had been used for a path and walls by prior owners of the site. New stone walls shaped different rooms, among them the kitchen garden, the herb garden, and the other pleasure gardens that

**5-17**

Garden.
Malibu, Los Angeles County, California, 2007.
Topographic garden.
[Jean-Pierre Gabriel]

**5-18**

Garden.
São Miguel, Azores, Portugal, 2008.
Fieldstone pool.
[Jean-Pierre Gabriel]

**5-19**

Garden.
São Miguel,
Azores, Portugal,
2008.
The microcosm
of plants.
[Jean-Pierre
Gabriel]

surround the house. The dialogue with the local people was very important; we wanted to have the artisans take pride in their work and to do the job well. I feel the dialogue with the people who build and maintain the garden is very important; in Belgium this often concerns the gardeners who will maintain and cut the hedges; in the Azores it concerned the masons who build walls in the traditional manner. While essentially a series of closed and protected outdoor rooms, in strategic points the walls open to reveal the landscape and the sea. We used a diversity of drought-tolerant plants like *Euphorbia*, *Erica*, and *Salvia* to provide accents of color throughout the seasons [5-19].

We have our own traditions in Europe that, unfortunately, we sometimes forget—like the decorated gazebo from the times of the baroque garden. We don't live in the baroque era anymore, of course, but we can adopt elements and practices from prior periods that may still provide us with pleasure. In this garden outside Brussels we constructed a palisade comprised of gingko trees. Their canopies have been clipped to create a hole through which we can see the sky [5-20]. While the void may at first appear like a Skyspace by James Turrell, I think of it more as a fresco by Giovanni Battista Tiepolo, with little birds—rather than angels or putti—flying in the lunette of the sky. These are the pleasures often missing in the garden, or those we often forget to experience.

In many projects we try to link the landscape design with architecture or with plants and forms sympathetic to the architecture of the house, particularly if the building has heritage value. Sometimes, however, I think this link is not necessary and that the garden design can stand on its own, more independently. For this old house in Germany we felt it was perhaps better not to design too much. We ordered some very large pieces of stone from a nearby quarry and hand-cut the slabs for the path on site, as if we had no machines. The stones were laid as natural paving with *Dianthus*, *Thymus*, *Polypodium*, and *Crocus* planted between them to conjure a sense of calm [5-21]. Walking on the pavement, one might fear stepping on a plant, and thus becomes more focused on the plants between the stones. This diversion may result in reduced stress—or so we would like to believe. Any mistakes made in the cutting or installation actually help create something new. With similar thinking, I proposed a monumental 8-meter-wide, 50-meter-long, approach to a new crematorium near Brussels. The effect of the promenade is, again, to produce distraction and calm, to remind you why you have come to that place. Here we nod to the power of nature. You begin to understand that your life is little when seen against all of nature. Perhaps that is consoling. Given the function of the crematorium, the primary issues in designing the landscape were psychological as well as functional, but the design was also an exercise in scale.

Topiary can be sculptural and may be read in different ways. One of my clients, a lady, said, "Erik, your topiary is so masculine, it should be more feminine." "OK, I will try," I replied. Responding to her concern made me smile. Of course, topiary can also be used to create a context of intimacy, filled with light, and graced by subtlety. Another client asked us to design a labyrinth. As the labyrinth is not really of our period, the problem was not only its basic configuration but also a question of what would occupy its center. Of course, as in older times, you could just put a statue of Diana or Venus in the center, or just a plant. Instead, we proposed putting a bench with a rock, inverted—in effect, a rock that represents both the center of the labyrinth and the center of the world. After reaching your goal you can sit on the rock, surrounded by plants, and experience the joy of nature. Perhaps you don't need much more than that in life.

**5-20**

Garden.
Ohain, Belgium, 2008.
Ginkgo palisade that forms an occulus.
[Erik Dhont]

**5-21**

Garden.
Coburg, Bavaria, Germany, 2017.
Naturalized perspective with new meandering stream and planted islands
[Jean-Pierre Gabriel]

# ADDRESSING DIVERSITY: PLANTING DESIGN IN THE BAY AREA

Andrea Cochran

6.

**All landscapes illustrated in this chapter have been designed by Andrea Cochran Landscape Architecture.**

—

Walden Studios. Geyserville, California, 2006. [Marion Brenner]

I moved to San Francisco in the early 1980s, never expecting to stay here for any extended period of time; perhaps I'd stay for a couple of years and then move back to the East Coast where I grew up. But over time the climate and the culture became a part of my identity and today I feel almost native. Although I first found its culture quite distinctive and very different from the culture of the East Coast with which I was familiar, the work of Andrea Cochran Landscape Architecture has reflected its location primarily in the San Francisco Bay Area. As I see it, Bay Area culture began to form during the Gold Rush, accompanying the influx of the 49ers who came to California in search of an improvement to their lives, immigrants from other parts of the country and from other parts of the world. They brought with them both the cultures and the prejudices of those places from which they came. But despite the cultural baggage that accompanied them, they felt that here in California they could enjoy a new beginning. It's no surprise then that in the 1960s, the Free Speech Movement gained momentum in the Bay Area. Or that the pioneering electronics companies found their origins in the Silicon Valley. In Northern California there has been and remains a culture holding that almost anything is possible. Certainly, the Bay Area has provided me with opportunities unattainable in any other place.

In my early years in San Francisco I would go to a party and people would ask, "What do you do?" and I would say, "I'm a landscape architect." If I had given that same reply in Boston, the response would have been something like, "Well, you know, my holly bush has some dots on the leaves. Do you know what's the matter?" And I would say, "Well, no, I'm a landscape architect, not a horticulturist. I design gardens." In the Bay Area, however, people actually knew about landscape architecture and could even name landscape architects. It was incredibly uplifting to live in a place where people understood the nature of a design professional. In terms of landscape architecture a large part of that awareness was probably due to *Sunset* magazine, which for decades had broadcast the idea of modern living—inside a modern house and outside in a modern garden. That focus was foreign to the lifestyles presented in magazines in most other regions in the country. Modern design and landscape architecture were really part of the public consciousness from the 1940s on, with celebrated works such as Thomas Church's Donnell garden and Garrett Eckbo's and Lawrence Halprin's residential and public landscapes. Modern landscape architecture was more advanced in the Bay Area than in any other part of the country, and as far back as the 1930s Eckbo had applied to landscape design ideas of space and structure interpreted from modern architecture and the paintings of Wassily Kandinsky: palm trees used as colonnades, overlapping spaces, and a nuanced and layered approach to defining space. And there were lessons from the agricultural landscape as well. California's Central Valley grows fruits and vegetables for much of the country and the greater world beyond. Passing through the fields and groves of the Central Valley you see row after row of almond, peach, and fruit trees of other species, all displaying a strong geometric order in their planting that for me recalls the landscapes of Dan Kiley. The grapevines of the Napa and Sonoma Valley vineyards drape themselves across the contours and encroach into the natural landscape, thereby constructing intersections between artifice and nature. In California modern landscape architecture has been diverse in expression, widely popular, and accepted as the norm. My own ideas and work have been shaped by these landscapes.

For a project on the site of a former prune packing plant in the wine country, we were required to raise the level of the building and the adjoining land about four feet above the floodplain, in the process creating a landscape that is highly artificial. That adjustment to the topography brought eye level above the vineyard and opened the views to a panorama that spanned the valley. As a totality, the result was a layering of agriculture and nature articulated by the addition of 300-year-old olive trees (*Olea europaea*) with sufficient weight to serve as punctuation marks in that greater landscape [6-1].

In the early part of the last century the entire valley would have been planted with orchards of prune plums. Trains on a local rail line picked up the dried fruit for shipment to the East Coast and Midwest. Today the entire landscape is planted with grapevines, of course. In our design we sought to recall the memory of that agricultural landscape in our plant selection by creating a bosk of Korean sun pears (*Pyrus fauriei* 'Korean Sun') that witnesses vivid seasonal change: yellows and russets in the fall, white flowers in the spring [6-2]. The landscape was also designed to harmonize with the architecture: Where does the one end and the other begin? To further the interconnection between building and agriculture, an allée of fruitless mulberry trees (*Morus alba* 'Fruitless') aligns with an entry door that leads out to the vineyard and creates an outdoor room for a communal table [6-3].

Incredible diversity in our environment and microclimates of the Bay Area accompanies the region's human diversity. Within an 80-mile radius of San Francisco, the annual rainfall can vary from 80 inches to only 10 to 15 inches, and at times the temperature might be 65° Fahrenheit in

**6-2**

**6-3**

Walden Studios.
Geyserville,
California, 2006.
[Marion Brenner]

San Francisco, while in the Napa Valley it may register 100° Fahrenheit or more on the very same day. In the summertime, heat from the Valley draws the cool air inland from the ocean, an interaction of hot and cold temperatures that produces the fog for which San Francisco is known. Wind, drawn from the ocean to land through gaps in the natural topography, is a very significant consideration when selecting plant species in the Bay Area.

Along the northern coast high rainfall nurtures the growth of redwoods; the conditions of drier inland areas produce oak woodlands, the savanna, and chaparral. Together, as in every specific ecological zone, these diverse conditions have generated and supported very different kinds of plant communities. Those differences in species and climatic zones condition a large set of microclimates that influence the method employed on each of our projects and provoke designs marked by diverse approaches and diverse types of visual interest.

In Northern California, we consider the oak savanna landscape to be our most representative type, and due to the ubiquity of this grassland ecosystem, we most often work in that environment. The grand scale of this landscape—far larger than the East Coast landscapes with which I had been familiar—also required an adjustment on my part after my move to California. Working with that larger scale allows for design ideas that can be minimal and powerful at the same time.

For Stone Edge Farm, a property near Sonoma, we were asked to create the landscape for a 3.5-acre site adjoining the client's 16-acre organic farm. Formerly the site of a dilapidated commune, the property sits on a deep alluvial plain adjacent to Carriger Creek. The site was flat, its only distinguishing feature an extraordinary stand of 500-year-old California coastal live oaks (*Quercus agrifolia*) and bay trees (*Umbellularia californica*). These trees were of incredible scale—the joined arms of five people could hardly circle the trunks of one of the bay trees. The challenge for the new design was to create a new landscape that would balance with the scale of the ancient trees.

Carriger Creek is filled with deciduous willows and in winter the neighbor's home across the creek becomes visible. To screen the adjacent property, we planted a long allée of 100-year-old olive trees (*Olea europaea*), referencing the oil produced on-site . The characteristic silver coloring of their leaves blurs the distinction between their leaves and the leaves of the willows in the creek—while creating a landscape that holds itself against the five-centuries-old trees in other places on the site. The technique we used recalls the idea of borrowed landscape: here the new planting dissolves into the native willows and makes the property feel larger than it is [6-4].

From April to October the entire property receives no rain. In winter, however, the site can be flooded by up to two feet of water. To divert the water around the buildings, we created a swale that directs the water into a seasonal creek bed that remains dry most of the year. To adapt to these seasonal variations of wet and dry, we planted Mauritius hemp (*Furcraea foetida*), which grows to nearly six feet in height, in addition to bearded irises, and other naturalized and native bulbs. In spring the landscape enjoys a burst of color [6-5]. As these early blooms fade, the very structured landscape reappears, a landscape with sufficient weight to hold itself against the ancient trees. In some ways the easy part of the project was to link the existing trees with the allées; the more difficult issue was how to treat the remaining two-thirds of the site that surround the building.

The Bay Area climate is Mediterranean, and this seasonal aridity, as noted above, has influenced my approach to landscape design—in fact, understanding the characteristics and effects of the dry months has been a necessity. Species must be selected carefully, choosing plants that will survive in the dry season and yet offer visual and sensual interest throughout the year. The coastal live oak native to the land neither requires nor appreciates irrigation in summer, and inappropriate planting around the oaks can actually kill the tree. For this project we worked with an arborist to devise a macrobiotically alive leaf litter that supports the life of those trees. Surrounding the building are bear's-breeches (*Acanthus mollis*), whose strong structure stands up well against the architecture and large trees with sculptural forms that include the native buckeye (*Aesculus californica*) [6-6]. The *Chondropetalum tectorum* planted near the swimming pool has a flower which at its tip matches in color the Corten steel panels sheathing the observatory adjacent to it. These shared colors create reciprocal references between the plantings and the architecture that establishes links between them. In all, through management and addition our work on the site has produced a landscape edited rather than created completely anew, a landscape sympathetic to the native vegetation [6-7].

The drought-tolerant meadow—an idealized planting reminiscent of the native grassland— serves as the landscape's principal feature and joins all the elements of the built

**6-4**

Stone Edge Farm. Sonoma, California, 2007. [Victoria Sambunaris]

**6-5**

Stone Edge Farm. [Marion Brenner]

landscape and connects with the surrounding environment. Employing a grass matrix previously recommended by the grass expert John Greenlee, the meadow evoked a "nature" as beautiful as the native species (while being strong enough to survive invasive weeds and adaptive to the climate). In this case, we mixed two grasses native to Mediterranean climates— *Pennisetum spathiolatum* and *Festuca mairei*— selected for their very similar thin blades. From afar, the grasses appear to be a monoculture, but two grasses actually interjoin throughout the meadow [6-8]. As it happens, the flowering times of the grasses overlap, with a golden color that begins earlier and ends later than either species if used alone.

Meadows and grasslands change form as well as color through the seasons. The vegetation emerges as small shoots in the spring and grows to a height sufficient to form ever-changing spaces thereafter. Above the grasses, the olive trees form a canopy that creates a space linking this new landscape to the landscape beyond. The chromatic tone of the meadow in spring is a limey green that plays well against the pink blossoms of the cherry trees (*Prunus serrulata*). The silver of the olive trees beyond fade into the distance; grasses prevail in the middle ground. In a smaller section of the property, the little bluestem grass (*Schizachyrium scoparium*) takes on a pinky cast in the fall and corresponds chromatically to the pink berries of the pepper tree (*Schinus molle*). Throughout the property the strong structural landscape supports a second landscape subtle and diaphanous [6-9].

Like landscapes by Peter Walker, the work of the minimalist artists like Donald Judd has influenced my thinking and designs. At Judd's Chinati Foundation in Marfa, Texas, for example, it's difficult to discern where the sculpture ends and the galleries begin, and the point at which the galleries join the fields beyond; they're all inextricably linked. Making connections like these is important to me. At times establishing these links is achieved simply by maintenance, for example, by cutting and removal.

For Baker Lane Vineyards in Sebastopol, the landscape design reveals connections among the historic Gravenstein apple orchards that grow in the western part of Sonoma County, the grape vines planted later, and the *Pennisetum spathiolatum* and gaura (*Gaura lindheimeri*) of the new landscape. Further up the hill, dwarf olive shrubs (*Olea* 'Little Ollie') ground the building in the agricultural landscape [6-10].

**6-6**

**6-7**

Stone Edge Farm. Sonoma, California, 2007. [Marion Brenner]

A house above the Napa Valley by architect Michael Maltzan was sited adjacent to the crest of a hill and configured so that the native grassland would pass through its center. The planting design blends the domesticated landscape with the wild landscape that provides the project its natural matrix, although the edge distinguishing the two remains fluid [6-11]. The foreground planting, of small cape rush (*Chondropetalum tectorum*), which we selected for its mass and dark evergreen foliage, provides structure and marks the path leading to the entry. Complementing this is a "no-mow" lawn of *Carex pansa*, a native grass with an unkempt appearance, which bleeds into the more native landscape beyond [6-12]. The meadow landscape designed by John Greenlee uses a mix similar to that for the meadow of the Stone Edge Farm, with the notable addition of *Epilobium canum* (California fuchsia).

The concept of allowing the new landscape to seamlessly blend with the native landscape also informed our design for a garden in St. Helena, also in the Napa Valley. A salmon creek running through the site required that all the planting along its banks be exclusively native. In addition to shrubs like ceanothus and coffeeberry (*Rhamnus californica*), we planted blue grama grass (*Bouteloua gracilis* 'Blonde Ambition'), which quietly moves in the breeze. Closer to the house the tall, non-native *Calamagrostis x acutiflora* 'Karl Foerster' screens an outdoor dining area. The softness of the grass bridges the gap to the native landscape, which results in a cohesive site design [6-13]. A zigzag path of steppingstones weaves through layers of grass and dwarf olive shrubs (*Olea* 'Little Ollie'), clipped as hedges to reference the larger olives trees behind them. Once again repetition, uniformity of color, and the contrast of gold and blue were basic to the design [6-14].

Low hedges of tightly clipped *Escallonia bifida* contrast with the riffled appearance of the working vineyard beyond. The pool fence is covered with Virginia creeper (*Parthenocissus quinquefolia*), whose leaves have a similar shape, texture, and color to those of the grapevines, especially in fall [6-15]. The plantings create distinctions between near and far, domestic and productive, but the edge between them is always soft and ambiguous—like a line drawn in the ground but partially erased. The structure of the planting remains very evident, but the selection of the species and the configuration in which they are planted renders that structure less distinct.

For a project in Michigan we applied lessons first learned working in California. Alongside the house is an area that

**6-8**

Stone Edge Farm. Sonoma, California, 2007. [Victoria Sambunaris]

**6-9**

Stone Edge Farm. [Marion Brenner]

**6-10** *(opposite)*

Baker Lane Vineyards. Sebastopol, California, 2006. [Marion Brenner]

**6-11**

**6-12**

Hilltop Residence.
St. Helena,
California,
2010.
[Richard Bloom]

**6-13**

**6-14**

Bella Oaks Vineyard. Rutherford, California, ongoing. [Marion Brenner, 2016]

traditionally would be occupied by an evergreen ground cover or low shrubs. In their place, we planted grasses that appear monolithic in form, yet move softly together in the wind. We again layered the planting so that it ultimately blends with the native landscape beyond [6-16]. A double row of river birch (*Betula nigra*) provides a soft foil for the architecture of the house, a bosk that casts light, dancing shadows on the white walls of the house. An underplanting of grasses adds a golden note of contrast to the greens of the birches and the white surfaces of the building.

It has been said that in California "everything grows here, but not everything belongs here." The landscape of the state has resulted from the contributions of many cultures and many horticultural traditions over time. The Spanish brought the grapevine; perhaps the Italians or the Italian Swiss brought the olive; the eucalyptus so prominent in the landscape has origins in Australia; and many ornamentals arrived from New Zealand and South Africa after World War II. The resulting landscape is a composite: although not entirely native, it feels right here. These different cultures inform our landscape designs and contribute a diversity of plant material. This is a very edited landscape, and also very sculptural and very quiet. In California, we have recently suffered through several years of drought. Australia has dealt with droughts for the length of its history and over the centuries many drought-resistant plants have evolved that also grow well here. One of them, *Lomandra*, looks almost like a grass and in some ways is perfect for our own dry conditions: It is an evergreen that demands little water. It's a good filler plant next to a building and serves as an edge that ties well with the larger landscape. Unfortunately, its color is a bit chartreuse in direct sunlight (although greener in the shade), so we usually set it against blue plants like the century plant to avoid an oversaturation of yellow-green. I happen to love eucalyptus trees and in this particular project on Telegraph Hill in San Francisco, the deck is cantilevered so that you can almost touch the bark of the trees [6-17].

Not everybody wants California to look like California, of course. Given the many diverse cultures in California, there are times when the design more particularly reflects the wants of the owners rather than the geographic conditions in which the project is located. The client for this garden in the Bay Area comes from the Midwest and wanted to have his garden look more European. Here littleleaf lindens (*Tilia cordata*) are flanked by hedges of boxwood and *Pittosporum tobira* 'Wheeler's Dwarf' used in layers as they ascend the hillside. The planting for the garden was itself drawn from several cultures: the chartreuse hydrangeas and boxwood that occupy the foreground are backgrounded by bay laurel trees (*Laurus nobilis*) and on the perimeter lavender is planted in rows; and then finally a row of Washington hawthorn

**6-15**

Bella Oaks Vineyard. Rutherford, California, ongoing. [Marion Brenner, 2016]

**6-16**

Dresner landscape. Birmingham, Michigan, 2014. [Marion Brenner]

**6-17**

Cliff House. Telegraph Hill, San Francisco, California, 2015. [Marion Brenner]

**6-18**

Belbrook Gardens.
Atherton,
California, 2008.
[Marion Brenner]

trees (*Crataegus phaenopyrum*). The lavender is particularly beautiful when in bloom, a purple-blue mass that on this large scale really packs a big visual punch [6-18]. The client for a garden in the Alexander Valley in Sonoma County wanted a landscape that recalled the fields of Provence. Rows of flowering quince (*Chaenomeles speciosa*) and lilacs stand behind the clipped balls of lavender and in turn join with lines of the native ceanothus [6-19]. Although we mixed and matched in creating the planting palette, the forms and characteristics of these two species combine well with our native landscape.

A hundred years ago, salt marshes dominated the shores of the San Francisco Bay, but over the decades these have been progressively filled as development has encroached on the water's edge. The idea for this garden at the new Mission Bay campus of the University of California, San Francisco (UCSF), was propelled by a memory of the former landscape and to recall what once had lived there. Like the parks proposed by Garrett Eckbo for the Farm Security Administration in the 1930s, a court of palm trees (*Phoenix canariensis*) shapes the north entrance to the campus. To the rear, we screened the temporary power plant with a vegetal structure that could balance the weight of this building for cardiovascular research—the landscape will exist only until the construction of a new laboratory building some time in the future [6-20]. Plantings of giant timber bamboo (*Bambusa oldhamii*) stand behind a diaphanous fence whose weight supports the plants and structures their volume. Before it, run bands of cape rush (*Chondropetalum tectorum*).

For the campus courtyard, we sought a landscape in which people could sit, reflect, escape, and possibly encounter one another. The courtyard faces south and is defined on one side by a west-facing wall. In many places and climates the afternoon sun is problematic, but in the fogs of the San Franciscan summer, temperatures can be so cold that protection from the wind is desirable and the sun is welcome. Rather than using trees—there is only one tree planted in the courtyard—the planting is developed as a layered composite of grasses: vegetation that will shift in the wind that accompanies the arrival of the fog [6-21]. Perhaps paradoxically, while offering protection we actually celebrate the wind rather than fight it. A screen wall of bamboo defines the space. Grasses are all planted in linear bands: *Juncus patens, Deschampsia cespitosa, Calamagrostis* 'Karl Foerster', and *Panicum virgatum* 'Shendandoah'. These lines span the courtyard and are tall enough to form spaces that are protected and feel safe. Rather than lawn grass, the design used a native grass meadow mix produced by Delta Sod. Meadow grasses yield a softer texture that suits the reinvented paradigms of beauty we thought appropriate for this landscape [6-22]. Unlike the precision of the planting in the courtyard, some of the meadow areas have a certain messiness to

**6-19**

Alexander's Crown. Healdsburg, California, 2005. [Marion Brenner]

them—but its a controlled messiness. In the Bay Area, autumn produces only small changes of color and texture in trees and plants, but like the reds in the grasses, however subtle, they can have a strong visual impact. Beneath the entire courtyard is four feet of permeable gravel that retains stormwater on-site to help maintain the water quality of San Francisco Bay.

Also on the UCSF campus is the landscape for its southern entrance, which fronts a building called Mission Hall and a new hospital. In our meetings, community groups requested flowering plants. We considered flowers like geraniums inappropriate. In their place we selected succulents that produce handsome flowers, and succulents that can withstand the wind that passes through the site: *Echinopsis pachanoi*, aloe, agave, and *Dasylirion carbapenopsis*, all of which are sculptural as well as drought tolerant. These have been planted in layers set against the of rows of Chinese elms (*Ulmus parvifolia*) [6-23]. After four years of drought we thought it was time to propose new paradigms of beauty proper for public places. If our design is judged to be successful, we hope it will inform people about a more appropriate direction than many of those followed in the past.

In reviewing our work for my talk, and now this chapter, I found that we have been selecting plants that might change the ways of considering what is appropriate and what is beautiful for the San Francisco Bay Region and Northern California. Using the right plant in the right place in the right configuration also has the ability to connect people to the larger environment and help them view the environment in a more informed way, even at small scale. This remains the goal for landscapes designed by Andrea Cochran Landscape Architecture.

**6-20**

**6-21**

Smith Cardiovascular Research Center. San Francisco, California, 2012. [Marion Brenner]

**6-22**

Smith Cardiovascular Research Center. [Marion Brenner]

**6-23**

Mission Hall: Global Health & Clinical Sciences Building. University of California, San Francisco, 2014. [Marion Brenner]

# HARSH BEAUTY: PLANTING DESIGN IN ARID CONDITIONS

Christine Ten Eyck

7.

**Unless otherwise noted, all landscapes illustrated in this chapter have been designed by Ten Eyck Landscape Architects.**

—

Arizona State University Polytechnic campus. Sonoran palo verde in bloom. Mesa, Arizona, 2009. [Bill Timmerman]

sun devil way
sun devil way
sun devil way
sun devil way
sun devil way
sun devil way
sun devil way

You could rightfully say that I work in what is still the Wild West, that is, the states of Texas and Arizona. To many people they are still the frontier, where they believe that the land is meant to be conquered. And I usually work with the guys who try to conquer it. In terms of idea and feeling I relate strongly to the work of the artists Robert and Shana ParkeHarrison, whose surreal photographs portray a person attempting to mend the broken technology-scarred landscape with humble contraptions that restore the landscape of his world. I share this plight. Many times we work with small budgets; at times we work with architects who take all the budget for their buildings and then say, "Work your magic," on what's left of the 16 acres that the building occupies. Often it seems that we are trying to accomplish memorable, responsive landscapes against all odds: the intense climate, the lack of care, and the minimal budgets we are usually provided.

I started my landscape architecture career in Texas. My dad worked for Mobil Pipeline, so my family was frequently transferred, moving to wherever a new pipeline was planned, which was mainly in the West. After finishing college at Texas Tech University in Lubbock, I moved to Dallas. Four years after this move, I went on a rafting trip down the Colorado River with some friends, and for me the magnitude of that ancient canyon in the wild desert riparian landscape was a spiritual experience. After moving yet again in 1985 to Phoenix, Arizona, I eventually opened my office there in 1997.

**7-1**

Sonoran Desert.
Saguaro National Park.
Tucson, Arizona.
[Marc Treib]

The work of our office has always been involved with the particulars of the place, principal among them the factors of heat and aridity [7-1]. The Sonoran Desert, with an elevation of about 800 feet, receives only about seven inches of rain annually. The Chihuahuan Desert, at an elevation of 4,000 feet, gets about nine inches—ten if it's a good year. In contrast, the Austin Hill Country, also at an elevation of about 800 feet, receives 34 inches annually. When I moved to Arizona, I quickly learned just how precious water can be and I'm not sure I would have reached that conclusion if I had lived only in Dallas my whole life. I came to appreciate the arroyos with their ephemeral water and the memories of that water when they went dry. I quickly learned that water always provided the challenge, and it remains a challenge anywhere I've lived in the Southwest: for a long period of time you may get no rain, no rain, no rain—and then comes an epic flood. And none of the cities in which we have worked has had stormwater systems that were, or are, adequate. One learns to accept these constraints.

Throughout my career I've been inspired by the Hohokam prehistoric map drawn by Omar Turney in 1929 on which are plotted the settlements and constructions of a prehistoric tribe that settled in the Salt River Valley in the area that is today Phoenix [7-2]. The Hohokam people dug miles and miles of canals, using gravity flow from the Salt River to irrigate thousands of acres of crops. For some reason still undetermined, over time this culture disappeared. In the late 1800s, among the settlers who arrived in the area was Jack Swilling, who discovered the remnants of the Hohokam canals and had them excavated for reuse. In the early 1900s, believe it or not, Phoenix was known as "The City of Gardens and Trees," with rows of trees lining all the freshly renewed canals. Sadly, after World War II, all the trees were cut down to give roads a wider right-of-way [7-3]. The result of those unfortunate efforts is the vehicular Phoenix of today.

After 22 years in Phoenix I realized that I wanted to return to where my mother and dad were living, to return to Texas. After some prolonged discussions I convinced my husband it was a good idea and we moved to Austin. A bit naively I thought that working and making landscapes there would be easy, far easier than it had been in arid Arizona. After all, Austin gets abundant rainfall each year: "Just imagine what you can do with all that water," I thought. In fact, shortly after we moved there, it began to rain, and it rained, and it rained. Our house turned green with mold. In contrast to the aridity of Phoenix, we really enjoyed the continued rainfall at first, but after a while we wondered if the rain would ever stop. There was major flooding. And then around 2011, we began to suffer from an epic drought. Fires were plentiful and persistent, and the lake that is the major source of the city's drinking water had shrunk by 50 feet to its lowest depth ever.

Another factor is the local geology. Much of Austin and Central Texas rest on Karst limestone that is topped by only a very thin layer of soil [7-4]. Beneath the surface the stone is permeated with voids and resembles petrified Swiss cheese; water quickly passes through it. In my own yard I can literally turn on the hose and just let it run: the water will never puddle. The water passes right through the substrate and ends up in a series of phenomenal springs, a geologic characteristic evident in the cross section of the Edwards Aquifer and the Balcones Escarpment [7-5].

Living in Arizona I fell in love with the desert and its qualities as a unique place. With a potential for rain at different times of the year, it's also one of the lushest deserts in the world. The net result is a landscape of incredible biodiversity that ranges from the lowland riparian mesquite bosks to the alluvial fans of the desert *bajada*. The Chihuahuan Desert, where we also work, lies at a higher elevation but is almost as dry and just as harsh—and it regularly freezes in winter. However, it is populated by small puddles, incredible *tinajas* or *huecos* filled with water that accompany the dry arroyos. Together they comprise a total canyon landscape that is home to all habitats: the *bajada* rich with desert spoon, then the rock ledges, farther down the mesquites, and still farther down the gravel. There are also the moist canyons where, if lucky, you'll see a maidenhair fern emerging from the limestone. And then you descend into the chasms abundant with plants that are found right outside Austin. Central Texas, in contrast, offers oak-studded grassland savannas. This has been my inspiration for connecting the urban dweller with the nature that lies beyond the city limits.

I love the desert, but I do not design deserts; instead, I design landscapes that are often directed by desert conditions. Unfortunately, where I work neither the climate nor the social values are conducive to making good landscapes. It's brutal out there and unfortunately, this is not a part of the country where people like to take care of things. Although many of the desert trees are abused, none are abused more than the *Leucophyllums* (sage). And even that horrible practice pales in comparison to the tortures inflicted on the saguaro cactus, the sentinel of the Sonoran Desert. Needless to say, chainsaws are not our friends. Add to this the lack of understanding or sympathy for desert conditions and the results are some very inappropriate and inhospitable places. Phoenix loves paving and produces lots of it. Never, never will the City of Phoenix streets department make the mistake of constructing tiny, narrow roads like their counterparts back East. Working in and around south-western cities such as these, with their lack of sensitivity to the pedestrian and preference for the vehicle, provides a continuous challenge.

Looking at the vernacular landscapes of Phoenix we can identify a number of differing landscape types: the Desert Oasis, the Cactus Garden, the Hodgepodge, and the Sun City Look [7-6]. All of these landscape types suggest that people do not really appreciate the presence of trees—or at least, it seemed that way when I began working there. Without doubt, Phoenix has made some enormous strides, and I don't mean to bash the city because it's really come a long way. I've also worked in El Paso, Texas. Many people think that El Paso is hardly a place you want to stop, and that you should only experience the city by driving through it on Interstate 10 on the way to one place or another. From the vantage point of Interstate 10, El Paso may not look

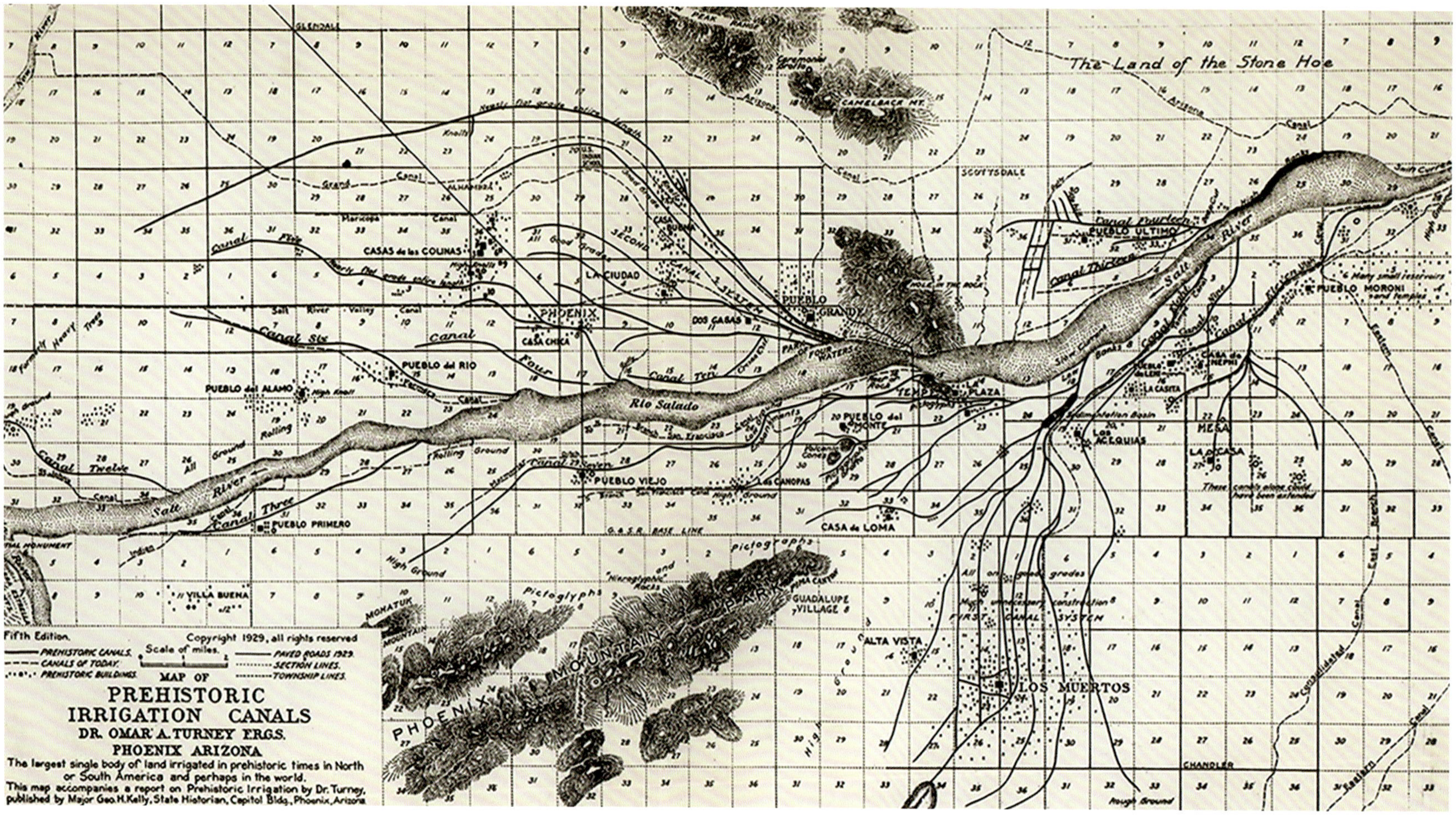

**7-2**

Dr. Omar A. Turney. Map of prehistoric Hohokam irrigation canals from the Salt River, 1929. [Geographicus]

**7-3**

Historic canal image. Phoenix, Arizona. Historic lateral irrigation canal lined with cottonwoods. [Photographer unknown]

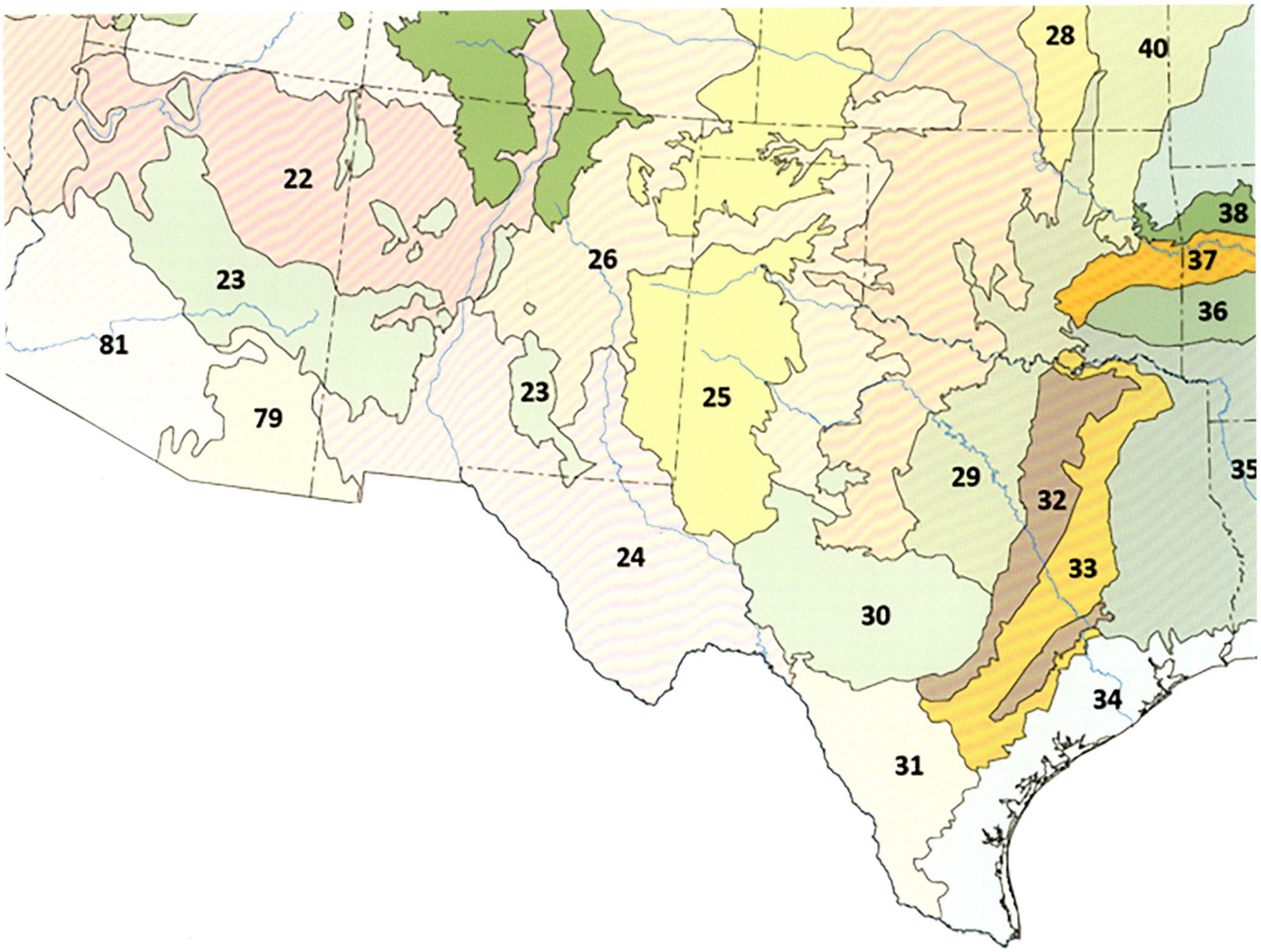


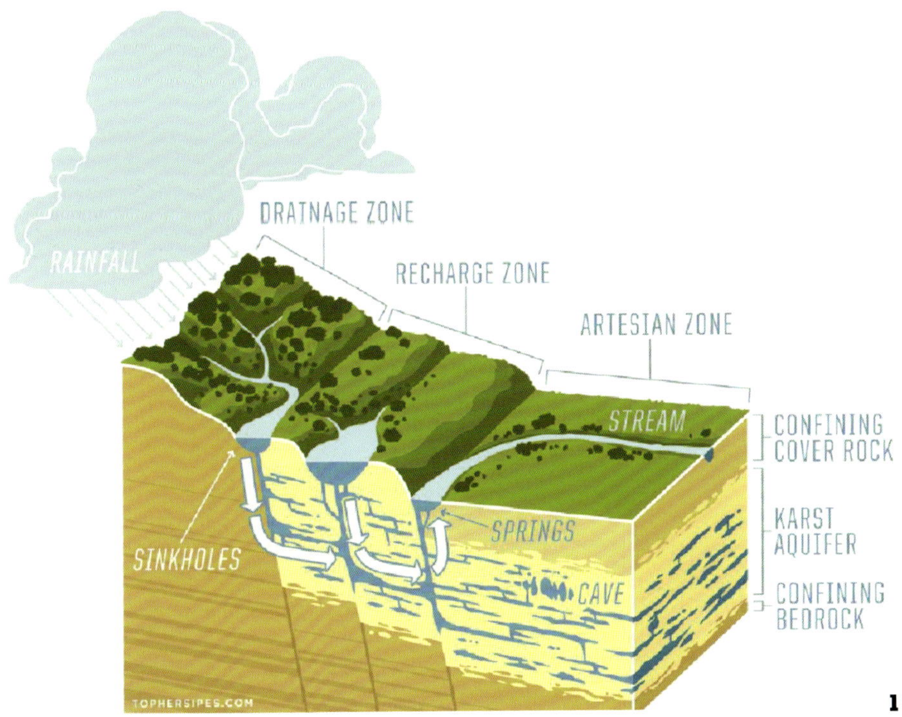


**7-4**

Ecoregions Soils Map of the Southwest. [Environmental Protection Agency]

**7-5**

Topher Sipes. Edwards Aquifer–infographic design. Austin, Texas. Cross section through Edwards Aquifer. [Topher Sipes]

very pretty but it is a city rich with history and filled with amazing people. And yet despite this heritage its landscapes are interpreted in just the same way as Phoenix to its west. The culture of Austin is different: it is the city of the lawn, the big lawn—and they also love their native trees like the Southern live oak (*Quercus virginia*) and cedar elm (*Ulmus crassifolia*) to name but two.

My colleagues and I share the search for connecting the urban dweller with nature, and each other. We feel that nature, especially in the cities in which we work, is missing and see no reason why we can't integrate nature into every aspect of the built urban environment. To us, shade and human comfort are paramount. We try to get people to own their geography. Given each region's unique character, we wonder why it has often been ignored. Perhaps I should have some major aesthetic concept governing my approach to planting design, especially within academic situations such as the original symposium. But honestly, I select the plants from those that will survive the harsh climatic conditions, survive the abuse of the maintenance staff who tend, or tend not to tend, the public landscapes. While what I say may be regarded only as platitudes, we really do want to create positive experiences for people in their everyday lives, whether it's walking down a street, or sitting in a plaza outside their school or office, or in the green oasis of a park—situations that provide people with good memories and experiences.

One of our first public projects was the Steele Indian School Park in Phoenix. For this commission we teamed up with Stantec, a large engineering firm, and worked with the city and all the tribes of Arizona whose children had been brought to this residential school. After Anglo settlement, Native American children were forced to attend the school to learn how to live in the white man's world. Although for many it constituted a very painful past, there were other former students who loved their experience there and were grateful for it. No matter the experience and memories, whether negative or positive, the descendants of those children considered the land sacred because their parents and grandparents had attended school there. The Indian School Park, a part of a broader municipal program, was programmed to be large enough for large civic celebrations such as the Fourth of July. Our solution for addressing the interests of the different constituents was a master plan that developed the total acreage of the site by dividing it into different programmatic areas [7-7]. The South Garden, measuring about ten acres, was dedicated to the memory of the tribes that had attended school there.

**7-6**

A vernacular Cactus Garden. Phoenix, Arizona. [Marc Treib]

A series of workshops with all the tribes attempted to resolve potential differences of attitudes concerning the park's master plan. For all the tribes, and especially for the Navajo, the circle represented never-ending life, and the circle was proposed to encompass the central heart of the park as well as the three historic buildings on the site; in response, we adopted the circle as an important geometric figure for our team's design. From our workshops we found that the community's main desire was that the ten-acre South Garden should be set down into the ground and surrounded by native plants; they also requested some means by which to connect with life-sustaining water. It took some effort but in the end we were able to convince the City of Phoenix to let us salvage all the old concrete pathways where the Native American children had walked in the past to create a spiraling retaining wall that follows the half-mile-long trail that descends to some 15 feet below grade at its lowest point [7-8]. The garden's planting changes from arid *bajada* to lush riparian as one descends deeper into the garden.

Designing this garden was my first experience using plants with meaningful associations. Most people in Phoenix, who have their own associations, refer to creosote as "desert scrub" and believe it is only there to be bulldozed. But creosote is one of the most prehistoric plants and for centuries has been used for its medicinal qualities. The initial *kiva* planting involved an austere grove of ironwood trees (*Olneya tesota*) and then changes to the *bajada* landscape of creosote, palo verde trees (*Parkinsonia florida*), brittlebush (*Encelia farinosa*), yucca, and ocotillo. In the mid-section chuparosa (*Justicia californica*) and turpentine bush (*Ericameria laricifolia*) mixed with lush mesquites. At the end of this labyrinthine path lined with a low wall of salvaged concrete, in the center of the garden, masses of grasses and stands of cottonwoods (*Populus tremontii*) and hackberry (*Celtis occidentalis*) accompany a reflective pool brimming with water. Perhaps my most moving personal experience there was when witnessing a young Native American family bless their baby in that water [7-9].

The site for the Biodesign Institute at Arizona State University in Tempe was flanked on one side of the road by a parking lot—the site of the new building—and on the other, a retention basin to collect all the area's stormwater. In truth, this was an ugly, neglected part of campus, although it sat just a quarter mile south of the banks of the Salt River. Thirteen feet below the surface lay river rock from the old floodplain of the river, the same material excavated by the Hohokam when they dug their canals. The retention basin wasn't

**7-7**

Ten Eyck Landscape Architects and Stantec. Steele Indian School Park. Phoenix, Arizona, 2001. Detailed concept master plan. [Christine Ten Eyck]

**7-8**

Ten Eyck Landscape Architects and Stantec. Steele Indian School Park.
Phoenix, Arizona, 2001. Spiral walk through entry garden through *Larrea tridentata* and *Encelia farinosa*. [Terrence Moore]

**7-9**

Ten Eyck Landscape Architects and Stantec. Steele Indian School Park.
Reflecting pool at low point off entry garden. [Christine Ten Eyck]

really within the scope of our project, but we were troubled by the lack of shade throughout the campus and the sterile character of these retention basins used only for functional purposes.

Our idea was to somehow recast the retention basin, paired with our project across the street, as a green gateway to this east side of campus. The architects had set their buildings on a plinth, elevating the first floor above the level of the street. In response, we proposed using different levels to showcase the differences between the desert *bajada* and the mesquite bosk. Along the walkways and the streets we planted palo verde trees in a more formal order. Next to the buildings and under its canopy the more formal plantings continued [7-10]. As the Biodesign Institute supports researchers who study the possible ways that plants can be used to cure human diseases, we also featured certain medicinal plants such as creosote, candelilla, and *Aloe barbadensis*. Although aloe originally comes from Africa, it was planted for its medicinal value, beautiful geometric form, and vivid yellow bloom in spring. In terms of plant selection, I'm not a purist and on occasion I use plants from other parts of the world with similar climatic tolerances. Planting design closer to the buildings on the plinth were more formal, but as visitors make their way down to the water harvesting garden the design becomes more naturalistic, marked by a studied carelessness. Rainwater collected from the roof flows into the garden as the terrain descends into an angular seating area. Here the metaphor was the arroyo, the dry canyon, a landscape that I have always appreciated for its microclimate and memory of ephemeral water [7-11]. The concrete *banco* seating is transformed into a water element of its own, that is, at those times when the irrigation valve is opened: the sculptural form wells up with water and flows down to the lowest part of the garden. The project is about 15 years old now and sadly has received very little attention and maintenance. Despite this lack of care, however, the landscape has survived and grown. And it definitely provides shade and a respite for those who venture out from air conditioning into the arroyo and desert heat for solitary activity and group celebrations.

In Tucson we encountered another building and were again given only leftover funds. We were asked to work our magic on surplus land and a parking lot whose situation was far from hospitable. During our site visits we noticed that the adjacent parking lot sloped directly toward our site. Although it may be hard to believe, we were actually inspired by the surface of the parking lot as a sloping vessel that directed water to our project. We were anxious to replace the existing heavy-handed concrete structures for managing the heavy flows of water from summer downpours with a greener solution. In response we proposed an immersive green bio-sponge landscape that would also serve as an outdoor learning laboratory for the students, and convinced our client to install an acrylic tank to store stormwater harvested from the roof of the new building. When filled, water overflows into the garden and makes its way through the bio-sponge before entering the stormwater system of the campus. In all, the landscape and outdoor spaces represent a complete stormwater system that also serves aesthetic and instructional purposes.

Creating shade in these hot locales has always been a huge concern. Here we planted mesquites to project dappled light and shadow onto the plaza; a sunken classroom receives a more riparian desert planting using grasses and Arizona sycamores (*Platanus wrightii*) [7-12]. In times of heavy rain and flood, the pond, set adjacent to the classrooms, recirculates the harvested water. In some ways, I believe that this project for the University of Arizona campus could become a model for downtown urban plazas in regions with similar climates. Each building would manage the flow of its stormwater and air conditioning condensate, and use that water to create hospitable places for people and plants.

The site for the Arizona State University Polytechnic campus in Mesa, Arizona, was a former Air Force base, whose two parts were divided by a street, and were troubled by a long history of flooding. In all truth, the campus was an overpaved, sterile place, and the university was having difficulty attracting students. With the San Antonio-based architectural firm Lake|Flato we proposed a complete redesign of the campus to accommodate a new academic village by demolishing some of the existing buildings, streets, and sidewalks, and to restructure the campus as a series of courtyards [7-13]. We removed the flood-prone street and transformed its path into a water-harvesting arroyo that teems with native plants; bridges facilitate movement to the other part of campus and truly connect people to the place.

In response to the idea for the symposium that led to this book I tried to consider the way in which we approach plants and planting design. I realized that we almost always work with a mixture of types, contrasting more formal areas with those more wild. I like both manners; I like the play between them—although I admit that a convincing naturalistic landscape usually requires more land. On the Mesa campus, we again relied on the opposition of areas more naturalistic and those more formal—each used

**7-10**

Arizona State University Biodesign Institute. Tempe, Arizona, 2004.
Plaza and seating with *Aloe barbadensis* and *Cercidium praecox* (Sonoran palo verde).
[Terrence Moore]

**7-11**

Arizona State University Biodesign Institute. Amphitheater nestled into water harvesting garden.
[Terrence Moore]

**7-12**

Arizona State University Biodesign Institute. Outdoor classroom shaded by *Prosopis chilensis* (Chilean mesquite). [Bill Timmerman]

**7-13**

Arizona State University Polytechnic campus. Mesa, Arizona, 2009. Outdoor classroom near *Platanus wrightii* (Arizona sycamore) and *Justicia californica* (beloperone). [Bill Timmerman]

where it seemed appropriate. In the naturalistic zones we brought in palo verde trees, bursage (*Ambrosia deltoidea*), brittlebush (*Encelia farinosa*), and cactus of various varieties. Along the malls and closer to the buildings, the arrangements became more structured and formal [7-14; see also chapter opening].

Given the climatic and soil conditions in which we work, we are always aware of the presence or absence of water, and have been influenced in our designs by the Spanish and Moorish garden traditions that celebrate the considered use of irrigation as a design feature. The courtyard for the School of Agribusiness uses the irrigation canal as its central element [7-15]. Water is not only used for ornamental purposes, however: the courtyards also collect the stormwater from rooftops and guide it to the main arroyo. The resulting landscape has completely transformed the former military base into a campus that recalls, but does not completely replicate, a natural arroyo. When the palo verde trees are in flower, the effect is spectacular. Really, who can't love the palo verde tree with its incredible yellow blooms?

The University of Texas at Austin was planned, for the most part, as a very formal campus, a significant part of which was designed by the architect Paul Cret in the 1930s. As it happens, former first lady Lady Bird Johnson studied at what is today the university's College of Communication, for which we were asked to design a new plaza to include an outdoor café, a lawn for performances, and an outdoor classroom. Our choice of planting uses only native species such as honey mesquite (*Prosopis glandulosa*), live oak (*Quercus virginiana*), bald cypress (*Taxodium distichum*), sage (*Leucophyllum frutescens*), Anisicanthus (*Anisacanthus quadrifidus*, var. *wrightii*), sideoats grama (*Bouteloua curtipendula*), red yucca (*Hesperaloe parviflora* 'Brakelights'), Mexican plum (*Prunus mexicana*), and possumhaw (*Ilex decidua*), although for the most part the compositions are formal [7-16]. To maintain the landscape we collect thousands of gallons of water from rainfall and condensate—the "sweat" of the building's air conditioners—and use it to feed the plaza's fountain. The condensate is recirculated and augmented by any stormwater that may fall. Permeable pavers soak up any excess water after which it is collected in four cisterns located to the rear of the building. Because a street near the building bears heavy traffic, the plaza provides the students with a refuge for study, where they can be among vegetation and listen to the sound of water.

As an aside I should note that maintenance is always a key issue, and we tend to be plagued by a lack of it for our

**7-14**

Arizona State University Polytechnic campus. Mesa, Arizona, 2009. Formal gardens near Student Union with Sonoran palo verde and *Muhlenbergia rigens* (deer grass). [Bill Timmerman]

**7-15**

Arizona State University Polytechnic campus. Mesa, Arizona, 2009. [Bill Timmerman]

projects. And it seems that the landscape is always at its worst when the photographer arrives to record it. In this case, the grounds crews had been instructed by their boss to cut off any yucca blossom that was not set perpendicular to the ground. Did they think there were just too many blooms? On days like these I think that maybe you just can't win. To top it all off, one day in winter, when the grasses and the bioswale at the bottom of the garden were brown, somebody flicked out a cigarette there and the bioswale caught fire and burned. Some Einstein inside the building pulled the fire alarm and all the people in the building came out into the fire and ravaged the landscape. Happily, the bioswale grew back, even better than before that unprescribed burn.

The Capri, in Marfa, Texas, was also originally a military building, but now the client wanted to transform it into a restaurant and a bar to serve as a community gathering place. In response, we proposed a beer garden set within a grassland planted where the parking lot used to be. A stain in the asphalt marked the path of the water runoff from the highway as it led to a small creek; we proposed to use its water as a feature of the design. The little beer gardens would be treated as islands surrounded by grass, accompanied by a larger, more formal court for weddings and intermissions during the concerts to be held on-site. The courtyard seating areas are planted with *Yucca rostrata*, live oaks, and Mexican elderberry (*Sambucus nigra*). And they're growing well.

Lake|Flato designed the building conversion; we did the site design, creating outdoor rooms with gabion walls filled with native stone and an arbor draped by 'Roger's Red' grapevines, which do very well in the desert [7-17]. The existing roof of the building sheds rainwater to both sides. We collected half the water in a bioswale that travels through the new garden into the adjacent creek, while the other half is distributed into a rainwater fountain [7-18]. At times of rain the water spills in celebration from the gutters into the trough of the fountain, and with heavy rainfall the trough overflows into the garden orchard and eventually to the creek. The bioswale in front and around the beer garden is planted with *Muhlenbergia emersleyii* and *Alkali sacaton* grasses. The *M. emersleyii*, native bull-grass, does well in these conditions. In the more arid parts of the site, we used what the ranchers call the king dagger, *Yucca faxoniana*, and various other yuccas and agaves [7-19]. Little kids love this garden, using it to play chase and hide-and-seek. Today we use what was learned in this project as a model for some family adventure gardens now in design, because we saw how children enjoy exploring a safe place, hiding in ephemeral creek ravines, looking at the flowers, and trying to catch butterflies. For the adults, it's a great place to sit outside and drink a beer while immersed in a native landscape.

The renovation of a ranch landscape in Marfa, Texas, addressed many of the properties of the site which had been lost over time. For years, vehicles had roamed freely; allowed to drive everywhere, they destroyed any sense of continuity in the immense grassland and damaged the soil. The design emphasized the vast horizontal sweep of the view, with most of the planting kept low to maintain the feeling of standing in an ocean of grasses. Our client was a young woman who was afraid of the wild; to be honest, I really don't know why she bought a 4,000-acre ranch. Our task then was to "civilize" the grasslands by creating a safe elevated plinth around the house while maintaining views and a sense of the greater landscape.

In response to the brief we created that "civilized" precinct around the house being renovated by Lake|Flato, who also designed a shade structure and a mirador. To root the new elements with the land, we borrowed the material that Frank Lloyd Wright called his "desert masonry," that is, concrete poured over local rock set within formwork. Bringing that grassland back up to these walls was our main intention. The garden was kept purposefully simple, planted with Mexican feather grass (*Nassella tenuissima*), butterfly plants, Apache plume (*Fallugia paradoxa*), the sacred Datura, and creosote (*Larrea tridentatc*) [7-20]. Set into a buffalo grass lawn the swimming pool was essentially a concrete trough integrated into the desert masonry walls.

In designing my own garden after my move to Austin, the challenge was to avoid all the clichés. We were attracted to the property because of its trees, and only later did we discover that the state of the house was in disrepair. But that's another story. The house is set back far from the street, which allowed me to test how shade plants respond to Texas conditions. Near the house, the planting is more formal and tailored. The front yard, however, is treated more naturally, that is, wilder. It's a rich palette, filled with pleasant contrasts, setting off geometric large agaves with softer grasses and dasylirions. By the street are *Agave americana, Yucca pallida, Nolina nelsonii*, with Mexican feather grass (*Nassella tenuissima*), zexmenia (*Wedelia texana*), and damianita (*Chrysactinia mexicana*) [7-21]. I've also been experimenting with understory plants that grow out in the forest, for example, *Eupatorium havanense*,

**7-16**

Belo Center for New Media, University of Texas. Austin, Texas, 2012. Permeable plaza beneath canopy of *Prosopis glandulosa* (honey mesquite). [Bill Timmerman]

**7-17**

The Capri. Marfa, Texas, 2010. View over rain fountain to arbor planted with 'Roger's Red' grapevine. [Adam Barbe]

**7-18**

The Capri. Rain fountain with *Sambucus mexicana* (Mexican elderberry). [Caitlin Atkinson]

**7-19**

The Capri. *Yucca rostrata* and *Chilopsis linearis* (desert willow) with gabion wall backdrop. [Caitlin Atkinson]

**7-20**

Ranch in West Texas. Marfa, Texas, 2011. Outdoor dining area in sea of *Nassella tenuissima* (Mexican feather grass), sacred datura, and *Fallugia paradoxa* under a grove of *Carya illinoiensis* (hardy pecan). [Terrence Moore]

a white native boneset, sedges, and also Turk's cap (*Malvaviscus drummondii*) and sea oats (*Chasmanthium latifolium*). Most Austinites are maniacal about blowing away all the leaves, but I let them stay and use them for mulch; sedges grow in the forests beneath the live oaks. The rear courtyard, which to me feels like a formal gravel river bottom, features American beautyberry (*Callicarpa americana*) and bamboo muhly (*Muhlenbergia dumosa*), possumhaw (*Ilex decidua*), and grasses.

**7-21**

Bridle Path Residence. Austin, Texas, 2011. A new native garden and path replaces a former circular asphalt drive and lawn through a forest of live oaks, *Eupatorium havanense*, and *Agave americana*. [Marion Brenner]

Our budget for the South Congress Hotel in Austin was poor, as was the soil, except near the street and one small area to the rear of the building. To address these limitations we filled gabions with soil and plants as living green walls that define the outdoor restaurant areas, giving them some privacy while maintaining views to the street [7-22]. The stack of gabions became, in effect, a vertical garden. To the rear of the hotel, where more soil was plentiful, we harvested the condensate from the hotel's air conditioning and ran it in a trough along the top of an eight-foot-high soil wall that we planted with maidenhair fern—it loves these conditions and thrives—and is reminiscent of the springs outside Austin. In the summer, however, supplementary drip irrigation augments the condensate.

The University of Texas at El Paso occupies a campus landscape whose design and maintenance have sadly been neglected for many years. One day after the university's original buildings had burned down in the early 1900s, one of the dean's wives was reading the magazine *National Geographic* and said, "Honey, I've got a great idea for the new campus. Let's build it to look like a Bhutanese village." And they did. They commissioned local architect Henry Charles Trost to design the first four buildings, intending that they should look just like the architecture of Bhutan.

The rugged campus terrain sits at the base of a major arroyo that extends down from the Franklin Mountains. Over the decades the arroyo had been very poorly treated on campus, having been pushed into tunnels or buried under buildings. The academic buildings have gotten larger and larger, and the engineers had gone rampant, paving extensive areas of the campus with asphalt. That description sums up the state of the landscape when we began, although every once in a while, you could still manage to see the mountain erupting up out of the asphalt. While there had been some grassed areas on campus before we began, the most prominent lawn area was set on an incline and difficult to use. In response to this unfortunate situation, we proposed a new ovular green heart for the campus, embraced by newly carved arroyos on either side. This is a place where students study, have community celebrations, throw a football, or just hang out. The university also holds campus events in this place surrounded by lush Chihuahuan Desert gardens on either side.

The administration was supportive and open to converting the existing roads into walkable pedestrian malls—so the roads were removed. Emergency vehicles still have access, of course, but all other traffic on campus has been banned. To regain lost tributaries we carved new arroyos on either side of the oval to link it to the mountains beyond. All the underlying boulders of andesite were salvaged and used for retaining grade and buffering the new arroyos. The resulting landscape reconnects the campus and the students to the native Texas landscape of which we felt it should be a part. For shade we planted some 700 new trees [7-23, 7-24]. Along the walkways and the pedestrian malls the feeling is formal, but the mix of the resulting species, textures, and colors reflects the particular character of the place. Due to the slope, the oval was cut into the hill, which allowed us to create amphitheaters at both ends that provide many places for small gatherings and large community events.

**7-22**

South Congress Hotel. Austin, Texas, 2015. Streetscape of *Platanus mexicana* (Mexican sycamore) and living wall of *Russelia equisetiformis* (coral fountain), *Carex divulsa* (grassland sedge), and *Tradescantia pallida* (spiderwort). [Mia Baxter]

In the arroyos the composition softens and becomes more naturalistic. We love the grasses of the Chihuahuan Desert: *Muhlenbergia emersleyii* and sideoats grama are contrasted with the spiky tall *Hesperaloe funifera*. Out there the wind is always blowing, at least as a soft breeze, and I am fond of plants that move in the wind. Although I love agave just about more than any other plant, I feel they should be used judiciously on public projects because of their short lifespan; in their place we use yucca because it is longer lived.

Who would have thought that when it rains, students would be able walk over a bridge along a burbling arroyo on their way to class? [7-24] The students and administration were very pleased with the resulting outdoor spaces, Chihuahuan landscape, and the new campus heart. They now say, "This is who we are; this landscape is us and it is beautiful and so are we."

**7-23**

Campus transformation project. The University of Texas at El Paso, 2015. Overview of campus transformation project and Centennial Plaza. [Adam Barbe]

**7-24**

Campus transformation project. The University of Texas at El Paso. A new bridge over a new arroyo connects students to the new heart of campus. [Bill Timmerman]

# PLANTING DESIGN IN THE SUBTROPICAL REGIONS: MEXICO

Mario Schjetnan

8.

**Unless otherwise noted, landscapes illustrated in this chapter have been designed by Grupo de Diseño Urbanos / Mario Schjetnan.**

—

Malinalco Residence. State of Mexico, 2011. [Héctor Velasco]

Landscape design in a subtropical region can be almost an overwhelming task, addressing broad issues such as climate, hydrology, solar exposure, soils, and altitudes. A basic definition of the subtropical condition in the dictionary describes it as "tropical relative to temperate zones" and "characterized with a warm climate with seasonal rains." Temperatures average between 27° to 33° Celsius in summer, which is marked by humidity, and between 5° and 12° Celsius in winter. This description represents a simple, perhaps oversimplified, definition because as we look more closely at all the variables and sets of relationships involved, the idea of "subtropical" becomes more complex, particularly when set against the other climatic regions of the world.

The subtropics occupy the band that extends around the globe between the Tropic of Cancer and the Tropic of Capricorn. That band enfolds parts of the Mediterranean, India, Africa, and South America, and includes Brazil, Peru, Ecuador, Colombia, Venezuela, parts of Argentina and Chile—but also South Africa and Australia. The zone also includes Mexico and Central America, parts of the United States and the Orient, including regions of China and Southeast Asia. According to Peter H. Raven, President Emeritus of the Missouri Botanical Garden, two-thirds of the world organisms (plants, animals, and insects) live in the tropical and subtropical bands: more than three million species, perhaps up to ten million.[1] Only 500,000 of these species have been cataloged scientifically. The subtropical regions hold approximately 25 percent of the world's vegetal biodiversity (roughly 265,000 species), an incredible wealth of plants that thrive in vastly different geographic conditions on several continents:

> *Of the roughly 265,000 species of plants in the world, about a third occur in temperate regions, a third in Latin America, and a third in the tropics and subtropics of Africa and Asia. Tropical forests are being destroyed very rapidly, as a result of the explosive growth of a record human population, extensive poverty, and an unwillingness to learn about and practice sustainable land use in the tropics. As a consequence, at least a fifth of the total plant species in the world, something on the order of 60,000 species, are threatened with extinction over the next several decades. Systematic botanists need urgently to devise comprehensive plans to inventory plant diversity, especially in the tropics. They should play a major role in making possible the utilization of this diversity for human benefit, and in conserving as extensive a sample as possible.*[2]

At the end of the eighteenth century and the beginning of the nineteenth, the German geographer, explorer, geologist and naturalist Alexander von Humboldt explored South America, Mexico, and parts of the United States and Canada. He carried out an incredible array of investigations related to plants and their growing conditions in the lands in which he traveled. He determined that rather than geographic location alone, it was climate that established the primary conditions for life of any plant species. For his publications, Humboldt produced a fascinating series of graphs and charts by which to concisely present his findings. One of his most revealing images is the chart that illustrates plant species relative to altitude [8-1]. In conversations we often use the category "subtropical" as if conditions were constant throughout all the lands and at all altitudes. In reality, however, even at the same latitude, environmental conditions differ, with plant species that have evolved in relation to the altitude, which adds considerably to the complexity of our study.

Humboldt and his traveling companion, the French botanist Aimé Bonpland, recorded the types and habitats of plants, what we now call biomes, that establish different floral regions of the world, and in addition traced along vertical scales productive plants such as fruits and vegetables. Bonpland identified and registered several plants in Mexico, particularly in Xochimilco, among them *Salix bonplandiana* (Bonpland willow), which characterizes Xochimilco's *chinampas*—the so-called, if misnamed, floating gardens. In *The Invention of Nature*, Andrea Wulf notes that in his *Essay on the Geography of Plants*, Humboldt published his celebrated chart, "Naturgemalde der Anden," in which he visualized his belief that the natural world of South America was organized as a set of "connections and unity." [8-2] In the book he examined the vegetal world within a wider context and viewed nature as a holistic entity between phenomena represented with a "broad brush."[3]

For instance, starting from Mexico City, whose latitude is 19.5 degrees north and at an altitude of some 7,000 feet above sea level, a journey westward will take you through environmental conditions that change from subtropical to low deciduous forests, then up the Western Sierra Madre to oak and pine forests, and finally to tropical conditions on the Pacific Coast [8-3]. While maintaining exactly the same latitude you will encounter severe changes of climate, vegetation, hydrology, solar exposure, and geology. Likewise, should you travel eastward from Mexico City along the same 19th parallel, you will encounter the Yucatan Peninsula. Due to its low elevation and adjacency to the Gulf of Mexico and the Caribbean Sea, the Yucatan possesses a tropical climate, hot and humid, that supports

**8-1**

Alexander von Humboldt. *Geographie der Planzen in den Tropen Landern*, 1803. [Wikimedia Commons]

low jungle and tropical evergreen forests, with frequent fogs and high humidity due to proximity to the Gulf of Mexico.

## The Land

Mexico has been graced by a rich vegetal bank filled with some 26,000 indigenous species [8-2, 8-3]. However, through four centuries of exchange—from the sixteenth to the nineteenth centuries—that number has easily doubled. This intensive importation and exportation of plants brought species in common use, very well adapted today in Mexico City and many parts of Mexico. For example, the jacaranda (*Jacaranda mimosifolia*), a beautiful flowering tree native to Brazil, is so ubiquitous many consider it native [8-4]. A similar regard holds true for the pepper tree (*Schinus molle*), native to Peru, which has persisted in Mexican paintings, photographs, and films as a "true" native [8-5].

**8-2**

Grupo de Diseño Urbano. *Catálogo de Vegetación* (Catalog of Vegetation), 2015. [Grupo de Diseño Urbano Archive]

Mexico is home to 10–12 percent of the world's biodiversity, with biomes that range from the mesophyllic mountainous forest to temperate forest, humid jungle, tropical evergreen forest, the xerophytic, and mangrove swamps [8-6]. The Chihuahua Sierra is not subtropical, but in the canyons of the Sierra, such as the Barranca del Cobre (Copper Canyon), deep down 1,000 or more meters (3,300 feet) below, the conditions are tropical. The pine/oak forest of the Chihuahua Sierra enjoys sparse rainfall (approximately 400 millimeters—16 inches—per year) and cold winters, including snow. In fact, Mexico is home to the largest variety of conifers and oaks on the globe, an asset few Mexicans realize.

Introduced species, rapid population expansion (Mexico presently has 130 million inhabitants and has doubled its population in the last 50 years), the greater demand for food, goods, and services—and very low protection for the environment—has caused a substantial loss of native flora. Deforestation and weather changes have caused the desertification of up to 500,000 hectares (1,235,000 acres) of land each year.[3] That is why it is critical—one might justifiably claim it is an emergency—that Mexico, Brazil, and other countries in Latin America protect and save their biodiversity.

## A New Paradigm for Planting Design

It is quite obvious that we must have a new paradigm for planting design in order to preserve water and soils, produce oxygen, retain rainfall, and attract birds—and to create beautiful, sustainable landscapes. Perhaps learning from Humboldt, we can determine a proper foundation for

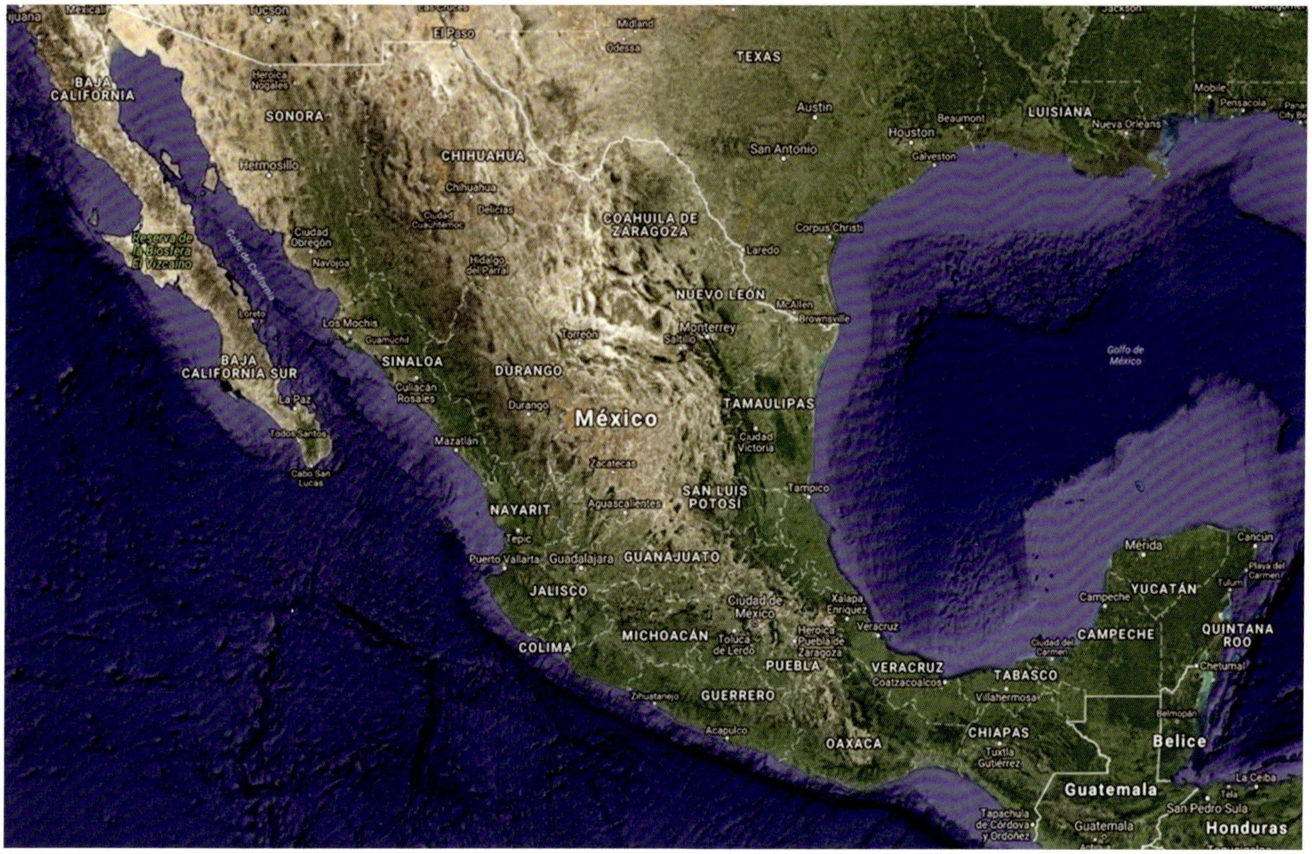


**8-3**

Geographical map of Mexico. [Vicente Díaz de León Acosta website]

**8-4**

Jacaranda (*Jacaranda mimosifolia*) in flower. Chapultepec Park, Mexico City. [Mario Schjetnan]

**8-5**

José María Velasco. *Pirú* (*Schinus molle*, pepper tree), 1860. [WikiArt–Visual Art Encyclopedia]

better understanding the conditions of the site and its vegetation. Looking more precisely at soils and water, orientation, microclimate, and altitude will aid in the design of gardens and parks that are more sustainable and resilient, but also beautiful.

In this respect we could then ask, "Should we consider only native plants in our designs? The interaction, introduction, and transportation of plants since the sixteenth century has been so intense, that today it is difficult to distinguish plants that by now have adapted and are considered part of the native landscape—for example, the jacaranda or pepper trees mentioned above—from those that are truly indigenous.

The great Brazilian landscape architect Roberto Burle Marx well understood the relationships among plants and used plant associations in his landscape designs. He was not averse to using foreign plants and imported species from North America, Mexico, South Africa, and Southeast Asia. He always spoke of "plant associations"; however, once associations were determined, or there was consonance among them, he considered color, texture, and form to compose or create his exemplary gardens and landscapes—and not their place of origin [8-7].

I feel this perhaps overdetailed discussion of climate, environment, latitude, and altitude is necessary for understanding the complexity of the Mexican situation in which I work—situations shared by many other places on the planet. In our practice we have tried to remain conscious of these factors that provide both restrictions and generate possibilities. There are only very few occasions, and very few reasons, to contradict what the site and climate provide. Instead, we work with them and transform these limits into assets. Luis Barragán used to say that only after defining the programmatic and technical conditions for a project do design and art truly begin.

**8-6**

Antonio Vizcaíno. Barranca del Cobre, Chihuahua. "Mexico Landscape and Spirit." [*America Natural*, 2010]

## Three Case Studies from Mexico

### *The Natura Botanical Garden, Parque Bicentenario Azcapotzalco, Mexico City*

Perhaps the greatest limits or constraints we have encountered on any site were provided by the project of the Bicentennial Park in the former Pemex oil refinery in Mexico City [8-8]. The refinery was closed in 1990, having produced oil, diesel, gasoline, and tar since the 1920s—at full production, it had provided most of the gasoline for Mexico City. When the refinery was built in the 1920s, Mexico City had one million inhabitants, but by 1990—when the refinery was closed—the population of the metropolitan area had risen to nearly 16 million inhabitants. Simply stated; the refinery was the powerhouse that provided energy for the region's motor vehicles, factories, and other uses. Imagine also the changes in technology during those 70 years and the amounts of pollution that resulted in layers and layers of contaminating liquids, gases, and solids that were deposited over decades, and the complex effects on the soil and subsoil that resulted. Fortunately, the refinery was built on top of an impermeable layer of clay some eight meters deep (23 feet) that sealed and protected the aquifers below.

**8-7**

Roberto Burle Marx
Sitio Burle Marx.
São Antonio de
Bica, Brazil, 1949+.
[Marc Treib]

After the plant's closure, all the metal structures related to production were demolished and removed from the site—everything except underground pipes, footings, and other elements of the plant's infrastructure. To reuse the 55-hectare (136-acre) site for a park, a complete remediation was required. After studies focused on the composition of the soil, several technologies were used to extract gases, clean the soil, and remove unwanted solids such as tar and liquids such as benzine. When the refinery was decommissioned, a presidential decree clearly established that the site should be converted into a public park with free access and that new structures must not occupy more than 10 percent of the land. The site remained polluted for 15 years. Remediation was accomplished in several phases over three years, with the land converted to a public park immdietaly thereafter.

For the comprehensive master plan, we collaborated with Legorreta Arquitectos, Sordo Madaleno Arquitectos, and the staff of the Children's Museum of Mexico City. Together we proposed a series of interconnected gardens based on certain themes: the Natura Garden as a botanical garden; the Wind Garden for major open-air concerts and sports; the Earth Garden for family outings, picnics, and free play; the Sun Garden with a museum of sustainable technologies (unbuilt); and a Water Garden with a lake, including a water treatment plant [8-9].

The entrance to Parque Bicentenario, which leads directly into the Nature Garden, is close to a preexisting Metro station. Although not in the original brief, we proposed a botanical garden, arguing that as a Bicentennial commemorative park, it should acknowledge the richness and diversity of Mexico's native flora. In general, Mexico has done a good job of preserving archaeological and colonial towns through the National Institute of Anthropology and History, but has been negligent in preserving the living environment

**8-8**

Parque Bicentenario. Azcapotzalco, Mexico City, 2010. Refinery site before park construction. [Grupo de Diseño Urbano Archive]

**8-9**

Parque Bicentenario. Aerial view, with entrance below center. [Sergio Medellín]

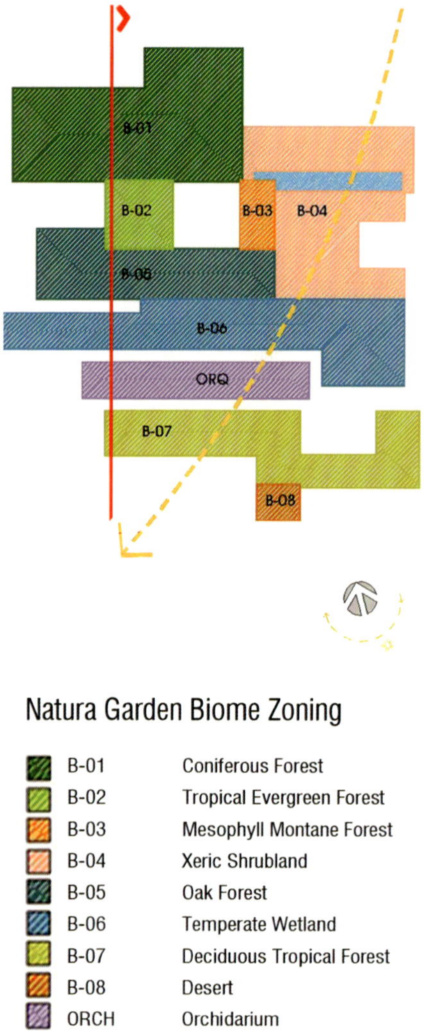


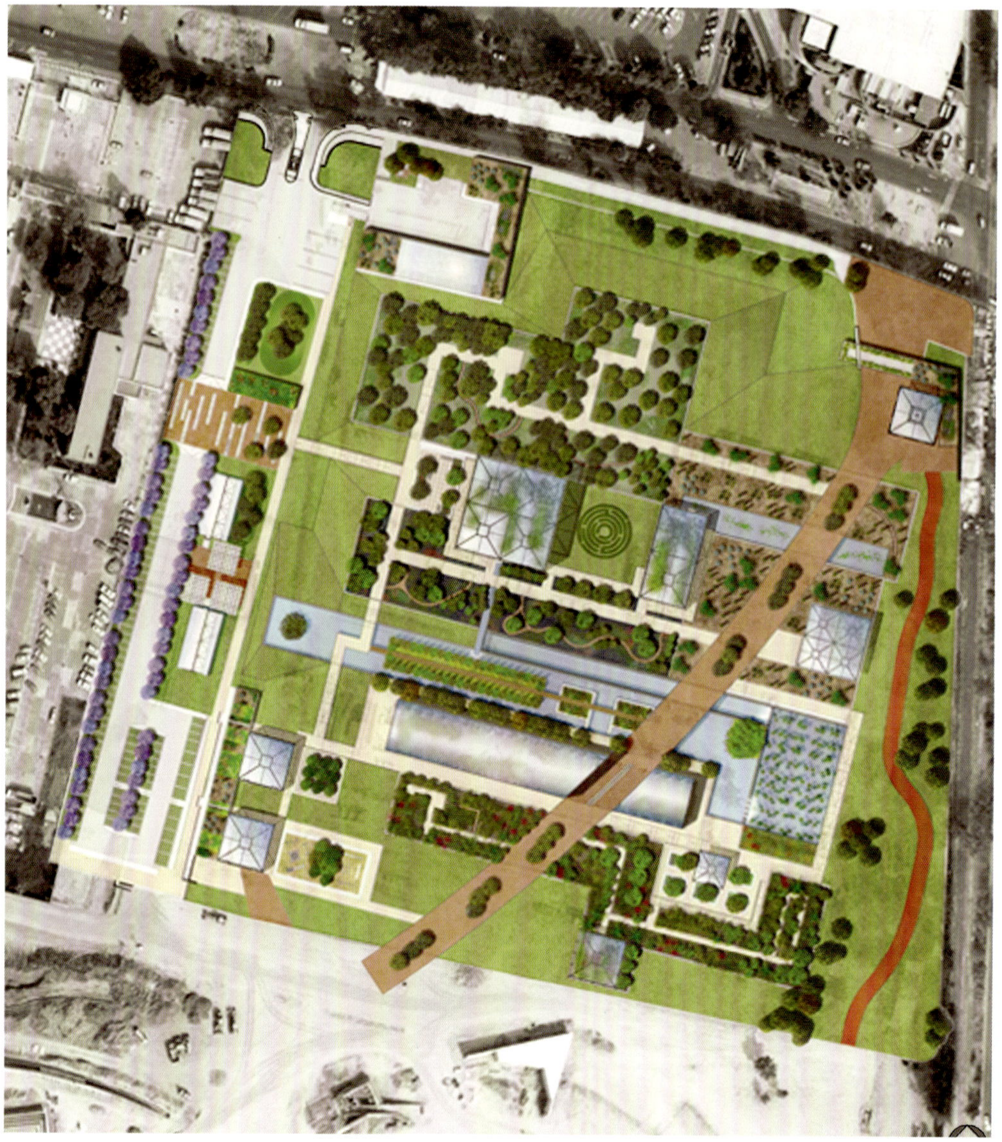

**8-10**

Parque Bicentenario. Azcapotzalco, Mexico City, 2010. Natura Garden. Site plan. [Grupo de Diseño Urbano]

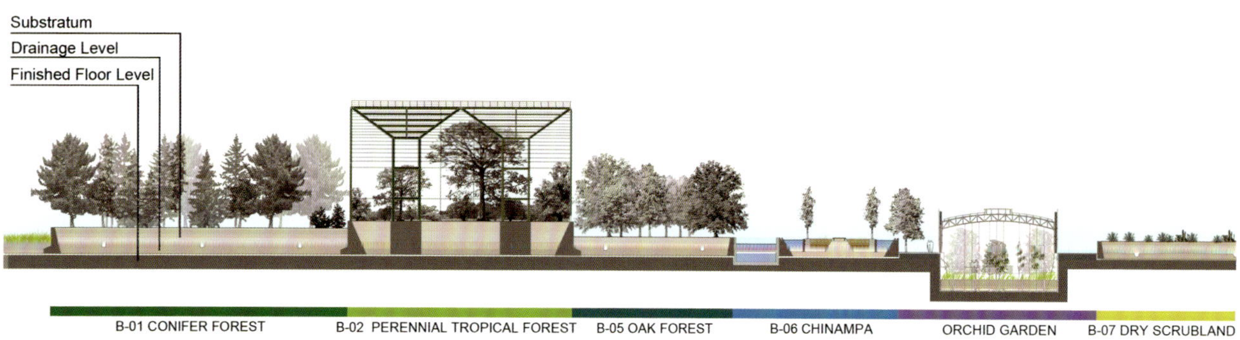


**8-11**

Parque Bicentenario. Longitudinal section. [Grupo de Diseño Urbano]

of diverse flora and fauna. The botanical garden, we believed, should be right at the entrance to the park in order to educate, and emphasize the importance of our land, and celebrate the beauty of our natural heritage. The preeminent location of Natura garden "invited" visitors to visit and experience it, even if their primary destination was the sports park, the skateboard park, or other gardens. Education and recreation should be integrated.

The Natura botanical garden incorporates an orchid house and eight biomes: coniferous forest, tropical evergreen forest, oak forest, mesophilic mountain forest, temperate wetlands, xeric shrubland, Sonoran desert, and deciduous tropical (low) forest [8-10]. The nine hectares of the garden are planted over a preexisting 40-centimeter-thick (16 inch) concrete slab that formerly served as the platform for the filling of tanker trucks [8-11]. Demolishing the slab would have been too costly and the resulting debris would have been distributed to other parts of the site. In response to these constraints, it was left intact. Gases existing beneath the slab were extracted and evaporated. What resulted from this restriction was one of the most interesting aspects of the botanical garden, since each biome required different soil depths and growing conditions. The varying depths of the soil were dictated by the needs of the individual plants and collectively produced a new above-slab topography.

Plants that could acclimate to the specific climatic and microclimatic conditions of Mexico City allowed us to create certain biomes outdoors: a coniferous forest, xeric shrubland, oak forest, temperate wetland (including a demonstration *chinampa*), and low deciduous forest were planted in the open. Other biomes, however, required an environment closer to their native conditions, which was provided by specifically designed glass houses [8-12]. These included the tropical evergreen forest, mesophilic fog forest, and Sonoran desert vegetation.

The form of 15 x 15 x 15-meter (16.5-foot) glass modules, topped by an inverted pyramidal translucent roof, garners maximum light [8-12]. Acting as funnels, they capture rain-water and divert it into the cisterns beneath them; excess water is directed to additional cisterns, where rainwater is filtered and thereafter flows to the aquifer some 80 meters below.

The temperature and humidity level of each glass house uses computer models to guide their bioclimatic design [8-14]. The tropical evergreen forest, for example, cannot survive in temperatures below 10 degrees or above 45 degrees Celsius or with low humidity (a minimum of 70 percent relative humidity is required). Humidity and rainfall are provided by suspended misters and sprinklers. Within the glass houses the soil depth is five meters. Now, some nine years after their planting, all the biomes have become fully established and today thrive—their success supported by good maintenance. Inside the glass houses, in fact, the trees have really grown too tall for the structure's 15-meter ceiling height, and some of them have had to be pruned. Entering the biomes one encounters a true piece of jungle, with its humidity, smell, and intense aura. It is an encounter difficult to describe in words and must be experienced personally.

The orchidarium is unique in its reuse of a preexisting structure from the old refinery: a large cistern (100 meters long x 15 meters wide x 5 meters deep) that was remediated, cleaned, and provided with a translucent roof over the entire space [8-15]. The sensory and visual impact of this interior garden results from the disposition and dense planting of orchids on different levels, guided by the idea to gradually "immerse" visitors within an inhabitable jungle as they walk along elevated walkways set above the dense forest floor. Orchids and bromeliads are set under and above the *passerelle*, planted in the ground or in planters hung from the new roof structure.

Adjacent to the orchidarium is the new *chinampa*, a land-scape type characteristic of Xochimilco, the lake still surviving from the original vast lacustrine environment of the Valley of Mexico. This *chinampa*, set within concrete tanks, displays the wetland environments and plants of Mexico's central high plateau [8-16]. *Chinampas* were artificial islands built on shallow lakes, whose mud and soil were retained by palisades of saplings and branches, reinforced by peripheral rows of Bonpland willows. The cultivation of maize, beans, squash, tomatoes, flowers, and herbs yields up to three harvests a year, a production that provided sufficient food for the Aztecs and supported their efforts to conquer other areas of Mesoamerica. The *chinampa*, implemented as early as the ninth century, was probably the most important indigenous technological invention by any Mexican culture and preceded the occupation of the Valley of Mexico and found its most extensive employ-ment in the lake of Xochimilco in the southern areas of the Valley. In the Parque Bicentenario, the *chinampa* is primarily a demonstration garden, but in an earlier project by our office, the Parque Ecológico Xochimilco and the restoration of the *chinampa* district of Xochimilco, the project involved study, restoration, and management. As an

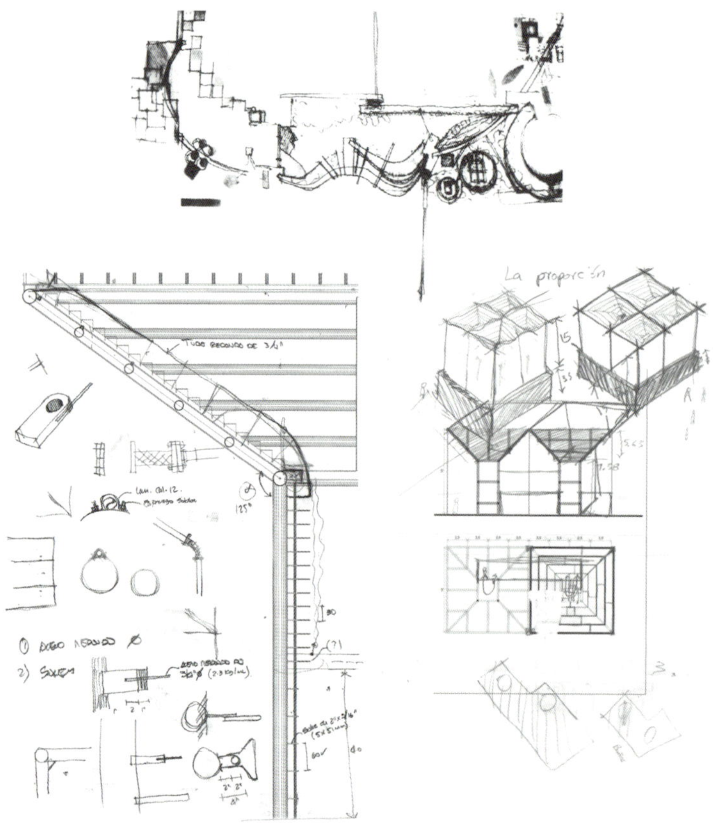

**8-12**

Parque Bicentenario. Azcapotzalco, Mexico City, 2010. Aerial view of glass houses, with the orchid garden to the right. [Francisco Gómez Sosa]

**8-13**

Parque Bicentenario. Study of glass house and construction. [Grupo de Diseño Urbano]

**8-14**

Parque Bicentenario. Glass house interior. [Grupo de Diseño Urbano]

**8-15**

Parque Bicentenario. Orchid garden. [Francisco Gómez Sosa]

**8-16**

Parque Bicentenario. Natura Garden. Azcapotzalco, Mexico City, 2010. The *chinampa* is to the right. [Francisco Gómez Sosa]

area of substantial historical and cultural importance in 1989 it was declared a World Heritage Site by UNESCO.

The Parque Bicentenario in the Azcapotzalco District of Mexico City has been a fascinating project for me and our office, a veritable environment from which to continuously learn about plants and their living conditions, the constraints placed upon them, and their needs for survival and growth. The Bicentennial Park provides a setting from which to continuously learn about the living environments of tropical and subtropical Mexico.

Over 20 years have passed since the park opened and today the vegetation is fully established. The park has gone from good maintenance to bad maintenance, but today it has recovered to some degree. Presently (2019–2020), the park is undergoing a further restoration, rehabilitation, and overhaul to address the problems caused by the years when the park suffered from the lack of maintenance and management of the various wetlands, lagoons, and other facilities. Our office is involved in the present rehabilitation, which presents a new opportunity to improve and protect the park for the future.

### *Parque Ecológico Xochimilco*
### *Xochimilco District, Mexico City*

The Parque Ecológico Xochimilco, designed and built from 1990 to 1993, with a surface area of 277 hectares, comprises four principal elements: the ecological park, a new lagoon of 50 hectares (124 acres), a sports park, and a large plant and flower market [8-17]. The ecological park included establishing several types of wetlands. Consulting with biologists from the National Autonomous University of Mexico (UNAM), we identified the plants and water depths necessary to attract various bird species, including migratory birds from other parts of North America; many of these plants were brought to Xochimilco from wetlands as far away as the state of Michoacán. These included tule (*Typha latifolia*), tulillo (*Cyperus seslerioides*), ninfa Mexicana (*Nymphaea mexicana*).

In the entrance plaza, rows of Bonpland willows (*Salix bonplandiana*) extend into the water to bind terra and aqua; eight gargoyles mounted on the piers of fieldstone spurt treated water into the new lake. Next, a long arc guides visitors to the embarcadero at the southern end of the park. Rows of Montezuma cypress (*Taxodium mucronatum*) and Bonpland willows occupy the various wetlands adjacent to the promenade.

One reason for the successive decay of the Xochimilco district was the extraction of clean water from its springs to feed Mexico City using aqueducts built in the early part of the twentieth century [8-18]. An essential part of the plan to rehabilitate the Xochimilco *chinampa* district (executed 1989–1993) was the construction of several water treatment plants to replenish the loss of springs that once flowed into the lagoons and canals. The introduction of treated water aided the recovery of historic water levels and supported the planting of the *chinampas*, in addition to restoring access and movement by the traditional canoes and flatboats.

### *Malinalco Residence*
### *Malinalco, State of Mexico*

On a far different scale from the two previous projects is a private garden in the town of Malinalco, two hours southwest of Mexico City, set at an altitude of 1,500 meters above sea level—which is almost 1,000 meters below Mexico City. The American owners of the garden spend half the year in Mexico, the other half in northern New York state, where winters are quite cold and the snowfall significant. Our clients selected this subtropical site for its temperate winters and asked for color, texture, flowers, and a sense of "tropicality" in their new garden [8-19; see also chapter opening].

The project is organized as a spectrum of gardens surrounding the existing house and an additional plot of some 6,600 square meters. Interestingly, a very ancient system of irrigation channels, *apantles* or *acequias*, could provide abundant water for the garden. (*Apantle* derives from the Nahuatl, from *atl*, or water, and *pantle*, a channel). However, due to ancient traditions concerning agricultural water rights, we could not use this liquid for irrigation in the garden. Instead, we could bring it inside the house and then return it to the communal *acequia*. Thus, the water channel first enters into a cistern surrounded by *Xanthosoma*, a beautiful plant with elegant, gigantic leaves. Next to the first garden are a paddle tennis court and a bamboo "room" open to the sky and surrounded by ground covers of agapanthus (*Agapanthus africanus*) and plumbago (*Plumbago auriculata*). An extensive lawn accompanies the bamboo "room." Along the *acequia* the path is planted with *Plumeria rubra* and ground covers of *sábila* (*Aloe vera*), *Euphorbia milii*, and other succulents.

A small lagoon three to four meters deep composes the central garden. The lagoon has been excavated to the level of the aquifer. The interior *acequia* terminates in the lagoon,

**8-17**

Parquo Ecológico Xochimilco. Mexico City, 1993. Aerial view of lake and wetlands. [Michael Calderwood]

**8-18**

Parque Ecológico Xochimilco. Water runnels and rows of Montezuma cypress (*Taxodium mucronatum*) at the park entrance. [Marc Treib]

but its overflow is again connected to the communal *acequia* outside the house. The lagoon is surrounded by *Equisetum* and papyrus and various kinds of *Nymphaea*. To the rear of the lagoon, the next garden, a preexisting wound of volcanic rock, contains beautiful large trees with sculptural trunks (*Spondias purpurea*, or tropical plum) [8-20, 8-21]. The ground is covered with two types of ferns: *Pteridium aquilinum* and *Dryopteris affinis*. Three large rocks were recovered from the excavation of the lagoon and were arranged to form a beautiful, peaceful spot with water issuing from between the rocks.

The transitional garden, joining the lagoon and the rear garden, takes form as a mound constructed from materials excavated to make the lagoon. It features large masses of colorful *Lantana camara*, whose bright orange flowers attract birds and butterflies. With the lantana are the large maguey plants (*Agave americana*) typical of this part of Mexico. The final back garden is a circular, concentric orchard of citrus trees that includes orange, lemon, and grapefruit. At the center of this circular composition is a red concrete bench enclosing a fire pit. Next to the citrus garden comes a herb garden structure, with elevated beds covered with dried branches, simulating large baskets.

Not all our efforts involve living materials and hardscape, and in closing, I would like to introduce a catalog our office has produced that records the names, qualities, and requirements for the plants we use in our work [see 8-2]. Ironically perhaps, despite the richness of plant species in Mexico, there are very few books that present sufficient technical information about their value as the material of landscape architecture. The book contains about one thousand plants that range in size from small flowers to large trees and describes their characteristics and their needs. We regard the book not only as a tool for our work but as a contribution to landscape architecture and horticulture in Mexico. While the material in the catalog informs our own design—we hope it will also benefit other landscape architects and garden makers designing good and appropriate places for Mexico, its climate, and its biomes.

**Notes**

1 Peter H. Raven, "Tropical Floristics Tomorrow," *Taxon* 3, 1988.

2 Andrea Wulf, *The Invention of Nature: Alexander von Humboldt's New World*, New York: Vintage, 2015.

3 Greenpeace México. "La deforestación y sus causas," Press release, México, 2017.

**8-19**

Malinalco Residence. State of Mexico, 2011. Lagoon and preexisting *Spondias purpurea* (purple mombin) growing in volcanic rock. [Héctor Velasco]

**8-20**

Malinalco Residence. Curving *acequia* with *Sempervivum* sp. (houseleek), *Agave attenuata*, *Xanthosoma sp.* (elephant's ears), *Plumeria rubra* (red frangipani). [Francisco Gómez Sosa]

**8-21**

Malinalco Residence. Acequia with *Philodendron selloum* and *Canna iridiflora*. [Héctor Velasco]

# PLANTING AND CULTURE IN THE FAR NORTH

Thorbjörn Andersson

9.

**Unless otherwise noted, landscapes illustrated in this chapter have been designed by Thorbjörn Andersson / Sweco Architects.**

—

Hyllie Plaza. Malmö, Sweden, 2010. [Kasper Dudzik]

Plants are probably the most critical material with which landscape architects work; both their very existence and their application derive from their geographical location. As a result, site and regional culture are basic to planting design. Plants inform us about a specific regional geography and how living systems survive and thrive there. Plants inform us about the physical world: how they are used tells us about our culture. If considerations of plants, site, and culture coincide, the landscape architect is given the means for creating an environment with a strong cultural identity [9-1].

## Roses

The Swedish author and polymath Carl Jonas Love Almqvist (1793–1866) composed music, painted pictures, and wrote both novels and nonfiction. As a cultural figure Almqvist shares certain parallels with Henry David Thoreau in the United States and Jean-Jacques Rousseau in France—and was equally controversial. Many of his writings were collected in a volume interestingly titled *The Book of the Thorny Rose*, and in that book Almqvist describes connections among culture, geography, and flora, using the rose as the primary vehicle for his argument.[1] In one section, he illustrates his thoughts by describing the various forms the flower has taken and discusses how these differences derive from responses to their native habitat.

Almqvist compares the rose growing naturally in his homeland of Sweden to the roses found in the manicured flower beds of southern Europe. The Swedish rose, *Rosa canina* (dog rose), has flat petals and a simple form [9-2]. Most of the varieties are white in color, although at times their flowers are graced with a pale pinkish rim that almost resembles a blush. The scent is subtle and difficult to discern; from a distance the plant is almost imperceptible. Its form is open and hides nothing. Its mild fragrance blends with the choir of scents experienced on land where meadow transforms into forest, and it is just at the edge between these two ecosystems that the *Rosa canina* grows as a shrub.

In comparison, Almqvist describes the flamboyant fullness of what he calls the Mediterranean rose [9-3]. Its color is often deep red and its flower is elaborate and multilayered. As opposed to the northern rose, its petals are plentiful and densely packed, and seemingly contain many secrets among them and within their hidden places. The Mediterranean rose has a strong, almost narcotic scent that dominates any other plant around it; it tolerates no competition; it does not participate in the choir. This rose is flamboyant,

**9-1**

Swedish landscape types: Forest. [Thorbjörn Andersson]

**9-2**

*Rosa canina*. [Thorbjörn Andersson]

**9-3**

*Rosa* sp. cultivar. [Thorbjörn Andersson]

like a flamenco dancer. The cultivated rose which Almqvist envisions before him exists in thousands of subspecies and cultivars: it has been crossbred, hybridized, and refined into numerous varieties. Of the *Rosa canina*, on the other hand, there is but one species, a horticultural limit that could serve as a symbol of Swedish plant life as well as its environment.[2]

## Poverty

Included in *The Book of the Thorny Rose* is an essay that bears the title "The Significance of Swedish Poverty" (Den svenska fattigdomens betydelse).[3] In his text Almqvist advances his belief that an aesthetic preference shared by a people derives from their geographical and cultural circumstances. The culture of Sweden has been shaped by its location in the far north and its limited natural resources; Almqvist terms this cultural trait "poverty." He tells us that poverty can, in fact, be a virtue, that virtues form values, and values form cultures. In the Nordic countries these values can be described as austerity rather than abundance, and necessities as opposed to possibilities. The ideas presented in "The Significance of Swedish Poverty" in many ways summarize Sweden's longstanding psychological attitude, as well as its cultural values and lifestyle. Poverty has also informed the country's design culture, which has not been without success when dealing with the greater world. If I were a businessperson, I would say that "poverty" has become a form of branding that has been used to market Swedish products from Volvo cars to Hasselblad cameras to Boda glassware [9-4].

These are all objects that own an elegance derived from restraint rather than ornamentation; however, this attitude also enfolds abstract values into the mix. Throughout the years, and the twentieth century in particular, "poverty" has fostered innovative thinking and catalyzed our means of finding a way. Poverty has created achievements in such fields as fashion design, furniture design, graphic design, ballet, filmmaking, music, and gastronomy. Poverty, here interpreted as simplicity, remains a basic value system that pervades the design fields and the arts, a value system that has become even more evident in today's world of global marketing. In the advertising for Swedish products, we repeatedly see environments wearing pale winter colors, snowy landscapes and endless spruce forests growing in the tundralike conditions of the very far north. The marketing message seems to be "This landscape is genuine, as are its people." A product from this land is genuine and trustworthy.

Many other writers have contributed to this Swedish worldview and its values, even those writing cookbooks. One of the earliest of these cookbooks was written in the middle of the eighteenth century by a woman named Cajsa Warg (1703–1769). She coined an aphorism, which Swedes still apply to all kinds of circumstances in modern life: "Use what is at hand." To accept what is at hand is a marker of acceptance, a reconciliation with the conditions given you. It suppresses greed and supports creative thinking, although some say it also suppresses ambition. In any case, this aphorism highlights what Almqvist identified as the significance of poverty in Swedish culture: accept what is available and maximize its potential.

**9-4**

Ingegärd Råman. *Farfars glasflaska* (Grandad's flask). glassware, 2017. [Vandalorum Museum]

## Landscape

The story of the two roses can also be taken as an explanation of Swedish gardens and landscape design, as well as their relation to the larger landscape and natural geography of the land. According to geographers, Sweden's eight distinct characteristics distinguish its landscape:

1. A mosaiclike character to its topography that comprises relatively small zones rather than forming grand lines
2. Poor growing conditions due to long winters and a harsh climate
3. Moraine over bedrock soil that drains quickly and results in meager soil quality
4. Characteristic rock outcroppings are also found in the lowlands, an unusual geographic phenomenon.
5. A topographic structure highly visible and marked by parallel ridges created by the inland ice that left the country 10,000 years ago. This has shaped the landscape in an unmistakable way.
6. Thin layers of soil with a low humus content
7. A vegetation belt that forms part of the broader taiga condition
8. A mix of the nemoral and boreal zones, a specific Swedish interweaving of deciduous trees and evergreen conifers throughout most of the country

## Paradise

Historically, Paradise has been conceived as a garden. Given its particular environmental conditions and its "poverty," what then might be Sweden's image of Paradise? In the biblical story of the Fall, Adam and Eve gained their universal knowledge by eating the apple, the forbidden fruit. In retribution they were expelled from Eden, from a landscape of liberty and abundance to a land of restriction and toil.

**9-5**

Swedish landscape types: Moraine ridge. [Thorbjörn Andersson]

**9-6**

Swedish landscape types: Marsh. [Thorbjörn Andersson]

**9-7**

Swedish landscape types: Grove. [Thorbjörn Andersson]

Outside Eden was wilderness. Outside Eden was unproductive land inhabited by the villain, the outcast, the leper. Outside Eden is not where you want to be: it is the shadow side of Paradise, a place where one must labor to exist. In Sweden, however, the vision of Paradise was reversed. Wilderness—nature—provided shelter, firewood, freedom of movement, land to explore, a place to restart one's life. In the Swedish mind, nature meant home, in complete contrast to visions of Paradise from the Middle East, the Bible's place of origin. The idea of garden versus nature represents a classic dichotomy in which the garden is cast as a dream factory or its realized vision. In the garden, physical needs can be tended and the mind fulfilled. In contrast to nature, however, the garden is manufactured and represents artifice. To maintain a garden requires an atlas of manipulations. A garden can seemingly be anything.

But not so in Sweden. Swedish landscape architects claim to address the conditions specific to the site, with plants used to render a place more legible. Plants in this context serve as a code for understanding a regional landscape [9-5, 9-6, 9-7]. The result, at best, is an optimized system of soil, temperature, light, and other factors that together create a relevant biological entity we can understand and mentally relate to. Over time, these landscapes reveal the cultural patterns that also shape the landscape. A few examples: Spruce (*Picea abies*) is found as dense forests on nutritious soils. Juniper (*Juniperus communis*) grows on dry, grazed land. Pine (*Pinus sylvestris*) thrives on dry land with thin soil layers. Alders (*Alnus glutinosa*) and birches (*Betula verrucosa*) grow in moist ground or by streams and brooks, as do willows (*Salix alba*). Swedish landscape architecture tends to follow these simple guidelines provided by the various species.

## In Film

Of all the austere landscapes in Sweden, some of those most telling are found on Gotland, a large island in the Baltic Sea lying off the east coast of Sweden [9-8]. The film director Ingmar Bergman (1919–2008) had his studio and home on Gotland, and there he shot many of his films. Among them was *Persona* (1966), whose simplicity prevented any obscuring of its content. In the film, Bergman traces the connection between the inner and outer landscapes. Shot in black and white, and restrained in its elements, the film features only two actors—Bibi Andersson and Liv Ullmann—and two settings, very little music, and restricted dialogue [9-9]. Bergman's investigation of the lead actress's silence is marked by an ambience of purity, frugality, thoughtfulness, and quiet interaction—and perhaps also ambiguity. From an aesthetic standpoint, Bergman's challenge was to walk the line between thrift and plenty, between necessity and possibility. In the best-case scenario, to resolve this dichotomy stimulates the spirit of life. It addresses "to have and to have not"; it is more a process than an image or a product. It is about finding the sublime, the Holy Grail of all aesthetic values. It is about defining something beyond the beautiful, about creating an aesthetic experience that touches our emotional lives—and not only our eyes. The landscape of Gotland serves as an appropriate backdrop for his quest and reinforces Bergman's artistic ambitions.

The Russian film director Andrei Tarkovsky made only seven films before he died in 1986. He shot his last film, *The Sacrifice*, that same year on what he called "the most beautiful place on the planet," a certain peninsula named Närsholmen, located on the east side of Gotland [9-10]. Närsholmen is a place almost completely lacking in prominent geographic features. Instead, its barren landscape pushes the imagination, both Tarkovsky's and our own. There is a horizon; there is a flat moor open to the sky; there are some low juniper shrubs (*Juniper communis*). Their forms tease our sense of scale and make the landscape appear larger than it measures. By this shift of scale we are transported far away, perhaps from a barren island in the Baltic to an African savanna. Another of Tarkovsky's films, *Stalker*, centers on the search for a place with those very effects, a transcendent place, a place that acts as a screen on which we can project our desires. In the film, three men trespass into a forbidden and dangerous area called The Zone, the aftermath of some traumatic event whose cause is unclear: perhaps a nuclear disaster or a climatic catastrophe. "It is a very complex maze of traps," says their guide, who is called Stalker; two of the other men are scientists; the third is an author. The three men explore the forbidden zone in search of a central place where Stalker has told them all things become clear, and all wishes are fulfilled. The Zone can be seen as a metaphor for the garden: "A place to indulge in spiritual and existential reflections," says the guide. In that way, Stalker's relation to The Zone bears similarities to that of a Zen monk in a Kyoto temple garden, or perhaps a Swede taking a walk in the woods.

If we transfer the idioms of austerity, scale, and sublimity into planting design, we transcend a focus on things decorative and ornamental and move into the realm of meaning, quality, and value, and probably also ambiguity. These are the aspects that unite many Swedish designers in what they hope to achieve in their work. Again taking Gotland as an

**9-8**

Landscape of austerity. Gotland, Sweden. [Thorbjörn Andersson]

**9-9**

Ingmar Bergman. *Persona*, 1966. Liv Ullmann (*left*) and Bibi Andersson. [AB Svensk Filmindustri / Sven Nykvist]

**9-10**

Närsholmen landscape. [Thorbjörn Andersson, 2018]

**9-11**

Flowering annuals along the road shoulders. Gotland, Sweden. [Thorbjörn Andersson]

example, the landscape here is "poor" in that broad-leaved grasses do not grow well here, which opens the potential for a different flora: a fragile, almost translucent, habitat of thin, miniscule flowers and annuals. These species do not thrive in rich soils and fertilized gardens but instead thrive on the moors and, surprisingly, on the shoulders of roads. As a result, Gotland's most intriguing flower beds color the paths of the traveler [9-11]. The formations of these environments are arbitrary; they arrive by chance. They resemble neither a Gertrude Jekyll herbaceous border from the early twentieth century, nor a Mien Ruys garden in the Netherlands from the 1950s, nor a Piet Oudolf perennial planting from the 2000s. Instead, they exist in response to the conditions of the landscape: its dry soil, the moisture of the mist, the shaping of the wind, the length of the day, and the climate. In some ways, these "gardens" are the products of the road engineers who accidentally created the conditions for the birth and survival of a very special plant habitat. After all, they were the ones who poured crushed aggregate over the chalky soil and created an unintended flower bed, absolutely dry and free of mulch. These accidental landscapes along the roads of Gotland have even received national prizes. They are, of course, public, and the plants can be picked by any passerby, anyone who appreciates their detail, simplicity, and authenticity—as well as those who believe that the public realm can also serve private uses. Examples of what we find there are the annuals *Centaurea cyanus* (cornflower), *Cichorium intybus* (chicory), *Echium vulgare* (blueweed), *Thymus serpyllum* (wild thyme), *Saxifraga granulata* (meadow saxifrage), *Viscaria vulgaris* (clammy campion), *Rubus caesius* (European dewberry), *Achillea millefolium* (yarrow), and *Vincetoxicum hirundinaria* (white swallowwort).

Although we may believe that a garden represents the dream of a private Paradise come true, Sweden as a whole is not a garden but rather a mosaic of natural landscapes of common ground rather than private domains. Inland ice shaped Sweden some 10,000 years ago; in contrast, the Dutch themselves made the Netherlands some centuries ago and since then it has become a machine for production. Much of the land occupied by cities, pastureland for dairy cattle, and tulip fields is territory regained from the sea. In that sense, the Netherlands is hardly natural. This geographic condition, I believe, influences Dutch landscape design, which is seldom subdued, usually inventive, and more often the result of endeavor rather than process. Still, there are links that join the two countries.

## Perennials

In the 1990s an international group of European plantsmen and plantswomen formed an informal group called Perennial Perspectives. Their aim, ideologically, was to offer an alternative to late-modernist landscape architecture and its attitude of treating plants only for their function: as shelter belts, spiky hedges of hawthorn (*Crataegus*) or barberry (*Berberis*) to prevent trespassing, and screens of fast-growing trees such as poplars and willows to create spaces and screen unwanted views. When I was a student of landscape architecture in the mid-1970s the book *Inte bara berberis* (Not Only Barberry) was required reading. The book advocated the expansion of plant applications beyond functional uses such as shelterbelts and poplar screens. Dutch landscape designers followed a similar train of thought. They looked north, beyond their national boundaries. There they discovered ideas about nature and wilderness, and found these northern plants beautiful because they were marked by seasonal change and were attractive even in decay. The book *Dream Plants for the Natural Garden* by plantsmen Piet Oudolf and Henk Gerritsen served almost as a manifesto.[4] A seminar prior to the book's publication was held in the Netherlands. One of the participants was Stefan Mattsson, director of parks for the town of Enköping, Sweden, who sat beside Piet Oudolf on the bus during a related field trip.

As a result of this encounter, Mattsson invited Oudolf to design a park for Enköping. This was Oudolf's first foreign work and it remains one of his largest projects, covering 3,000 square meters (32,000 square feet) and using almost 250 different species of plants. The Dream Park, as it is called, opened in 1995 [9-12]. At the park's inauguration, with Stefan Mattsson on the podium—not without pride—stood seed producer Rob Leopold and Piet and Anna Oudolf. In Oudolf's short talk, he listed what he regarded as the three keys to good planting design: (1) homogeneity (as opposed to mixtures); (2) rhythm and repetition; and (3) structure (often created by pruned hedges; in Enköping these were hornbeam (*Carpinus*). Grasses typically served as a sort of glue between the homogeneous surfaces of species. In the Dream Park, 24 different grasses were used, all of which came from Oudolf's own nursery in Hummelo.[5]

The Dream Park represents only one way to use nature to guide planting design. Among those many ways to work with nature, I will note four; there are certainly others. For the 2009 conversion of the old rail yard to a park at Südgelände south of Berlin, the landscape architects Planland with Group Odious left the switchyard as it was, allowing

natural growth to prosper, adding only pathways and some small structures. That strategy might be called *abandon*. The British filmmaker Derek Jarman *decorated* his gravel garden with materials such as driftwood and detritus found on the beach near his house. At the Novartis pharmaceutical company in Basel, Switzerland, Günter Vogt chose to build nature as authentically as possible above the underground parking garage at the entrance to the complex. This represents a *mimetic* reproduction of nature—almost completely lacking in interpretation or transformation; it is an extremely sophisticated landscape but stands apart from the urban landscape around it. A different kind of elegance is found in the gardens of Japan, also said to be an imitation of nature, but in its treatment of plants and basic miniaturization it is more an *interpretation* and *transformation* than a true copy. Thus, all the strategies of *abandon*, *decoration*, *mimesis*, and *interpretation* form a grammar for planting design using nature as their point of departure.

Planting design is often about making beautiful and/or useful compositions by mixing different types and species of vegetation. In Sweden, landscape designers generally take into account the complex natural systems as well as the cultural and regional factors, and produce designs that paradoxically appear as a simple, or even simplistic. The most decisive factor directing Nordic planting design is relevance to the context, in contrast to the garden cultures in many Mediterranean countries. Two projects of my own design illustrate a Nordic attitude: Hyllie Plaza in Malmö, in which only one species of tree was used, and the Physic Garden at the Novartis research campus in Basel, Switzerland, where we planted as many as 83 species on a much smaller site. Despite their differences in size, both fall within the category of interpretation described above.

## Planting

For the Hyllie Plaza in the southern Swedish city of Malmö, only a single species of tree was planted, namely *Fagus sylvatica* (European beech). The geography of this part of Sweden is not very representative of the country's greater landscape, as the soil is sedimentary and the presence of granite is muted. The landscape, flat and almost without any single identifiable character, serves primarily as farmland and more closely resembles the landscape of Denmark than the remainder of Sweden to its north. Apart from the coastlines with their pretty beaches, only one feature stands out in this southern landscape: the medium-sized forests of beech that dot the territory.

**9-12**

Piet Oudolf, with Stefan Mattsson. Dream Park. Enköping, Sweden, 1996. [Marc Treib]

The design idea for the plaza was to create a stylized beech forest with a rhythmic play of open glades for rest and shaded areas assigned to circulation. The plan shows 32 beeches set in slots in the paving. As a composition, the trees cohere as a forest; in the clearings, seating is provided [9-13; see also chapter opening]. The trees used were already 35 years old, selected a year before being planted in Malmö. Ironically perhaps, the trees were not purchased from local sources but came from a derelict nursery in the former East Germany. As they grew, the trees had been left unpruned and had acquired more individualistic shapes and branch structures than usual. In winter, complete with their frozen root balls, they were transported to Malmö and planted in their new habitat.

Beech proved to be a challenging choice of species, if not quite a poor one. As it has a sensitive root system, beech does not like pavement: It needs direct exposure to soil, nutrients, and air. It does not like changes in its habitat. It feeds on its falling leaves and other organic debris, in a way cannibalizing itself. When developing the design, we hired an army of the best experts we could find to consult on issues of soil, growth, nutrition, transporting large trees, and other risk factors. The consultants developed a structural soil applied over some 19,000 square meters (205,000 square feet), the largest of its type in northern Europe [9-14]. To ameliorate the soil quality, we imported large bags of mycorrhiza, the mycelium of a fungus that enters into a symbiotic association with the roots of the plant to become highly active in planting beds. Truckloads of lava stone, useful for both its porosity and its ability to retain moisture, were also brought in. Charcoal fills the voids in the structural soil, with remarkable results in terms of the microbiological life in the planting beds.[6]

Hyllie Plaza is paved with large slabs of Swedish granite, although importing granite from China would have cost only half the price. Like the selection of species, the choice of stone tells us something about the region. At the start, we had wanted the floor of the plaza to be so elegant that people would take off their shoes and walk on it in their socks or bare feet [9-15]. Parallel cuts in the granite permit air and stormwater to enter and exit the subgrade, while granting the plaza a graphic regularity. As a whole, the plaza is like a giant sandwich with layers of materials, tubes, and pipes, comprising a life-support system for the beech trees. In its use of substantial resources, it is not a very Swedish project. The concept of nature could not be sustained here, due to the lack of natural features on the site. Instead we constructed an interpretation of nature with the help of

**9-13**

Thorbjörn Andersson / Sweco Architects. Hyllie Plaza. Malmö, Sweden, 2012. [Kasper Dudzik]

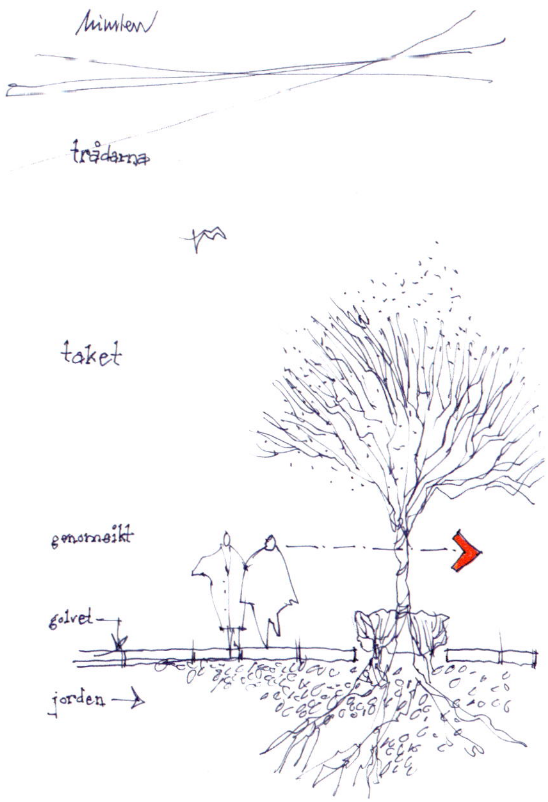


**9-14**

Hyllie Plaza. Section. [Thorbjörn Andersson]

high-tech biological tools. We tried to underline the artificial aspect of the plaza in various ways, making evident that this is, in fact, a site of manufactured nature. For instance, 50 feet in the air above the granite paving are three kilometers of cable on which 3,500 LED diodes are attached [9-16]. The effect is that of a digital sky. Even heaven can be interpreted.

The beech is a handsome tree—tall and proud—with many qualities, including longevity. It keeps its golden-brown leaves in wintertime. It has a horizontal branch structure that makes it quite sympathetic to architecture. As an individual, it has a smooth silky trunk resembling an elephant's foot. As a forest, it has foliage that screens out light and makes the ground beneath almost sterile. It is a monoculture. It is one of few habitats that already looks designed in nature. Nonetheless, that there were so many issues involved with ensuring the survival of the beeches on Hyllie Plaza taught us certain lessons. When we realized the difficulties of using the beech, we considered changing the species. However, Rune Bengtsson, professor at the Swedish University of Agricultural Sciences and one of Sweden's foremost experts on trees, suggested that we should use the beeches as a subject of research. The project opened in 2011, and after nine years, only one tree has died; it was replaced from the reserve of six trees we keep on the side. Hyllie Plaza is probably the only public space with a stylized beech forest as the main feature.

The Physic Garden on the Novartis Campus in Basel contains 83 species of plants in an area only one-fifth the size of Hyllie Plaza [9-17]. Because Novartis is a major producer of pharmaceuticals, the design idea proposed a garden that featured plants significant for their healing properties. In that sense, the Physic Garden can be said to represent the core of the company's activities. Its design also relates to the medieval monastic garden in which monks learned about the medicinal properties of plants, knowledge that laid the foundation for today's advanced research and production efforts.

The Physic Garden is organized as a theater, with backdrop provided by yew (*Taxus baccata*) and hornbeam (*Carpinus betulus*), each with a different shade of green and whose presence remains strong in winter. A sunken planting bed in the center of the garden is organized as a series of stripes containing 32 of the most important pharmaceutical plants [9-18, 9-19, 9-20]. Viewed from above, the bed reads as a colorful and textured painting or carpet. Bridges of light construction span the sunken bed and permit visitors to

**9-15**

Hyllie Plaza. Malmö, Sweden, 2012. [Robert Kjellén]

**9-16**

Hyllie Plaza. The Digital Sky: LED lights at night. [Åke E:son Lindman]

**9-17**

Physic Garden.
Novartis Pharma
campus.
Basel, Switzerland,
2012.
Seen from above.
[Jan Raeber]

**9-18**

Physic Garden.
Novartis Pharma
Campus.
[Thorbjörn
Andersson]

**9-19**

Thorbjörn Andersson / Sweco Architects. Pål Svensson, sculptor. Physic Garden. Novartis Pharma campus. Basel, Switzerland, 2012. [Thorbjörn Andersson]

**9-20**

Physic Garden. Novartis Pharma campus. In flower. [Beat Rösch]

more closely examine the plants. Among the plant species are wooly foxglove (*Digitalis lanata*), cornflower or bachelor's button (*Centaurea cyanus*), field poppy (*Papaver rhoeas*), and autumn crocus (*Colchium autumnale*).

## Conclusion

Sven-Ingvar Andersson (1927–2007), a legendary Swedish landscape architect, once pinned a sixteenth-century engraving by Jan Breughel the Elder to his office wall [9-21]. In elaborate detail the engraving shows us that a knowledge of plants—how to care for them, how to grow them, how to compose them—was already well developed in prior centuries. Knowledge of the forest was important to the hunter; knowledge of cultivation was critical to those who became settlers. Symbolically, the garden and its plants formed the cradle of civilization, whether in the Garden of Eden or the celestial gardens of Islamic culture. The Persian word for garden is *Paradezia*, which we recognize in its inherited form as Paradise. A sign on the front door of the office of the German landscape architect Dieter Kienast read, "Paradise is where you are," an expression that easily could have been Swedish. Living a harmonious life includes considerable degrees of acceptance, but some aspects of life can be influenced, for instance, by landscape and planting design. How we grow, treat, and work with plants—whether for pleasure or for food, unifies almost all cultures over the world. Within that shared framework of needs and desires, however, are substantial and remarkable differences. Plants and the landscape designs in which they are used produce and embody our culture and should be made with care, and with a profound understanding.

**9-21**

Pieter van der Heyden (after Jan Brueghel the Elder). *The Seasons: Spring*, ca. 1570. [Metropolitan Museum of Art, New York, Wikimedia Commons]

### Notes

**1** *Törnrosens Bok* (The Book of the Thorny Rose) is a compilation of Almqvist's writing, consisting of 14 volumes. It has had two overlapping editions: the shorter Duodes edition published in 1833, and the longer Imperial Octave edition that followed some years later.

**2** The Swedish botanist Hugo Sjörs (1915–2010) has shown that it is possible to classify the complete Swedish landscape by identifying only 12 plant habitats.

**3** "Den svenska fattigdomens betydelse," in *Törnrosens bok*, Duodes edition, volumes 8–11, Stockholm, 1833.

**4** Piet Oudolf and Henk Gerritsen, *Dream Plants for the Natural Garden*, London: Frances Lincoln, 2011.

**5** When I interviewed Stefan Mattsson while preparing my text in 2017, he noted that Oudolf charged no fee for his design work, only for the sale of plants, which arrived in Enköping on three large trucks.

**6** As we learned from Brazilian studies of the *terra preta*, their black soil.

# BOTANICAL STORIES FROM THE ANTIPODES

Kate Cullity

10.

**Unless otherwise noted, landscapes illustrated in this chapter have been designed by Taylor Cullity Lethlean (TCL)**

—

TCL with Paul Thompson.
Royal Botanic Gardens Victoria.
Cranbourne, Victoria, Australia, 2012.
Australian Garden.
[John Gollings]

The practice Taylor and Cullity was founded in 1990 by Kevin Taylor (my late husband) and myself, with Perry Lethlean joining us in 1994 to become Taylor Cullity Lethlean: today TCL. While we all shared the pursuit of landscape architecture, our backgrounds and interests varied. Kevin had a degree in architecture, Perry a master's in urban design, and I had a degree in science, majoring in botany with studies in the visual arts. A colleague of ours once said that we had the "ability to disagree productively." There have certainly been lively debates over the years, and of course, they continue.

For many years now, TCL has involved far more people than just the three founders. Today we have three additional directors and many enthusiastic and talented people working with us. We maintain the climate of an open studio, and ever since our inception we've been keen collaborators. Why try to do something by yourself when you know there are other people who can do it so much better? We often collaborate with architects, artists, historians, writers, various designers, scientists, and horticulturalists. We lure people to our studio with the prospect of lively design sessions, food, and a drink at the end of the day.

The firm and its works are obviously Australian, and over the years we have often been inspired by authors like Tim Winton, a well-known writer from Western Australia where I was born, grew up and studied. Winton wrote that Australia is "surrounded by ocean and ambushed from behind by desert, a war of mystery on both sides."[1]

I grew up in Western Australia's capital city, Perth, which is one of the most isolated cities in the world—as well as one of the windiest and driest. Perth is defined by both its scarcity and abundance of water; it's edged by ocean, sits on the generous Swan River, and has a Mediterranean climate; as the rainfall is minimal, the climate is somewhat like that of California. Although the sandy soils are ancient and impoverished, the southwest of Western Australia is one of the 25 original global hotspots for wildlife and plants, and the first one so identified in Australia. The region is about the size of England. England has about 1,500 species of vascular plants, 47 of them found nowhere else. By contrast the southwest of Western Australia harbors an astonishing 7,239 vascular plant species, with almost 80 percent of them endemic. The ancient *Xanthorrhoea*, the grass tree, is just one example of the prolific, diverse, and abundant species that grow in this region.

I grew up with a mother who had also studied botany and was and—now at 90—is still a keen gardener. She and my grandfather were very involved in Kings Park, an almost 1,000-acre Australian native landscape adjacent to the city, graced with large areas of indigenous "bush" and cultivated landscapes that showcase the native flora. The park had a huge impact on me and was a magical playground in which to learn about plants.

In this chapter I will discuss plants and the narratives they convey through the lens of TCL's projects, with each varying in overall approach and planting design. The particular design approach can be described in these ways:

- *As Found*: Minimal intervention, on the Uluṟu-Kata Tjuṯa Cultural Centre in Central Australia.
- *As Artifice*: Cultivated by Fire, a permanent display garden for the IGA Berlin redevelopment.
- *As Abstraction*: The Australian Garden, dedicated to the display of indigenous plants.

## Landscape as Found / Minimal Intervention: Uluru-Kata Tjuta Cultural Centre

In Aboriginal Australia there are approximately 245 language groups of which 150 remain in daily use [10-1]. Of these 150 languages, only 13 are being taught to children; thus many of them are highly endangered.

The Uluṟu-Kata Tjuṯa Cultural Centre, completed in 1990, was a rather daunting project involving complex social and environmental issues. Uluṟu, a geological formation formerly known as Ayers Rock, is an important sacred site for the Anangu—its Aboriginal traditional owners—and an Australian icon that each year attracts thousands of visitors from around the world. In designing a new Aboriginal cultural center landscape for the national park that encompasses Uluṟu, we felt it important to express the rich living history of the traditional owners and to understand their deep and continuous commitment to, care for, and connection to their land, as well as to one another. In addition was the need to incorporate and explain the law (Tjukurpa) that is passed down as spirit stories to succeeding generations. At the time we began our work, visitors still climbed the rock, a practice the Aboriginal people abhorred. An advertisement for the Sails in the Desert Hotel at the nearby Ayers Rock Resort proudly proclaimed that for guests at their resort, "being in the desert was nothing like being in the desert." In stark contrast to this message, we wanted the cultural center landscape to center on experiencing the desert, and to instill in visitors an understanding that in the Aboriginal way of thinking, plants are intricately intertwined with all aspects of everyday and spiritual life.

To better understand the geography, people, and flora, we spent about a month living in the Mutitjulu community (a housing settlement for both the Anangu and park rangers). We walked through the desert, discussed the possibility of different building sites, listened to Anangu stories and aspirations, and worked with the joint management of the national parks. The Anangu expressed themselves through interpreted conversations, taped monologues, drawings on sand, paintings of possible building ideas, and road trips into the park. One of the paintings that resulted from these conversations depicts the Tjukurpa of the creation of Uluṟu, in which Liru (a poisonous carpet snake) and Kuniya (a python) fight, forming marks and indentation on the rock face [10-2]. A second painting featured horseshoe shapes that represented Anangu sitting during a ceremony; dots in lozenge forms possibly depicted the first Aboriginal representation of cars.

**10-1**

Artist and date unknown. Aboriginal painting depicting the mosaic patterns formed by lighting low intensity fires known as "firestick farming" or "fire mosaics." [Peter Emmett]

Through experience it became obvious that structured meetings were an anomaly to the Aboriginal culture, so in their place we set up an open-door studio filled with photographs, drawings, and models to encourage informal encounters. I worked with the women, especially regarding their cultural connection to plants. Early in the project an Aboriginal elder walked us through the site, pointing to the ground, passing around the spinifex, noticing the nuances and minutiae of land, and the ephemeral marks painted by animals and plants. When explaining the experience she wanted visitors to have traversing the site, she pointed and said, "*MInga* walk around touching trees, one by one, slowly, not just look at Rock." The Anangu call tourists *minga*, their word for ants, as they look like ants in a line as they climb the rock.

As part of our site analysis Kevin Taylor wrote this poem, *Walking In*:

*Walking with Anangu*
*Gently, around the grasses, past the warrior oaks, to this place*
*Anangu*
*Plain*
*Earth*
*Stories*
*Law*
*Rock*
*Space*
*Open spaces, all not filled*

**10-2**

Barbara Tjikatu and Nipper Winmati, Aboriginal elders. Painting commissioned by the Uluṟu Kata Tjuṯa Cultural Centre project, depicting the dreaming story of how Uluṟu was formed by two snakes in conflict, 1990. [Gregory Burgess, Uluṟu Kata-Tjuṯa National Park Australia]

**10-3**

Uluṟu seen from the air, 2019. The massive rock sits on a plain of shifting sand dunes. [Kate Cullity]

*Sparseness*
*Seeing the value in what is there*
*Using what is there*
*Making do*
*Watching where you walk*
*Patterns*
*Sand*

At the time of our working on the project we were told that the average visitor's trip to Uluru is approximately a day and a half, and other than climbing the rock and standing in car parks to view the sunset and sunrise, most of them do not walk in or experience the desert other than looking at it from air-conditioned cars and buses [10-3]. Our aim was to assist the Anangu in their inviting visitors to experience and respect the traditional owner's culture and perceptions of the country. We wanted to immerse the visitor in a visceral, and perhaps even metaphysical experience; we wanted them to not only see the landscape but to experience it on a deeper level—and like us, to appreciate on many levels the beauty and care for the land.

After much consultation, collaboration, and analysis, a preferred site was chosen about one kilometer from Uluru. It was a site of low shrubs, spinifex, and desert oaks (*Allocasuarina decussata*), when juvenile trees known to Anangu as the Liru warriors due to their narrow, tall spear shape (the juvenile tree keeps this form for approximately 20 years until its taproot hits water but spreads when mature) [10-4]. The sinuous, snakelike building would enfold a large, significant if dead, desert oak. We collectively decided that no trees would be removed, and any removal of vegetation would be minimal; no additional vegetation would be planted. During the early stages of consultation, a number of park rangers proposed including a selection of the more spectacular plants from elsewhere in the park in a garden near the building. This was rejected in favor of fully appreciating what grew on this particular site, and to respond to the subtle beauty of the immediate landscape. This approach, we believed, would also imbue an understanding and appreciation of both Anangu culture and that particular place. The mass and character of Uluru create a delicate microclimate, the immediate landscape being marked by the intermittent presence of water shed by Uluru and how it is dispersed. The bloodwoods (*Eucalyptus terminalis*) occupy a very thin strip of land around the rock and grow to a height of about 20 meters (roughly 75 feet) [10-5]. The Aboriginal people use the tree's red sap as a disinfectant and as an inhalant. Seen against the mass of the rock, the bloodwoods provide a sense of scale and reveal the enormity of Uluru.

As even micro changes in grade affect this fragile landscape of shifting sand dunes, we decided there would be no changes in levels and no construction of swales or curbs. To avoid disturbing any trees, great precision was required when staking out the pathways and car and bus parks. To achieve this, the paths were marked out on-site by Kevin Taylor and the engineer Peter Yttrup—while suffering under 113–119$^{o}$ Fahrenheit heat and a plague of flies. The allowable site perimeter for the new building was allowed to penetrate only about one meter beyond its walls [10-6]. Our desire was that the site would remain as close as possible to its indigenous state. The Dutch landscape architects Karres en Brands once said in a manifesto something along these lines: "Although the act of design is very enticing, sometimes not designing is the best answer." Over time we also came to realize that not overdesigning on this site was the best answer.

In order to give the visitor an experience of being in the desert, the car and bus parks were held back 165–330 meters from the cultural center. Winding paths of compacted site sand, edged by branches collected on-site, encouraged visitors to slow down, to observe the patterns of the plants, and truly regard the memory of environmental activity etched in the red sand [10-7]. In all, this was walking as a conversation with the land, the visitors' cadence in rhythm with the surroundings. Albeit briefly, perhaps they would be immersed in the landscape rather than only viewing from the car or conquering the land through the "climb." This extended walk gave visitors time to become attuned to their surroundings and prepare for the Tjukarpa (Anangu dreaming) stories told in the Centre. This slowing down is another important means of encouraging a more careful and cultivated respect for and reverie of the Anangu's living history and the fragile, if seemingly robust, desert environment [10-8]. The landscape juxtaposes the "fast" time of speedy Western life and travel in cars with the "slow," continuous time of an ancient living culture. The walk encourages a cultivation and depth of understanding between the visitors and the Anangu.

The process needed to produce a sensitive design for the Uluru-Kata Tjuta Cultural Centre had a profound impact on Kevin Taylor and me, and our experience there in many ways informed our approach to the Australian Garden, a project begun five years later, discussed below.

**10-4**

*Allocasuarina*. Uluṟu Kata-Tjuṯa National Park, Australia. Local Aboriginal people refer to juvenile desert oaks (*Allocasuarina decussata*), columnar and spear shaped, as Liru warriors. They usually require about 25 years to find an artesian water source, at which time their canopy begins to spread. [TCL]

**10-5**

Bloodwood trees. Uluṟu Kata-Tjuṯa National Park. *Eucalyptus terminalis* grow around the perimeter of Uluṟu where they receive water as it cascades off the rock during rain periods. [Kate Cullity]

**10-6**

TCL with Gregory Burgess Architects. Uluṟu Kata-Tjuṯa Cultural Centre. Very little vegetation and no trees were removed during construction of the project. [Mark Rogers]

**10-8**

TCL with Gregory Burgess Architects. Uluṟu Kata-Tjuṯa Cultural Centre. The building was sited around a dead desert oak (*Allocasuarina decussata*) and a small grove of juvenile desert oaks. [Gregory Burgess] Architects]

**10-7** *(opposite)*

TCL. Uluṟu Kata-Tjuṯa Cultural Centre. Uluṟu Kata-Tjuṯa National Park, 1995. The path edges are lined with branches and sticks collected from within the wider park. [TCL]

**10-9**

TCL with kl Landschafts-architekten. *Cultivated by Fire* garden. Berlin, Germany, 2017. Design and plant selection were inspired by the ancient Australian Aboriginal practice of firestick or mosaic farming. [Nico Nowak]

**10-10**

TCL with kl Landschafts-architekten. The diverse planting expresses the regrowth that occurs after fire. [Lena Giovanazza]

**10-11**

TCL with
kl Landschafts-
architekten.
*Cultivated by Fire*
garden.
To propagate
kangaroo paw
(*Anigozanthos* sp.)
requires smoke from
fires.
[Leña Giovanazza]

## As Artifice: *Cultivated by Fire*

The garden *Cultivated by Fire*, completed in 2017, is a permanent display at the IGA Berlin, a high-density housing development located on the outskirts of the city [10-9]. The garden design explores how Australia's Aboriginal people use fire to manage land. This sophisticated practice known as "firestick farming" increases fertile growth, provides abundant edible plants and grasses for the wildlife they hunt, and by lowering available fuel loads also reduces the likelihood of destructive wildfires. The regions where this technique was—and is still—practiced form a mosaic of different burnt landscapes of varying ages. In the aftermath of a fire, its destructive beauty can actually appear quite sublime. Then follows the regeneration of the plants adapted to the fire that is necessary for their regrowth—grass trees and eucalyptus are blackened but endure, and in fact thrive. A verdant explosion of vegetation as well as flower color often follow a number of months after a fire.

The installation *Cultivated by Fire* abstracts and distills this practice of "firestick farming" to create a mosaic garden composed of elements reminiscent of both the burnt and rejuvenated Australian landscape. These include actual fire (although, at the authority's request, the flame is protected by a glass shield), charred poles, and a tracery of burnt branches. Eucalyptus seedlings and floriferous garden beds of Australian native plants embellish the artifice of post-fire regrowth. A startling red walkable ground plane of crushed red brick replaces the fiery red sands found in central Australia.

The German horticulturalists did not believe that our native grasses would survive the Berlin winter, and so European grasses that most closely resembled Australian grasses were used, including *Pennisetum*, *Poa*, and *Calamagrostis* species. Of course, true Australian plants have also been planted; these include foxtails, *Ptilotus*, the wonderful kangaroo paw (*Anigozanthos* ssp.), fan flower (*Scaevola aemula*), and the wonderful bird's nest Banksia (*Banksia baxterii*), all of which need to be replanted each year or put in a hot-house over winter [10-10, 10-11]. The cider gum trees (*Eucalyptus gunnii*) were planted with great German precision and fitted with heaters in their pots to ensure their survival over the winter [10-12]. So artifice once again. The *Cultivation by Fire* garden is a landscape primarily for display and goodwill. For a project on a real site and informed by myriad social, cultural, and environmental factors, we return to Australia and to the desert.

## Abstraction: The Australian Garden

The Australian Garden at the Cranbourne branch of the Royal Botanic Gardens Victoria is located about 30 miles south of downtown Melbourne. The project was our first undertaken in collaboration with Paul Thompson, a landscape architect with extensive experience and an encyclopedic knowledge of the Australian plants he selects and composes with amazing sensitivity. The site for the new Australian Garden was a former sand quarry set within a much larger landscape of quite pristine indigenous vegetation. During the design phase we made extensive studies of appropriate species, excluding several that would have been regarded as attractive had they not been invasive or troublesome in some other way. The brief for the project was magnificent, probably the greatest brief we've ever been given. There was no requirement to mimic or "recreate" the ecosystems of Australia; in fact, the administration invited us to abstract the landscape and design and sculpt the land to be expressive of our times [10-13; see also chapter opening]. At root, we at TCL wanted the garden to display the wonder, magnificence, and variety of Australian flora. Unlike in California, where eucalyptus are rather invasive, we have the native pests to keep them under control, which is good because we have a love affair with them. The eucalyptus family includes some very beautiful trees like the ubiquitous river red gum (*Eucalyptus camaldulensis*) and broad-leaved paperbark (*Melaleuca quinquenervia*); there are also the fabulous boab (*Adansonia gregorii*) and bottle trees (*Brachychiton rupestris*), and the great members of the *Proteaceae* family such as *Banksia* and *Grevillea*. Adding to the indigenous palette are the curiously expressive kangaroo paw and ancient grass trees (*Xanthorrhoea*), which sprout spearheads after fire and can live for thousands of years. There are also the ephemeral plants that emerge only after rain. In all, a walk through the 26 hectares (65 acres) of the Australian Garden presents an abstracted presentation of a walk through Australia, its colors, its textures, its richness, and perhaps even its sounds.

**10-12**

TCL with kl Landschaftsarchitekten. *Cultivated by Fire* garden. Berlin, Germany, 2017. *Eucalyptus gunnii* provides shade adjacent to the black plinth seating. A heating system surrounding their pots assists their survival in the Berlin winter. [Kate Cullity]

George Seddon, a great academic and writer on the Australian landscape, once noted that "we are still learning to see our own land and ... forgive it for not being England."[2] And in a sense, that's what we were really doing in designing the Australian Garden. The site as we found it was a somewhat blank canvas except for prior efforts to create a lake from the former sand quarry within the very rich envelope provided by the indigenous woodland. The client's requirements directed the ways in which the garden would be used. Our response was a design that explored the age and conditions

**10-13**

TCL with Paul Thompson. Australian Garden. Royal Botanic Gardens Victoria. Cranbourne, 2012. Dedicated to the wonder and diversity of Australian flora, the highly stylized landscapes are surrounded by remnants of indigenous flora. [John Gollings]

**10-14**

TCL with Paul Thompson. Australian Garden. Royal Botanic Gardens Victoria. The Red Sand Garden is an abstraction of the desert landscapes of inland Australia. Discs are planted with saltbush (*Rhagodia* sp.), the North Line with everlasting daisies (*Helichrysum* sp.). [Peter Hyatt]

of the Australian continent and the continental edge that borders the ocean. We felt that the gardens representing the continental edge could be fertile, immersive, urban, and recognizable; the landscapes expressing the desert and dry areas could be confronting, distant, and striking. The Australian Garden employs a landscape design approach that communicates geographic, scientific, and cultural narratives via experience and immersion rather than didactic signage.

The design expresses these narratives of the Australian landscape through the artistic modes of abstraction, distillation, sculpted forms, repetition, and patterning rather than by recreating landscape types or ecosystems. The primary narrative is the journey of water, from the arid center of this vast continent to its fertile continental edge. This journey of water is also a principal orientation device for visitors navigating their way within the garden. Visitors enter the garden through a quite understated forest of *Casuarina* trees. Passing through the visitor center designed by architect Kerstin Thompson, the great vista of the Red Sand Garden greets the view [10-14]. On its edge are exhibition gardens designed by others, the Dry Creek Bed Garden, and the Eucalypt Walk. Those areas were all part of Stage One.

Our journey to Uluṟu inspired the inclusion of the Sand Garden—a garden intended to evoke the sublime qualities of grandeur, the awe and vastness of the desert. It calls to mind Australian's love/hate relationship with the desert, a relationship of wonder and fear. We were inspired by Australian artists, in particular Fred Williams, whose staccato, minimal, expressive gestures presented aerial and plan views as one, all with an ever-present ground plane. Williams also spoke of a lack of focal point in the Australian landscape. The Red Sand Garden expresses the desert land of spinifex and low shrubs where each plant sits in its own shadow. The strong minimal patterning, abstraction, and repetition of the Red Sand Garden with its circular patterns of saltbush (*Rhagodia spinescens*) and sculptural installation Ephemeral Lake by Mark Stoner and Edwina Kearney distills and intensifies the sublime experience of the Australian desert.

A sense of reverence for the magnificence yet ecological fragility of the desert is expressed by prohibiting visitor entry to the garden. As in a Japanese sand garden, the viewer maintains a respectful distance and is invited only to contemplate the scene in a way that does not interrupt the garden's powerful elemental experience. The saltbush circles also decrease in size, a device used to intensify a

**10-15**

TCL with Paul Thompson. Australian Garden. Royal Botanic Gardens Victoria. Cranbourne, Victoria, Australia, 2006. Rockpool Waterway. Lines of apple gum (*Angophora costata*), with low plantings of *Dianella* and *Lomandra*, are interspersed with stone plinths. [Ben Wrigley]

**10-16**

TCL with Paul Thompson. Australian Garden. Royal Botanic Gardens Victoria. Melaleuca Spits. Parallel bands of paperbarks (*Melaleuca linariifolia*) accompany abstracted sand spits. [John Gollings]

**10-17**

TCL with Paul Thompson. Australian Garden, Royal Botanic Gardens Victoria. Cranbourne, 2012. The Eucalypt Walk evokes the patterns found on the trunks of scribbly gum (*Eucalyptus haemostoma*). [Peter Hyatt]

**10-18**

TCL with Paul Thompson. The Weird and Wonderful Garden. Australian Garden, Royal Botanic Gardens Victoria. This garden hosts some more unusual floristic forms such as bottle trees (*Brachychiton rupestris*). [John Gollings]

**10-19**

TCL with Paul Thompson.
The Weird and Wonderful Garden, Australian Garden.
Royal Botanic Gardens Victoria.
Cranbourne, Victoria, Australia, 2012.
[Paul Thompson]

**10-20**

TCL with Paul Thompson.
Australian Garden.
Royal Botanic Gardens Victoria.
Grass trees (*Xanthorrhoea sp.*) are very slow growing but can live for hundreds of years.
[John Gollings]

sense of distance and space. The line planted with ephemeral daisies creates a slash through the center of the Red Sand Garden and refers to the north point, the navigational necessity for European explorers of this harsh land.

Moving away from the Red Sand Garden to the eastern side, the escarpments of Uluṟu and other Australian rock formations, such as in the Flinders Ranges in South Australia, provided the inspiration for the Escarpment Wall alongside the Rock Pool Waterway. Here the water pulses, sometimes full and sometimes a trickle, just as the myriad of dry creek beds and dry rivers do in the dryer Australian landscape [10-15]. Lines of Sydney red gum (*Angophora costata*) order the landscape and create boundaries for the Exhibition Gardens. On the western side, bands of different eucalypts and *corymbias* such as peppermints (*Eucalyptus radiata*), stringy bark (*Eucalyptus obliqua*), lemon-scented gums (*Corymbia citriodora*—my favorite), and ironbarks (*Eucalyptus sideroxylon*) create the Eucalypt Walk. At the end of the walk is a clearing with a serpentine pathway inspired by the calligraphic markings of the scribbly bark Eucalyptus (*Eucalyptus haemastoma*) that encourages visitors to detour from the major pathway.

Paul Thompson feels that the most important ingredient of any garden is the process of creation because the plants change over time. In reflecting on our process, Paul realized that the design for the Australian Garden involved three types of planting: planting as *structure*, planting as *support*, and planting as *display*. Structural planting supports the strength of the design with plants that will remain for many years. These plants are very reliable and will survive with minor changes and little care. Support planting displays more diversity and enriches the primary structure with visual and ecological richness. Some risk about their long-term durability is acceptable and the design intent can tolerate some change. The third type of planting is the icing on the cake, species that express seasonal visual appeal; they are about display. If they fail, another species can be planted in their place. On the garden's opening day of Stage One in 2006, unexpectedly 6,000 people turned up on a rather cold and rainy day and caused a traffic jam, which encouraged the premier of the state of Victoria to immediately fund the second stage. The lesson for us was that if you want funding for your landscape project, just get a lot of people to cause a traffic jam.

Stage Two, which opened in 2012, focuses on the continental edge and gained inspiration from the wetter environments of Australia. By using a larger expanse of water, a series of journeys adjacent to or on the water are created. These include the Arbor Walk with its vine-covered support structures, and the startling white concrete forms of the Melaleuca Spits, where the paperbark melaleucas have been clipped to express in an abstracted way the repetition of the interval and quality of their trunks [10-16, 10-17]. The Weird and Wonderful Garden is a rock garden of idiosyncratic trees such as the bulbous bottle tree (*Brachychiton rupestris*). In certain areas of the garden, the vertical stone formations create a microclimate for other plants as they grow over time. [10-18, 10-19] The varied gardens and journeys create a myriad of ways to navigate a way beside and through the plantings. About the Australian Garden Kevin Taylor wrote in his diary, "Walking through the Australian landscape is a journey of waves, shifts and jumps, one never travels in a straight line, the flora always gets in the way." [10-20]

One final thought: gardens take time and the Australian Garden will not be fully realized in our lifetime; it will continue to evolve well into the next generation. I have also realized, particularly in regard to plants, that the more I know, the more I realize I don't know, and how much more there is to know. That's one of the realizations that keeps me fascinated with the world of plants.

**Notes**

**1** Tim Winton, "The Island Seen and Felt: Some Thoughts about Landscape," speech to the Royal Academy of Arts, London, November 2014.

**2** George Seddon, *Swan River Landscapes*, Perth: University of Western Australia, 1981, p. 3.

# VERTICAL PLANTING: TECTONICS AND AESTHETICS

Richard L. Hindle

11.

—

Raderschallpartner, landscape architects; Burkhardt + Partner, architects. MFO-Park. Oerlikon, Zürich, Switzerland, 2002. Interior space in summer. [Marc Treib]

Vertical surfaces have been a component of garden-making since the first woven fences separated cultivated ground from wilderness. Vertical planting, however, represents a departure from the archetypal forms of the garden, as designing with plants in an upright orientation often requires structural support, artificial soils, and precise hydroponic systems to maintain them. Although vertical planting admittedly consumes intensive resources, it allows designers to achieve new effects with living plants, effectively integrating vegetation with architecture, and rapidly creating verdant and colorful urban spaces without the time required for achieving large trees and shrubs. Three unique design challenges and opportunities accompany vertical planting and raise some critical points of inquiry into its history, representation, and design. These include (1) the experiential and representational anomalies relative to the ground plane, and the issues raised by designing in elevation; (2) the theoretical origins of vertical planting in the modern era as viewed through the work of Stanley Hart White; and (3) the importance of depth and pattern when designing the planting medium (soil or composition substrate). Although these subjects are by no means exhaustive, their discussion will hopefully initiate discourse on an as yet poorly theorized form of garden-making.

## Plan, Elevation, and the Ground Plane

For centuries, the planting plan has been used to graphically depict the spatial organization of plants on a designed landscape, and like other plan drawings represents the ground orthographically, as viewed from above. Vertical planting therefore inverts, or more precisely rotates, the once stable relationship between ground and designed plantings. Rotating the axis of the planting plan perpendicular to the ground plane technically renders the vertical planting plan an elevation drawing, and alters the eye-level experience of the design. Although this may sound at first like a wonky distinction, the perpendicular shift of projection throws the widely accepted axioms common in planting design—mass, line, texture, and color—into disarray.[1] In many cases, this results in flattening the planting into a surface pattern, or more kindly, an expansion of the plants into new spatial dimensions.

Drawings and photographs of the 2013 Oasis of Aboukir in Paris by Patrick Blanc and a garden at Lindisfarne Castle designed in 1911 by Gertrude Jekyll in Northumberland, England, clearly illustrate the tension effected among plan, ground, elevation, and vertical planting. The notational styles of the plans for both gardens are similar, each utilizing drifts and masses of plants; yet certain peculiarities between the two nevertheless result. The voids/apertures in the planting plan of the Oasis of Aboukir (also known as Le Mirage Vert) are actually the windows of the adjoining apartment building; the openings/voids in the plan for Lindisfarne Castle are the paths that facilitate movement through the garden [11-1, 11-2]. In addition, the eye-level reading of the drifts of vertical planting appears as a graphic pattern on the building's façade; the drifts of the earth-bound Lindisfarne garden retreat in the distance as the varied heights and transparencies of the plants become layers that mask one another [11-3]. This resulting shift of orientation between viewer and designed planting creates both opportunities and challenges for spatial design and its representation. As suggested above, many vertical planting plans are in fact elevation drawings. Therefore, vertical plantings permit viewers at a distance to observe the expanse of the garden in a single glance and at full scale—a "bird's-eye view taken from the ground." In his essay "On Plans," Marc Treib notes that "a plan presents a view that never exists in reality" although it gives us a "coherent idea [of the order] at the expense of spatial experience."[2] Perhaps this is why many vertical gardens possess such a "thin" graphic quality—like a veneer, pattern, or camouflage—when compared to conventional gardens experienced from eye level.

Designing vertical planting involves certain anomalies and unique representational and structural challenges—but also opportunities—that exert an impact on the spatial qualities of the planting and the experiential qualities that result. MFO-Park in Zürich, Switzerland, and the CaixaForum in Madrid, Spain, neatly illustrate the issues involved. MFO-Park utilizes a steel frame and extensive trellising to support the growth of a mixture of climbing plants [11-4]. Although the beds for these plantings occupy minimal square footage, today the vines completely inundate the structure with foliage and flowers. Alternately, at CaixaForum, the plants grow from a thin felt substrate supported vertically by a building façade and create a sheet or mat of vegetation that appears as a surface veneer. Both projects employ vertical planting, yet MFO-Park presents a series of intricate spatial volumes, while the CaixaForum laminates the planting to the building façade and reads only as surface, like a wall of greenery.

MFO-Park was designed by Raderschall landscape architects and architects Burkhardt + Partner around 2002 [11-5]. The vine-covered structure occupies a former industrial block of the Maschinenfabrik Oerlikon, a Swiss manufacturing company involved in various aspects of mechanical engineering, including the early production of electric trains. Given that the plan would have been ineffective in communicating the overall planting design, the landscape architects studied its

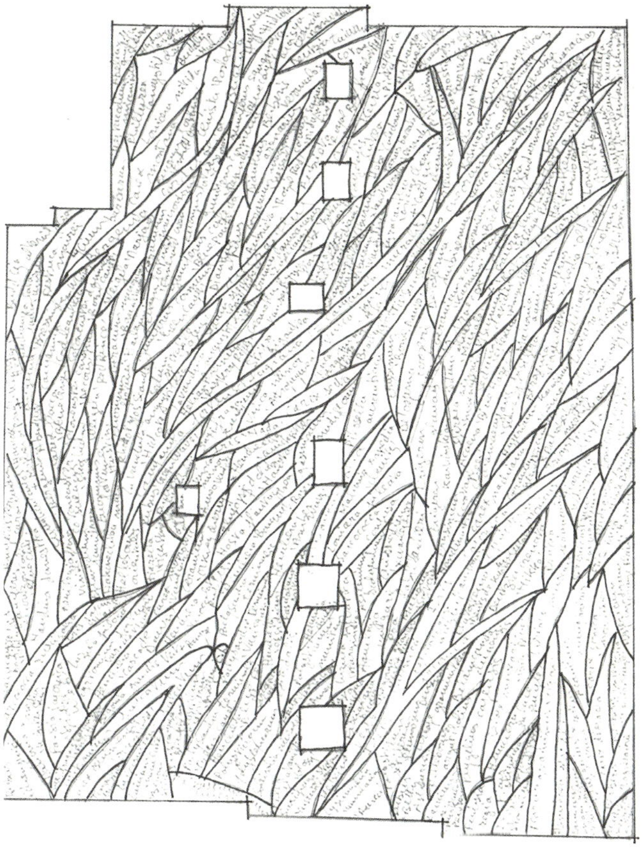

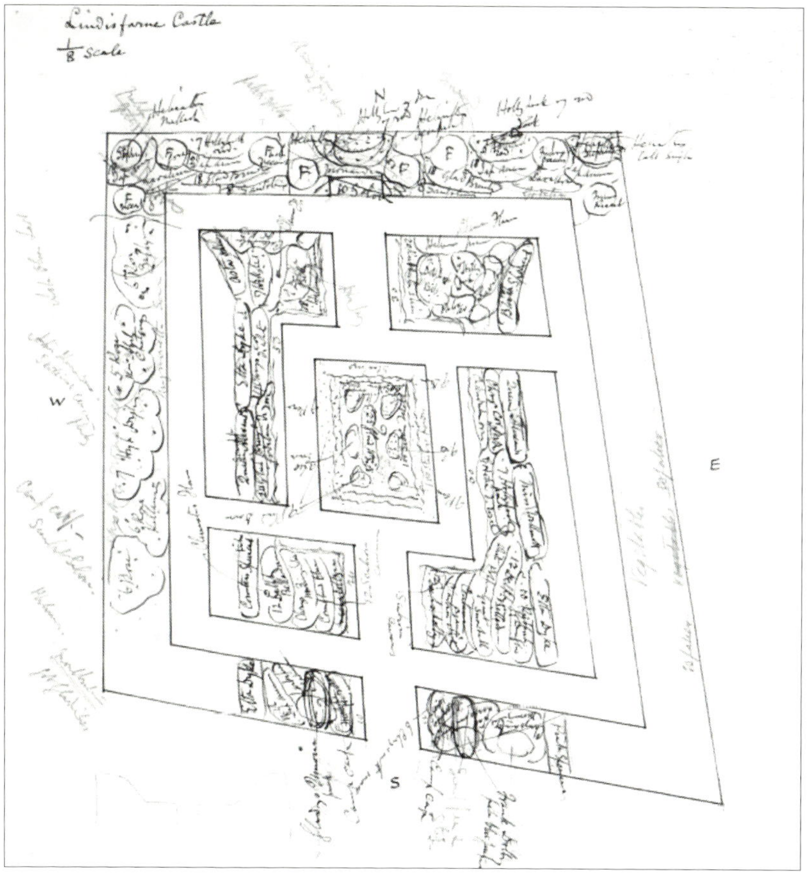

**11-1**

Patrick Blanc.
L'Oasis d'Aboukir.
Paris, France, 2013.
Planting plan/elevation showing the vertical distribution of plants on the wall surface.
[Redrawn by author]

**11-2**

Gertrude Jekyll.
Lindisfarne Castle garden.
Holy Island, England, 1911.
The planting plan delineates the arrangement of plant species.
[College of Environmental Design Archives, University of California, Berkeley]

**11-3**

Gertrude Jekyll.
Lindisfarne Castle garden.
The spatial arrangement of plants seen from eye level.
[Marc Treib]

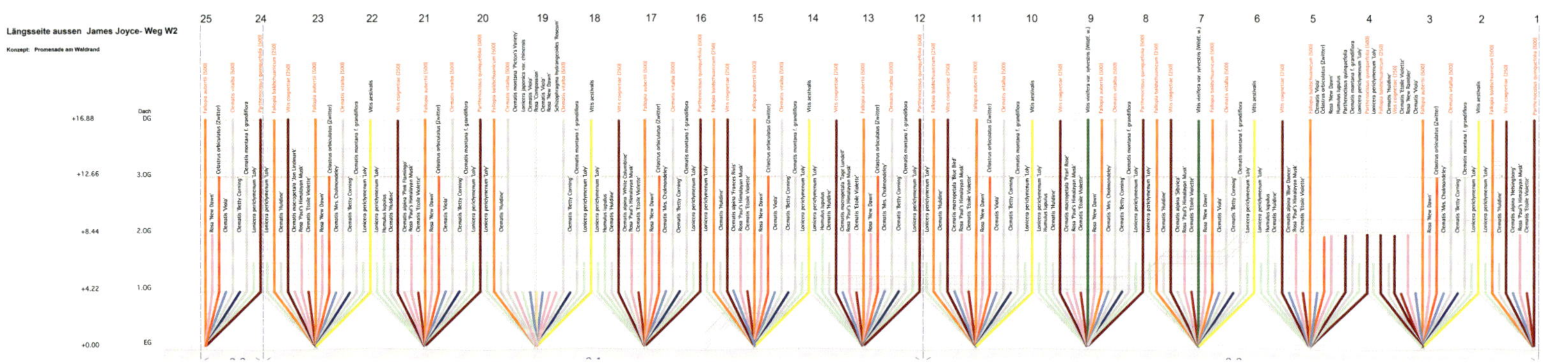
Längsseite aussen James Joyce- Weg W2
Konzept: Promenade am Waldrand
25 24 23 22 21 20 19 18 17 16 15 14 13 12 11 10 9 8 7 6 5 4 3 2 1
+16.88 Dach DG
+12.66 3.OG
+8.44 2.OG
+4.22 1.OG
+0.00 EG

**11-4**

Raderschallpartner, landscape architects; Burkhardt + Partner, architects. MFO-Park. Oerlikon, Zürich, Switzerland, 2002. Interior planting in autumn. [Joachim Kohler Bremen, Wikimedia Commons]

**11-5**

Raderschallpartner, landscape architects; Burkhardt + Partner, architects. MFO-Park. Interior space in summer. [Marc Treib]

**11-6**

Raderschallpartner, landscape architects; Burkhardt + Partner, architects. MFO-Park. Elevation showing the distribution of plant species. [Roland Raderschall]

design primarily in elevation diagrams [11-6]. Elevations of the project reveal the intimate relationship between plants and structure by articulating the anticipated vertical arrangement of plants as well as the structural framework. The architectonic system of cable trellising and steel frame supports the masses of varied clematis species, climbing roses (*Rosa 'Albertine'*), porcelain berry (*Ampelopsis brevipedunculata*), and other species that have today grown into a rectilinear volume of living plants. The elevation drawings reveal the hybrid of vegetation enfolding the elaborate trellis works; in many places, the vines prevail and are especially vivid at certain times of year, in autumn, for example. The planting is highly volumetric, ultimately mimicking or paralleling the structural form established by the architecture, yet on the ground the planting barely draws notice.

The vertical planting at CaixaForum, designed by Herzog & de Meuron in collaboration with the botanist and landscape designer Patrick Blanc in 2008, derives from a far different spatial and compositional idea [11-7]. The public space and adjoining plaza are bounded on two sides by historic structures: on one side stands the Corten steel façade of the former electrical substation designed by the architects; on the other, the green wall planted by Blanc. The plants used—including genera of *Carex* sp., *Iris* sp., *Sedum* sp., and *Delosperma* sp.—sheath the adjacent wall and have adapted successfully to their vertical orientation and the thin planting medium [11-8]. The felt substrate that covers the apartment block façade reorients the plane of the "soil" and thus the plane of the planting. As a result, the planting and its substrate, almost invisible when viewed in plan, dominate the elevation and read as a component of the building façade.

At the CaixaForum, the planting becomes an ornamental skin for the apartment building and simultaneously a garden for the adjacent public space [11-9]. The collaboration between Blanc and Herzog & de Meuron is noteworthy in this regard, as it brings together similar garden and architectural languages premised on exquisitely detailed building envelopes and bold geometry. Jeffrey Kipnis summarizes the seductive power of this approach in his article "Cunning of Cosmetics."

> *Ornaments attach as discrete entities to the body, like jewelry, reinforcing the structure and integrity of the body as such.... Cosmetics are erotic camouflage; they relate always and only to skin, to particular regions of skin. Thinness, adherence and diffuse extent are crucial to the cosmetic effect, which is more visceral than intellectual, more atmospheric than aesthetic.*[3]

MAESTROS DEL CAOS:

**11-7** *(opposite)*

Herzog & de Meuron, architects; Patrick Blanc, planting design. CaixaForum. Madrid, Spain, 2008. The Corten steel façade and the green wall bracket the plaza. [Edmund Gall, Creative Commons]

**11-8**

Patrick Blanc, planting design. CaixaForum. Tapestry of species. [Marc Treib]

**11-9**

Herzog & de Meuron, architects; Patrick Blanc, planting design. CaixaForum. A felt substrate supports the thin planting on the building façade. [Marc Treib]

This reading of the Herzog & de Meuron architecture also provides a critical lens through which to regard vertical planting as façade and cosmetic blush for a generation of "green" buildings. At the CaixaForum, the technique is particularly salient, as the cosmetic treatment of the vertical planting screens the space in manner akin to Herzog & de Meuron's metal façade—yet it lacks the perspectival depth and spatial layering offered by earth-bound gardens of similar scale and dimension.

## Tectonic and Theoretical Origins of Vertical Planting

MFO-Park and CaixaForum reveal the unique spatial and representational opportunities provided by vertical planting, its tectonic and structural hybridity—but also its limits. For example, gardens by Patrick Blanc, usually composed of veneers of felt and vegetation, also conceal involved technological devices for cultivating plants on vertical surfaces required for evoking awe and wonder from an impossibly thin green wall. Conversely, the open tensile structure of MFO-Park creates a volume that explores the tectonics of landscape architecture and the heliotropism of plants. Each approach has radically different implications for the ground plane, design in elevation, and space-making. This suggests that vertical planting should always be discussed in terms of the interrelation of building technology and living materials. History provides some examples and inspiration.

For at least four centuries, plants and structure have coevolved, many advances in architectural technology instigated by the pursuit of raising exotic plants. For example, the orangeries and winter houses built in Europe during the seventeenth through nineteenth centuries were necessary to create supportive climates for the cultivation of fruits and vegetables in northern latitudes.[4] These structures developed over time in a reciprocal relationship with plants that they housed, providing temporary shelter, or idealized artificial climates for the tender plants brought to Europe from distant colonies. These innovative structures represent an inextricable mutual relationship between plants and architecture that continues today in vertical plantings and their structural supports. No single point of origin for the coevolution of plants and structure can be determined with any degree of accuracy, of course. Yet within this vast field of inquiry we might include the ivy walls of storied universities, the sod roofs of Scandinavian folk architecture, the ornate and functional espaliers of France, agricultural glass-house technology, and the structural and botanical experiments of the Baubotanik ongoing at the University of Stuttgart in Germany. What unifies these precedents is the search to configure environments that foster an intentional symbiosis of plants and structure. Viewing vertical planting from the perspective of vegetal/structural coevolution leads to some uncanny interpretations of the "green" buildings that pepper contemporary cities. One Central Park, in Sydney, Australia, designed by Ateliers Jean Nouvel, has ostensibly more in common with nineteenth-century conservatories than with the urban ecology and sustainability often used to justify vertical vegetation in cities [11-10]. The treatment of the building's glass façade and arrangement of plants yields a curious hybrid in which indoor and outdoor spaces profit from structural innovation and adaptation of building systems that facilitate the survival of the plants. In a like manner, Stefano Boeri's Bosco Verticale in Milan sheaths a multistory structure with an unlikely coating of arboreal greenery [11-11]. This squarely situates the architectural design in the lineage of advanced glass-house technology that stems from Joseph Paxton's 1851 Crystal Palace, but has continued in modernist glass-wall construction that has fostered the creation of voluminous light-filled spaces.[5] Although no longer at the peak of fashion, conservatories provide fascinating precedents for the complex reformulation of architecture to accommodate vegetation as well as the domestic, social, and commercial lives of their patrons and visitors. Historically, the structural elements of many conservatories—such as support columns—were used to foster plant growth and create well-composed spaces for human enjoyment. This, I would argue, also represents the highest ambition of vertical planting—and not its function as a simulacrum of ecology.

Vertical planting in the urban landscape has tectonic origins and has been a part of the landscape architect's tool kit for more than a century. A "hedge-fence" designed by the landscape engineer John McLaren adorned the entrance to the 1915 Panama–Pacific International Exposition in San Francisco [11-12]. The fair, which among other things showcased a model of the Panama Canal, a transcontinental telephone, and other icons of Western technological progress—included, apparently, vertical planting.[6] The hedge-fence surrounded the fair's exhibition spaces with a 36-foot-high green enclosure, a feat achievable in very few months and far from the centuries of care and growth needed to grow a yew hedge or ivy wall of similar dimension. The hedge-fence was a grand piece of civic architecture designed to provide a threshold for the fair, rapidly assembled on the exposition site. The support structure comprised shallow trays six feet long, two feet wide, and two-and-an-eighth inches deep, filled with soil and planted with ice plants (*Mesembryanthemum spectabilis*). Replacing the use of traditional hedges, these boxes provided an arched threshold for the fair; they were

**11-10**

Ateliers Jean Nouvel, architects; Patrick Blanc, planting design. One Central Park. Sydney, Australia, 2013. [Marc Treib]

**11-11**

Stefano Boeri. Bosco Verticale. Milan, Italy, 2014. Each floor of the building supports large planters for trees, creating a vertical forest. [Marc Treib]

used in other configurations throughout the grounds. The expediency of this horticultural structure provided the perfect metaphor for the rapidly expanding and urbanizing West.

The hedge-fence at the Panama–Pacific International Exhibition made etymological reference to the miles of boundary fences that crisscrossed the American Midwest before the mass implementation of barbed wire in the late nineteenth century. Early American hedge-fences of the Middle West combined tensile steel wire and unique forms of joinery to weave living enclosures for the agricultural and ranch landscapes [11-13]. Although they varied radically in form and function from their urban counterpart at the San Francisco exhibition, these rural applications shared the common root of combining vegetation with inert structures, thus inventing a third condition in which tectonic elements augment the natural performance of living materials.

Other noteworthy vertical planting precedents include the walled enclosures used by Gertrude Jekyll, who planted the joints of stacked stone retaining walls to support her turning of plant growth from the ground plane to the vertical surface. Jekyll's wall gardens profited from the joinery of stone elements and exploited the cracks to cultivate rock-loving plants in a stereotomic configuration, through which mass and arrangement of the stone allows for growth of the plants in the open masonry joints on both vertical and horizontal surfaces [11-13]. These precedents, in combination with the historical forms such as espalier, arbors, and vine walls, provide the context in which to discuss today's vertical planting.

Permutations of vertical planting, from dry stacked wall to tensile systems to veneer, suggest that the structural origins of the type may also yield insights. The history of vertical planting and its aesthetics is primarily a trace of tectonic and technological innovation in relation to the selection and application of plants in tandem with the evolution of their substrates/soils. Or to put it more succinctly, in reference to vertical plantations: tectonics become aesthetics. For example, Jekyll's walls utilized plant species that were well adapted to rock outcrops and fissures. The midwestern hedge-fences interwove wire with vegetal species such as Osage orange (*Maclura pomifera*) and sea buckthorn (*Hippophae rhamnoides*), two plants that graft and fuse easily. Arbors and ivy walls exploit the capability of plants to attach to architectural construction. In contrast, the hedge-fence of the Panama–Pacific exhibition overlaid a skin of plants well adapted to shallow soils and drastic fluctuations in moisture. The structures that supported this green veneer allowed designers to surpass the limits characteristic of

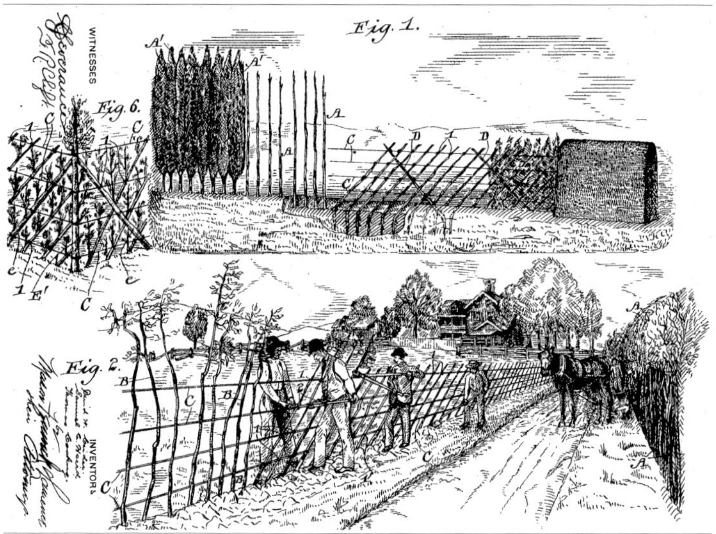


**11-12**

John McLaren. Hedge-fence. Panama–Pacific International Exhibition. San Francisco, California, 1915. The foreground shows the hedge-fence and the hollow wall that supports the thin veneer of planting boxes. [San Francisco Public Library]

**11-13**

David W. Crider and Samuel C. Heird. "Combined Hedge and Wire Fence," U.S. Patent #588,400 (1897). Hedge-fences were common in this era before the invention of barbed wire. [U.S. Patent and Trademark Office]

**11-14**

Gertude Jekyll. Hestercombe. Taunton, Somerset, England, 1904. Garden planting and wall enclosure define the garden space. [Marc Treib]

living plants and augment their growth rate. Increasing the possible heights achieved by these species fostered new compositional possibilities, an evolution that necessitated innovations in areas beyond structure. The advent of hydroponics, formulated by William F. Gericke at the University of California, Berkeley, in the 1920s, challenged preconceptions about the composition and need for natural soil, and liberated plants from their earthly bond. The artificial felt utilized by Patrick Blanc, as well as other lightweight substrates, has led advances in artificial nutrients and irrigation technology.

The structural and horticultural origins of vertical planting are relatively easy to retrace, yet the theoretical origins remained sketchy. In his notes for a 1931 lecture on the modern garden at the University of Illinois, Stanley Hart White conceived a modern vertical garden characterized by modified lightweight substrate and hydroponic irrigation. His lecture notes and sketches of the era reveal two distinct ideas. First, that the "green wall" should incorporate the elements of the landscape—among them soil, plants, water, and birds—composed on a vertical plane rather than on the ground [11-14]. Secondly, structural garden elements supporting plant growth should allow for the free movement of occupants encouraged by a suitably open plan. White advanced this thinking on the subject in an essay titled "What Is Modern?" in which he theorized gardening on the vertical plane in order to free the ground plane for the practice of modern living. "In the first place, there is little reason for introducing extreme decoration into the ground plan," he writes.

> *New ideas of living call for such absolute simplicity that if the plan is perfectly plain it may be best in character. In the next place, a vast field of possibility lies open for development, of the walls in a modern garden and it's conceivable that fabricated metal compost filled walls with interior irrigation might be easily devised to produce fine sheets of greenery or color in which the most fanciful imagination of the designer could be expressed in insets of lights, sculpture, or bird cages, fish globes and any other extravagances.*[8]

White was not alone in his preoccupation with vertical dimensions in the modern garden. Experiments in volume and spatial layering led to the creation of new garden prototypes, such as the temporary sculpture garden at the Museum of Modern Art by John McAndrew with Alfred Barr Jr., built in 1939. Garrett Eckbo pioneered theories of the "garden as stage" in his hypothetical project for "Small Gardens in the City," published in 1937, in which garden designs were developed using axonometric drawing conventions that prioritize vertical elements and spatial layering. Perhaps echoing White, in 1937 Eckbo declared that every "garden is a stage and every person and actor." For White, the solution to this modernist paradigm of the free plan and an increasing reliance on technology were walls tectonic and verdant, and in 1938 he even patented his design as the "Vegetation-Bearing Architectonic Structure and System"—or "botanical brick," as it was referred to, perhaps sarcastically, by his brother E. B. White [11-15].

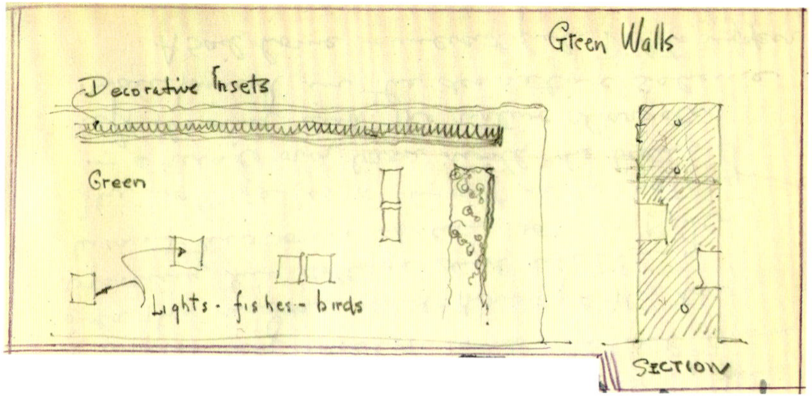


Tectonically, White's invention was a peculiar inversion of the stone or brick construction utilized by Jekyll in her wall gardens, where the face of the masonry provided the support for the plant. In White's design, a steel frame carried the loads. The utilization of the steel frame to construct buildings of greater height emerged in Chicago near the end of the nineteenth century, when skyscrapers by Louis Sullivan and Daniel Burnham left the ground to seemingly defy gravity. White deftly adapted this structural idea to create the first "modern" vertical garden that set off a chain reaction in which his students and collaborators obtained their own patents for new structural plant hybrids. These included the "Vegetation-Bearing Cellular Structure and System" by William M. MacPherson and the "Vegetation-Bearing Display Surface and System" by Elmer Hovendon Gates also in 1938 [11-16]. A review of patents for other of the era's vegetated structures reveals a diverse set of structural adaptations—after all, modernism sought a "total design" in which every element of architecture and landscape could be reinvented, manufactured, and produced to suit the diverse modes of modern living and, later, rapid postwar urbanization. Modernist principles were not restricted to architectural construction but also propelled the invention of landscape elements that included frames, trellises, and other armatures for hedges; bricks that integrated soils and living plants in the courses of masonry walls; and an array of other planting technologies [11-17].

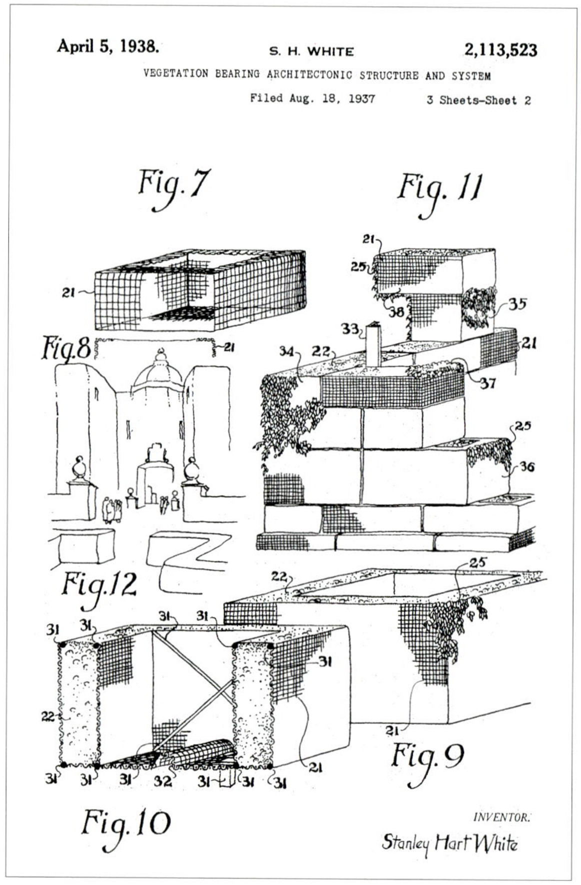


## Thickness, Thinness, and the Role of Substrates in Vertical Planting

The structural hybridity of vertical planting is not strictly limited to aboveground growth. The planting mediums (i.e., substrates) and spatial configuration provide the essential elements for cultivating plants—water, oxygen, and nutrients—in addition to the structural support for botanical architecture and an anchorage for the plant roots. The volume, thickness, and orientation of the substrate play an integral role in structuring vertical planting as they dictate the location of

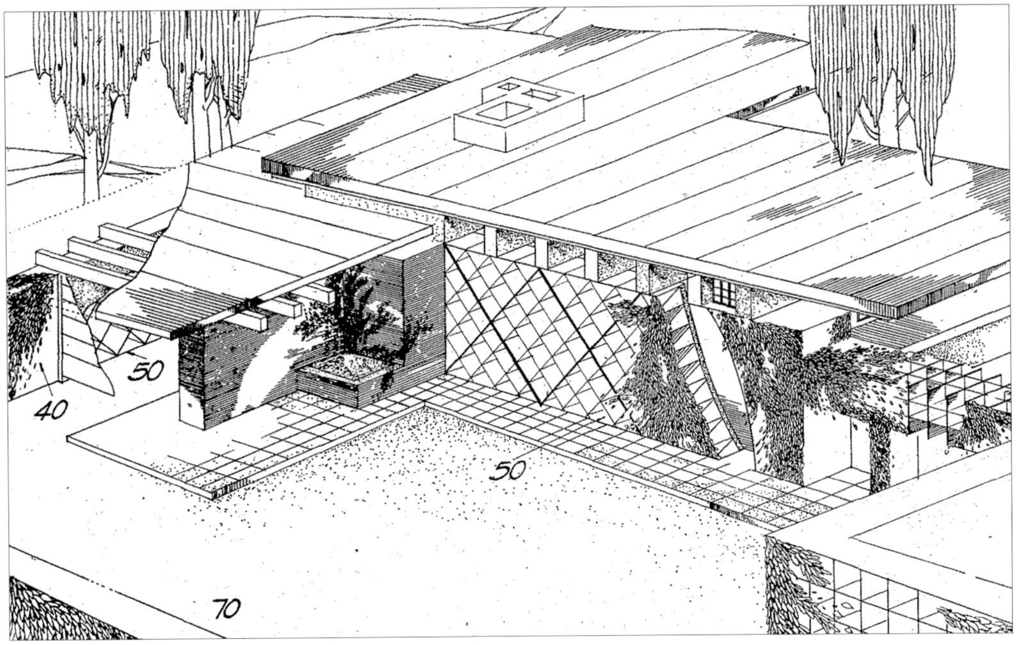


**11-17**

William MacPherson. "Vegetation-Bearing Cellular Structure and System," U.S. Patent # 2,121,173 (1938). Planting substrate and integrated structural system. [U.S. Patent and Trademark Office]

**11-15**

Stanley Hart White. Green walls, 1932. A conceptual skotch showing plants and voids for lights, fishes, birds, and irrigation. [University of Illinois Archives]

**11-16**

Stanley Hart White. "Vegetation Bearing Architectonic Structure and System," U.S. Patent #2,113,523 (1938). Drawing of a "botanical brick" and system of assembly. [U.S. Patent and Trademark Office]

**11-18**

Clyde Burney. "Plant Growing Block for a Decorative Fence Construction," U.S. Patent #2,514,536 (1947). A modified concrete unit in which the planting substrate fills the voids and plants grow from the apertures. [U.S. Patent and Trademark Office]

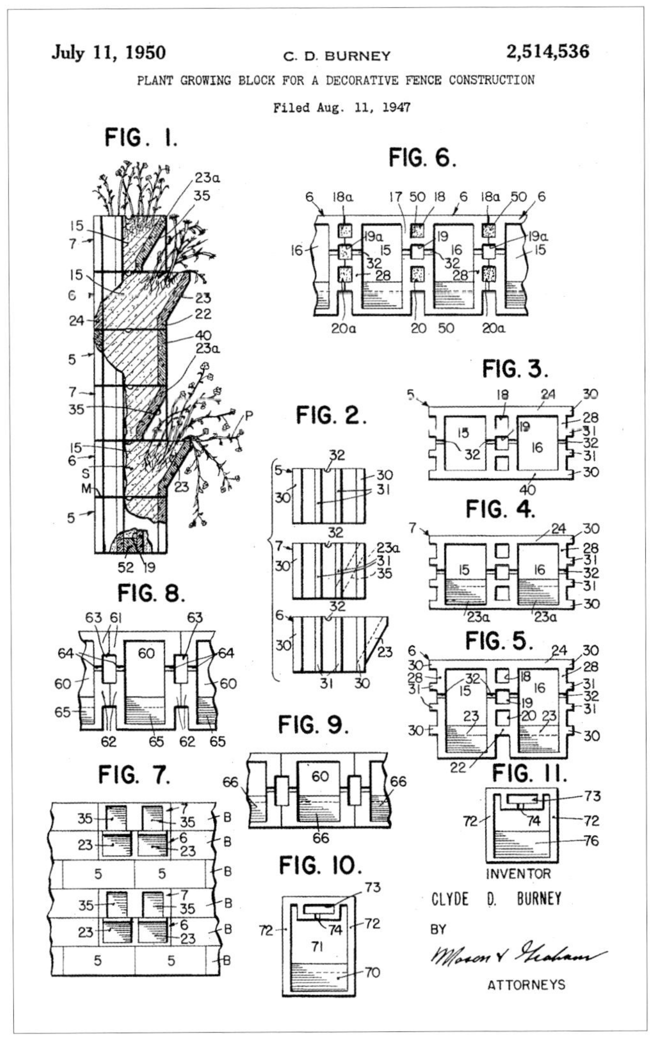

**11-19**

Jeff Koons.
*Puppy*, 1992.
Guggenheim Museum Bilbao. Bilbao, Spain.
Plants grow on a thin structure of stainless steel.
[Marc Treib]

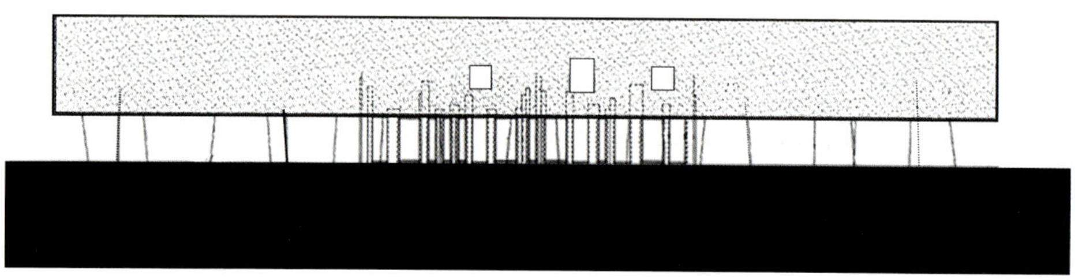

**11-20**

Édouard François and Duncan Lewis, architects.
Gites Ruraux.
La Chauvinière, Jupilles, France, 1997.
The drawing shows the relationship of the ground (black) to the vertical structure (hatched) that bounds the planting.
[Richard Hindle]

the plant's root volume and therefore the organization of the planting as a whole. Although substrates and mediums are often masked by living vegetation, when foregrounded the configuration of the planting substrate becomes an important design component that is unfortunately often left unstudied and underrepresented—especially in relationship to aesthetics and plant composition.

Vertical planting can be studied in terms of the relationship of plants to their substrate, and substrates to their structure and/or vessel. Vertical planting on terra firma easily coaxes upwards plants supported by a structure. In addition, vertical planting can also be accomplished by using thin substrates such as felt mounted on a load-bearing wall, or with elevated planters of varied geometrical forms filled with modified planting mediums. Studying the thickness, orientation, and mass of vertical elements hearkens back to the architectural reference to poché (i.e., representation of thickness)—retrieved from Beaux Arts methods as a counternarrative to modernist theories of thinness and transparency. Spence R. Kass has written that

> *If recognition of the poché has helped to reestablish a dialogue between the wall and the plan, it may be expedient to divert some attention to effects of poché on the vertical surface as well, and initiate an argument for façades not as autonomous screens, but as integral to the wall matrix behind. Poché, then, is seen not merely as planar organization, but as a three-dimensional cement that merges throughout the building mass.*[9]

Although anachronistic, arguments for thickening walls may be particularly salient to the discussion of vertical planting. Substrates used in vertical planting may be understood as a three-dimensional material integrated into structure that organizes the distribution of plants through its position and relative thickness.

Four works clearly illustrate these relations among elements and allude to the possibilities of designing with substrate (more accurately, its vessel) as an architectonic element: *Puppy* by the artist Jeff Koons, re-erected in 1992 at the Guggenheim Museum in Bilbao, Spain; the 1996 Gites Ruraux, by Édouard François and Duncan Lewis in France; the 2013 Wall of Hope (Kibo no Kabe) in Osaka, Japan, by Tadao Ando, and the "I'm Lost in Paris" House designed by R&Sie(n) Architects in 2008. To create distinct forms, each project used the volumes of substrate/soil in radically different ways.

*Puppy* was adorned with 60,000 petunias, impatiens, marigolds, and other annual bedding plants. The vegetation was planted in a thin modified soil retained by a geotextile and wire frame that covered a primary structure of stainless steel. The thinness of the soil and relatively low height of the annual bedding plants were appropriate choices for covering the frame [11-18]. On its web page, the Guggenheim Museum Bilbao describes *Puppy* in this way:

> *With* Puppy, *Koons engaged both past and present, employing sophisticated computer modeling to create a work that references the 18th-century formal European garden. A behemoth West Highland terrier carpeted in bedding plants,* Puppy *employs the most saccharine of iconography—flowers and puppies—in a monument to the sentimental. Imposing in scale, its size both tightly contained and seemingly out of control (it is both literally and figuratively still growing), and juxtaposing elite and mass-cultural references (topiary and dog breeding, Chia Pets and Hallmark greeting cards), the work may be read as an allegory of contemporary culture.*[10]

Beneath the overly saturated color of the planted surface, a thinly veiled layer of soil masks the technological mastery that makes the sculpture possible, and provides not only an enduring critique of culture and its architecture, but also a critical window into many vertical plantings and their greenwashing. The Gites Ruraux, designed by Édouard François and Duncan Lewis in 1996, utilized a different approach. These tourist cottages, situated far from the city center, are set among agricultural fields and a forest of mixed species. The designers of the buildings brought forest planting into dialogue with the structure by surrounding the building with a densely planted bosk, enclosing the planting within an architectonic frame. The trees that accompany the building are planted in soil and their foliage becomes a vertical composition that blurs the line between bosk, frame, and façade. This relationship shapes a distinct perspective on vertical planting, that is, using terra firma as the substrate and the structural frame to organize the form of the aboveground parts of the planting [11-19].

Tadao Ando's 30-foot-high, 312-foot-long Wall of Hope in Osaka, Japan, spans a public space at the base of the Umeda Sky Building [11-21]. An architectural frame supports its planting with woody shrubs, flowers, and ground covers. Lines of elevated boxes positioned at each level of the structure feed the woody plants that cover a massive construction that exceeds the growth potential of any individual plant. Pruning follows the guide provided by the architectural frame, creating the impression of a clearly shaped rectilinear mass [11-22]. Horizontal banding is created by the plant species in relationship to the arrangement of the planting troughs. Although masked by foliage, these boxes of soil express the arrangement of plants within the

**11-21**

Tadao Ando. Wall of Hope (Kibo no Kabe). Osaka, Japan, 2013. A green wall 30 feet high, and a 250-foot-long vegetated wall seen from the street. [Richard Hindle]

**11-22**

Tadao Ando. Wall of Hope (Kibo no Kabe). Section showing the distribution of planters, substrate, and plants within the structural frame. [Richard Hindle]

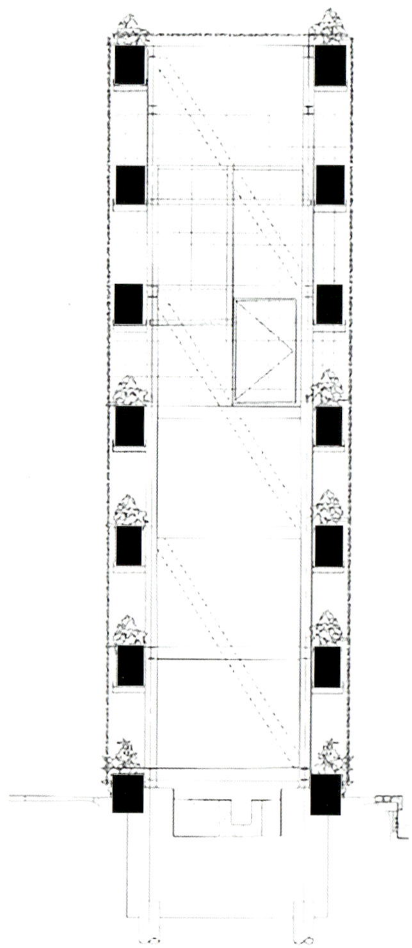

structure. The "I'm Lost in Paris" House, designed by R&Sie(n) Architects in 2008, enshrouds the building in a blanket of ferns supported by a tensile mesh separated from the concrete walls of the building by a moisture barrier and stanchions [11-23]. Pots, attached at the intersection points of the mesh, are filled with ferns and watered by a concealed system. The result is an integrated mix of vegetation, substrate, and irrigation whose repetitive elements and structure evoke a woven textile, a textile that wraps in greenery the building's volume.

## Conclusion

Vertical planting creates unique challenges in terms of spatial design, challenges that necessitate hybrid frameworks and muddle widely accepted practices in planting design. In essence, vertical planting rotates the direction of the surface, and upsets the once stable relationship between ground plane and vegetal compositions. In addition, in rotating the planting plan, the elevation represents an experience modified from the one secured at normal eye level. As a result, certain designs feel thin, while others read as volumetric and highly spatial. These shifts are often made possible by the tight bonds between plants and architecture. When considered broadly, we can trace the evolution of solutions that combine plant and structure that date to early glasshouse experiments, espaliers, sod roofs, and other precedents. Although vertical planting has been part of the designer's repertoire for more than a century, its more theoretical aspects emerged only during the modern era, as formulated by Stanley Hart White. In his patented green wall designs, White integrated vegetation with structure in novel configurations, positing that the vertical garden was the backdrop for the "pageantry of modern living." Whether or not we will turn more fully to vertically orientated planting in the future, opportunities for new configurations exist for restructuring ground plane, plants, and support. This will require new forms of thinking, new substrates, and new structures to support these vertical gardens.

## Notes

**1** Florence B. Robinson, *Planting Design*, New York: McGraw-Hill, 1940.

**2** Marc Treib, "On Plans," in *Representing Landscape Architecture*, London: Taylor & Francis, 2008.

**3** Kipnis, Jeffrey, "The Cunning of Cosmetics," in Herzog & de Meuron," *El Croquis 84*, Madrid, 1997.

**4** John Hix, *The Glass House*, London: Phaidon, 1996.

**5** Brent Richards, *New Glass Architecture*, London: Laurence King, 2006.

**6** Laura A. Ackley, *San Francisco's Jewel City: The Panama–Pacific International Exposition of 1915*, Berkeley: Heyday; San Francisco: California Historical Society, 2014.

**7** William Frederick Gericke, "Water Culture Experimentation," *Science*, 13 October 1922.

**8** Richard L. Hindle, "Stanley Hart White and the Question of 'What Is Modern?,'" *Studies in the History of Gardens & Designed Landscapes* 3, 2013, pp. 170–177.

**9** Spence R. Kass, "The Voluminous Wall," *Cornell Journal of Architecture*, 1986, pp. 44–55.

**10** Guggenheim Collection Online, Jeff Koons, *Puppy*, https://www.guggenheim.org/artwork/48.

**11-23**

New-Territories, R&Sie(n), architects. "I'm Lost in Paris" House. Paris, France, 2008. Substrate and vessel are arrayed on a tensile steel mesh, allowing for the distribution of plants over the building envelope. [François Roche, New-Territories, R&Sie(n)]

# THE TREE IS NOT AN ISOLATED SUBJECT

Alexandre Chemetoff

12.

**Unless otherwise noted, landscapes illustrated in this chapter have been designed by Bureau des Paysages / Alexandre Chemetoff.**

—

The banks of the River Meurthe. Nancy, France, 1993 [Alexandre Chemetoff, 2011].

## Le bureau des paysages

I work as an architect, an urbanist, and a landscape architect; my office is called Le bureau des paysages because in my opinion the landscape (*le paysage* in French) is a serious matter. Our bureau is an office for designing inhabited landscapes, cities, houses, and gardens, but it is also a place reflecting my philosophy and aesthetics of design: *une situation construite*, a showcase [12-1]. My practice is located in France, which is not an isolated country among the nations of Europe, and I identify with being a European. I studied landscape architecture at Versailles in the early 1970s, at the Section du paysage et de l'art des jardins, which later became L'école du paysage. However, I feel, and hope, that I am still learning. I was particularly pleased to participate in the symposium from which this book derives, and to learn from its presentations and informal discussions. On my visit to Berkeley in 1989, I visited the Donnell garden by Thomas Church and I still have very precise memories of that experience. My most significant memory is Church's belief that "gardens are for people."

**12-1**

Alexandre Chemetoff. Bureau des Paysages. Gentilly, France. 1993–2019. *Une situation construite*, a showcase. [Arnauld Duboys Fresney, 2003]

## Les eaux et les forêts

*Les eaux et les forêts* (Waters and Forests) could be the title of a novel by Marguerite Duras, but it also summarizes the subject of my contribution to this book. The theme of waters and forests will recur in this chapter, but I will begin with water in Nancy, a city in northeast France. In the last decade or so, our office has been working on a site between the River Meurthe, whose name sounds almost like *meurtre*—"murder" in French—and the canal leading from the River Moselle to the River Rhine. Industry with mixed productions formerly occupied this tract of land set between these two lines of water. It was a district that Shane MacGowan, lead singer of the Pogues, might have called a dirty old town.

> *Dreamed a dream by the old canal*
> *I kissed my girl by the factory wall*
> *Dirty old town*
> *Dirty old town.*

It was not a place people wanted to live or even visit.

## Nancy, a City of Many Parts

By the time we began our work in the 1990s, almost all the buildings on the site had been destroyed. We did not choose to design this new housing district—our commission—in isolation, but instead as a new part of the city, following the traces, the footprints of the former industrial plants. Nancy is a city of many, many historical parts that include Ville Vieille, the old town; the city of Charles III; the city of Stanislas (Leszczynski); the city along the railway; the hillside city; the forest city with le Plateau de Haye—a project we are currently working on—and the Water City. Our proposed regulating plan, like any map of Nancy, shows the relation among these districts of the city, constructed over many centuries. Maps also render obvious the geometrical changes and transitions between existing urban quarters and the new district we proposed; the geometric consequences of our urban *parti pris* is obvious in the master plan that served as our guide [12-2].

### *The Water Garden*

The Water Garden that stands by the canal provided the foundation stone for this new part of Nancy I call the Water City, La ville de l'eau. The official name of the neighborhood, however, is Rives de Meurthe, which refers to the banks of the river of that name. For the city and for the developers, the main purpose of the garden, the earliest part of the project to be realized, was to announce the transformation of the land from industrial to residential use [12-3]. In the design we attempted to engage the water and geometry of the canal, as well as the pattern of the existing streets, and to make visible and understandable the abstraction embedded in our urban plan. In that sense the Water Garden served as a tool for comprehension as well as a sign to mark the place of the neighborhood within the greater region.

### *Seven Pools*

The Water Garden (le Jardin d'eau) comprises seven pools that due to the roughly triangular shape of the site vary in dimension, shape, and plantings. The first pool relies on irises; the second is devoted to reeds; the third pool to bulrushes (*Typha latifolia*). Somewhat differing from the others, the next pool features its surface as a mirror, while the fifth is animated by a high jet of water. "One hundred fountains" animate the sixth pool, while the seventh is filled with water lilies. In 1996, when the Water Garden was realized, almost no new buildings stood on the site. The garden was intended to fix on the ground the geometric structure for the future neighborhood then being constructed according to our urban plan.

The linear first pool, which lies adjacent to the architecture school designed by the Ticenese architect Livio Vacchini and the lift bridge that links the banks, echoes the line of the canal. It is planted with irises, the beloved flower of the painters of the École de Nancy, who worked in the region at the end of the nineteenth century [12-4]. In planting these pools, we selected aquatic plants that would generate interest and beauty without requiring complex patterns, plants that would survive with little care. Plants line the edges of the pool; only in specifically determined places did we plant trees. The triangular shape of the reed pool derived from the shift in geometry between the Stanislas City and the Water City. One cannot always control what will happen to a landscape after its realization, which was the case here. After the initial plantings of reeds, duckweed (*Lemna minor*), invaded the pool and over time came into dominance. The pool of bulrushes (*Typha latifolia*) is lined along the perimeter with arrowheads (*Sagittaria latifolia*) and accompanied by bulrushes planted in linear containers set below the surface of the water. The water in the Miroir d'eau and the water jet pool, whether still or animated, strengthens the relationship between the gardens and the buildings alongside them. While vegetation originally played a smaller role in these gardens, more recently the wisteria has come to cover the low fences and the Caucasian wingnut (*Pterocarya fraxinifolia*) and to dominate the square. The Hundred Fountain Pool is today bounded by what have become large trees—bald cypresses (*Taxodium distichum*) —and from certain viewpoints the garden appears almost natural.

### *Nature and Culture*

Today, it is obvious that the buildings that followed the construction of the Water Garden have responded to its geometrical pattern [12-5]. On the other hand, as the plants have matured, augmented by those that have invaded, the garden produces a quite specific atmosphere that at times appears to be the work of nature. Even the structures within the garden have been naturalized by its plantings. The gardeners' structure, for example, was built as boxes of wood; today its volumes and all the railings around it are completely engulfed by wisteria [12-6]. For educational purposes, enamel metal signs precisely identify the vegetation in the garden so that every visitor can recognize the plants in and around the pools, and most of the squares and pools are, in fact, named for the plants featured there.

### *Urbanism Began with Landscape Architecture*

Before the site was developed, this quarter adjacent to the canal was regarded as one of the worst in the city. The development of the Water City not only provided housing and commercial space for the new district but fundamentally changed the way the people of Nancy regard the quarter bordering the river and the canal; in actuality, this new neighborhood has become one of the city's most desirable places to live. In all, the Water Garden was not only the foundation stone for a new urban development, it also transformed the way people looked at their city and its waterways. The gardens came first, and from the canal and the new landscape architecture began the urban design and broader

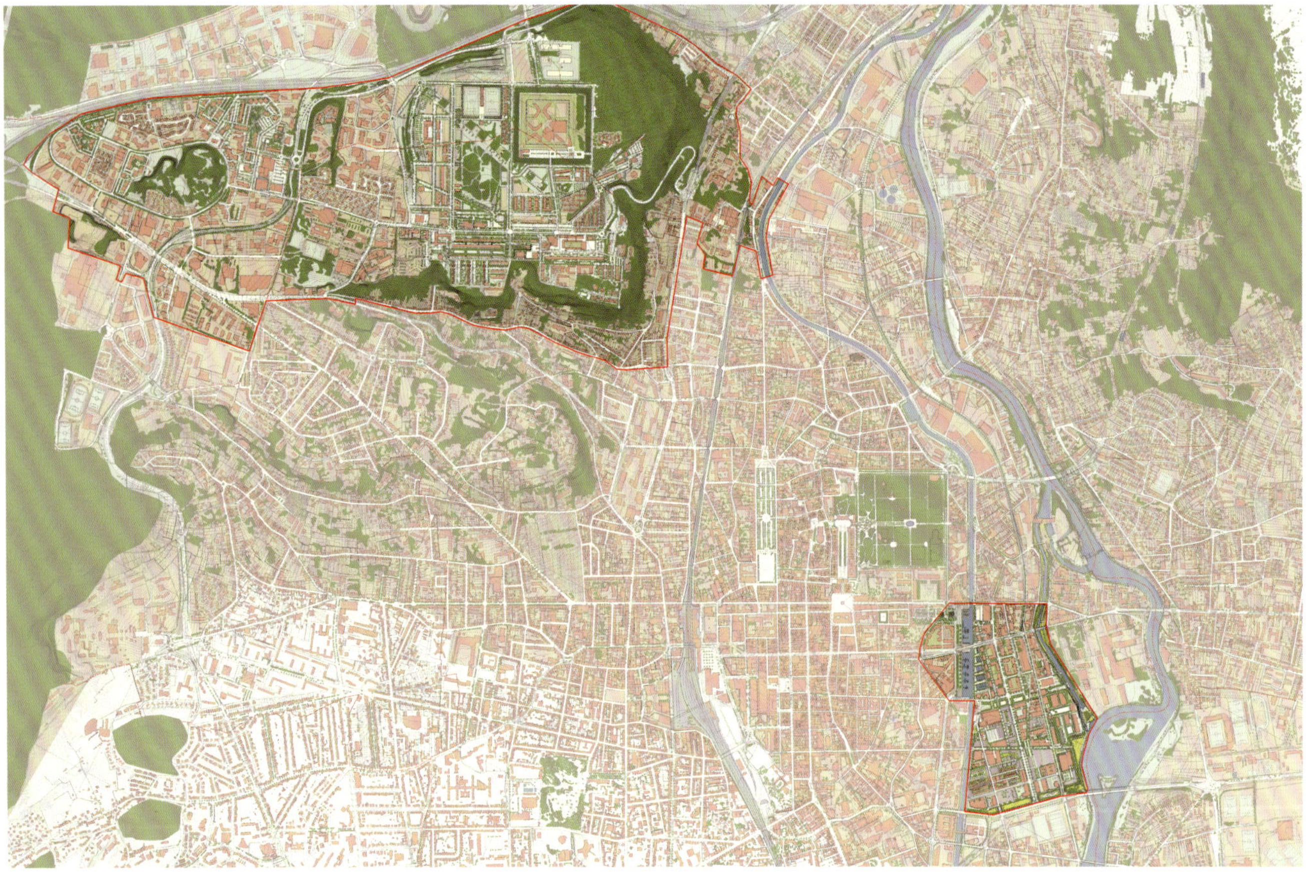

**12-2**

La Ville de l'eau (Water City) and le Plateau de Haye. Nancy, France. Site plan, November 2019. The Map and the Territory: The red lines show the limits of the two project areas. [Alexandre Chemetoff & associés]

**12-3**

Le Jardin d'eau (Water Garden). Nancy, France, 1996. The Water Garden was the foundation stone for a new part of Nancy: Les Rives de Meurthe, or the Water City. Photo taken shortly after construction. [Arnauld Duboys Fresney, 1996]

**12-4**

Le Jardin d'eau (Water Garden). The Iris Pool adjacent to the canal. [Arnauld Duboys Fresney, 2007]

**12-5**

Le Jardin d'eau (Water Garden). The adjacent architecture responds to the geometric pattern of the Water Garden. [Arnauld Duboys Fresney, 2007]

**12-6**

Le Jardin d'eau (Water Garden). Wisteria engulfs the gardeners' structure. [Arnauld Duboys Fresney, 2007]

scale development of the quarter between the river and the canal. Here, urbanism began with landscape architecture.

Our design work has been ongoing since the beginning of 1991; the construction of the gardens followed in 1996. We continue to work on the site. But from the Water Garden came the inspiration and principles for the overall urban plan, the vocabulary of trees and spaces along the streets, and the street design. That is to say, the garden provided the starting point and elementary vocabulary for designing the entire neighborhood [12-7].

### *Public Space*

Throughout the neighborhood, swales collect rainwater and feed the willows (*Salix alba*), maples (*Acer saccharinium*), and alders (*Alnus glutinosa*) that line the streets; no irrigation systems are used. In other places, for example, around an office building of our design, we adopted the species of the existing pine trees (*Pinus nigra*) and used it to replace what had been proposed in the original urban vegetation plan [12-8]. Much of the planting for the streets was carried out before the buildings were designed and constructed, as were most of the public spaces. We also paid particular attention to those places ordinarily regarded as insignificant, like the entrance to the underground parking. There, a sunken allée of silver maples (*Acer saccharinium*) invites people to visit the place and drivers to enter the parking zone. The stairways that face the access ramps to the garages have been purposely made quite wide to lead residents and visitors to the gardens, canal, and other aboveground destinations. Here we sought to grant a place normally regarded as having no interest—like an entrance to a parking garage—with some significance, elevating it to become a prominent part of the master plan. New streets were also planted with wild cherry (*Prunus avium*) to add color in the springtime and to attract birdlife.

### *Designing with Existing Conditions*

The entire site has been completely transformed; today the canal district has become a thriving neighborhood that adds a new chapter to Nancy's long urban history. When we began our work, as noted above, all the industrial structures had been completely demolished; the ground was essentially flat. Over time the Water Garden was made, the streets planned, buildings erected, and trees and other vegetation planted; today everything has grown significantly, including the number of buildings under our authority as urbanists. It is obvious that the place has changed from its prior life as an industrial site. But hopefully, someone who has been away from the city for some years may still recognize the place, not only because the promenades along the canal have remained as they were, but also because we have designed the new plan based on the traces left by the urban pattern of the former industrial district. The environment has changed, but the memory of the place has been retained, at least to some degree. The budget for creating the landscape was quite limited: only about 100 euros per square meter (about 11 dollars per square foot), which had to include services, roads, sidewalks, furniture, lighting, and vegetation. To keep costs down we used young plants like the willows that line the Promenade des Canaux, the swales, and the subsidiary canal. Not only have the willows grown, but so too the relationship between the private sites and the public spaces. The plan for the new neighborhood has stimulated the growth of new restaurants and their terraces that soften the edge between inside and outside—and serve the entire city.

### *An Emerald Necklace*

A second industrial canal, used to modulate flood surges, was transformed into a second promenade using very few elements, primarily the trees planted along its banks. Although dry before the start of the project, the water today flows freely through it once again. The banks of the Meurthe have been reinforced against flooding by a substantial retaining wall, and a lower quay now serves as a lower promenade set at water level. Although this area was originally planted with bald cypresses, reeds have invaded the site. That was not a part of our original plan, but I like the idea that an artificial design using natural elements such as trees can introduce an unexpected result, natural and dynamic [12-9; see also chapter opening].

To increase public understanding of our plans for the district, we created a very large map, some 800 square meters (86,000 square feet) in surface area, installed on the floor of a former warehouse [12-10]. Visitors are allowed to walk on the map, and perhaps by walking upon it they can visit or revisit the territory that was transformed—but also can imagine the territory not yet redesigned. In all, we read the flow of the process: the initial work to create a plan for the neighborhood; then we enlarge our scope to embrace the "resource of the river;" then on to the surrounding territory, and even beyond, to the "territory of data." The map is not the territory—of course, it can never be exactly congruent—but it is of sufficient size to be understood.

## Bièvre, a Forgotten River

The name of the River Bièvre, is the old French word from which the word "beaver" in English derives. The Bièvre has its source near Versailles, in Saint-Quentin-en-Yvelines, and passes between the higher lands of the Villejuif and Bagneux before entering Paris [12-11]. The river, which passes quite

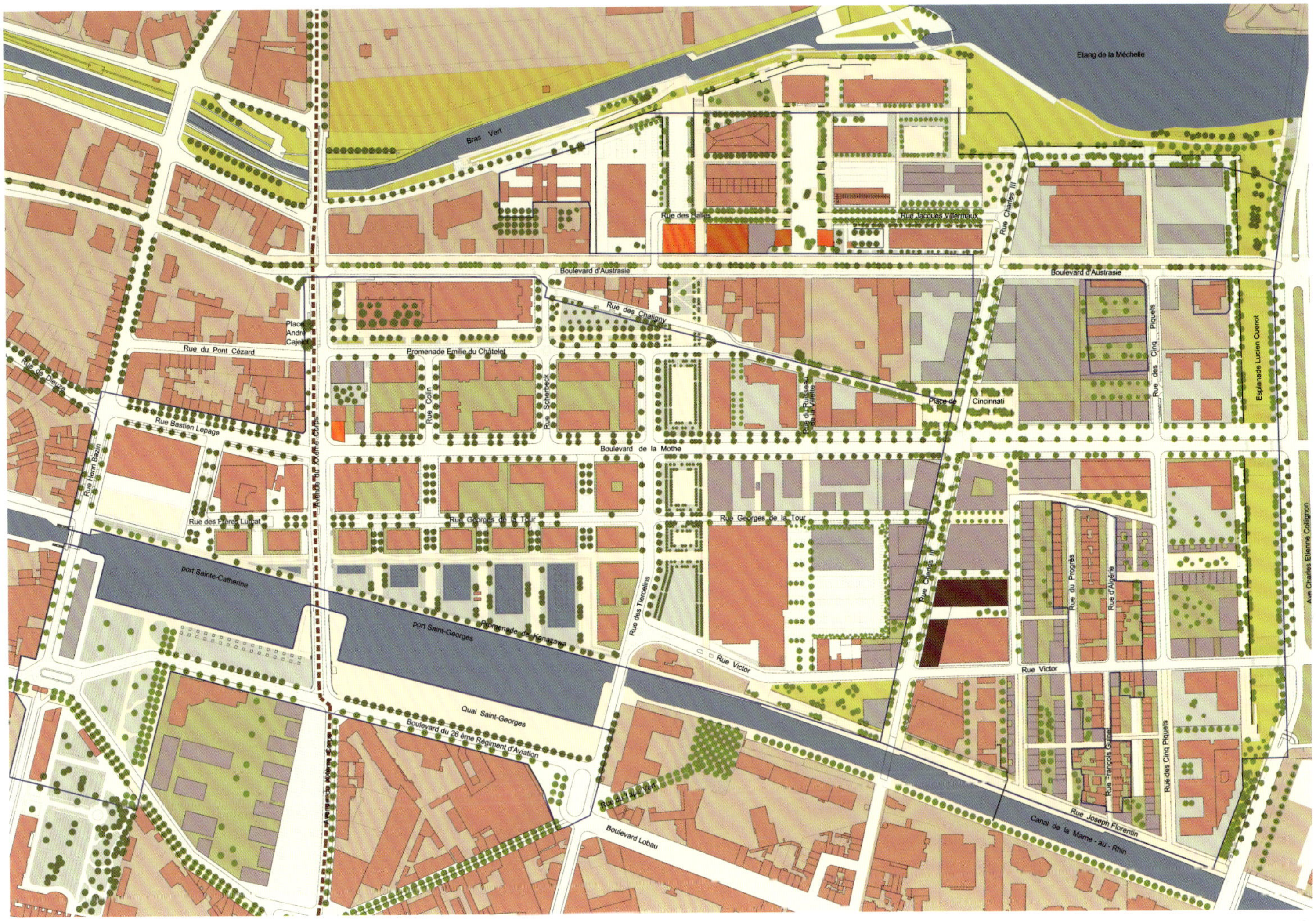


**12-7**

Les Rives de Meurthe. Nancy, France, 2013. Site plan. The Water Garden provided the starting point and basic vocabulary for designing the neighborhood. [Alexandre Chemetoff & associés]

**12-8**

Les Rives de Meurthe. Médiaparc office building and public spaces. Nancy, France, 2007. Existing pine trees surround an office building of our design. [Arnauld Duboys Fresney, 2017]

**12-9**

The banks of the River Meurthe. Nancy, France, 1993.
The lower quay was planted with bald cypresses, but reeds have invaded the site. [Alexandre Chemetoff, 2011]

**12-10**

Les ressources de la rivière. Nancy, France, 2013.
Walking upon the map, visitors can perhaps visit or revisit the territory. [Arnauld Duboys Fresney, 2013]

close to our office in Gentilly, geographically links the outskirts of Paris, *les banlieues*, and the historical parts of the center city. But what the river really says, what its geography tells us, is that the *banlieues* are as historical as the city's core. In addition, the river narrates its own geography, and demonstrates that no boundary divides the topography and history of the periphery from the geography and history of the center.

In Bagneux, on the slopes of the Bièvre Valley we built the Butte des feux d'artifices (Fireworks Park), so named because the artificial hill provides an ideal location for observing the fireworks shot into the sky from the center of Paris on July 14th, Bastille Day. On most days, however, the view falls on the land rather than the skies. From that viewpoint you may also observe the three aqueducts that have brought water to Paris over the centuries: the almost-destroyed Roman aqueduct, the Medici aqueduct built at the beginning of seventeenth century, and the aqueduct constructed in the middle of the nineteenth century by the civil engineer Eugène Belgrand. At the end of that century the Bièvre, as shown in photographs by Eugène Atget, was lined by a mélange of elements, such as the characteristic wooden structures and tanneries that exploited the river for industrial purposes.

### *Landscape and Memory*

After the First World War, however, the river had been covered and paved as it passed through the center of Gentilly. Although our design for the river significantly transformed the center of Gentilly, we were unsuccessful in our efforts to reopen its waters to the sky. It was just not possible at that time, but we nonetheless prepared a plan to reopen the river one day, and to make comprehensible the language of the suburbs—to understand why a church from the thirteenth century stands adjacent to certain industrial structures or houses [12-12]. Along the river, willows accompany your walk, and perhaps from these trees you may imagine that one day the river will see daylight once again [12-13]. We also needed a signature, a symbol by which to make visible the forgotten river. For this purpose we planted *Ginkgo biloba* along the streets, along the valley, along the river. The shape of its leaves also provided the theme and motif for the urban furniture, the cast iron bollards, tree grates, and railings placed along the buried river.

One early morning in autumn, I noticed the carpet of ginkgo leaves that had fallen upon the suburban sidewalk. It was a beautiful sight, this brilliant yellow set against the dark concrete made wet by rain. The colors made me consider this natural phenomenon in relation to the economic state

**12-11**

Bièvre Valley. Val-de-Marne, France, 1988. Model of Bièvre Valley between Antony and Paris. [Alexandre Chemetoff & associés, Nathalie Massenet, model maker]

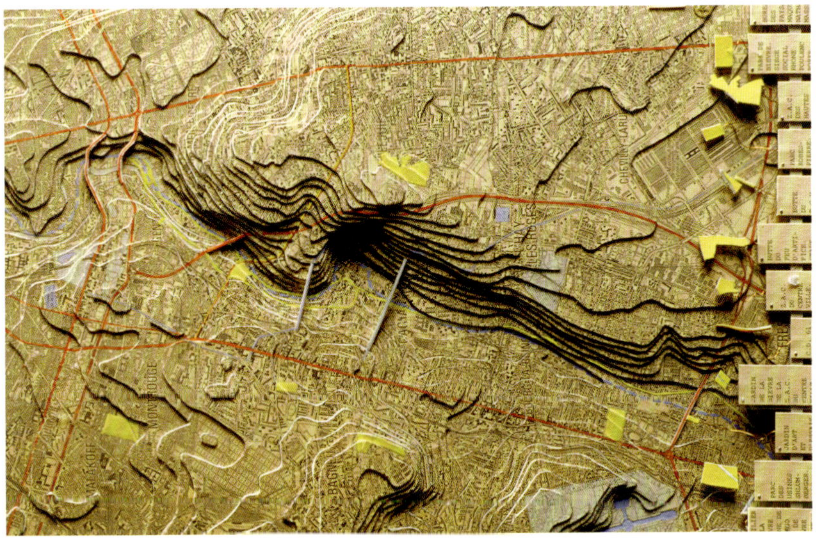

**12-12**

The River Bièvre at Gentilly, France, 1945. Why does this church from the thirteenth century stand by this river? [Robert Doisneau, *La Bièvre à Gentilly* (The Bièvre River at Gentilly)]

of the suburb—both poverty and abundance—and a symbol of the changes made to the image and fabric of the town.

## The Forest City

But now we will leave the rivers and their waters and return to Nancy, to consider the forest and the Forest City and to observe that a tree in a forest is not an isolated subject, and that the real treasure of the forest is the soil itself.

For this neighborhood from the 1960s on the edge of the forest we were asked to transform 4,000 units of social housing and their services that stood on land some 150 meters (500 feet) above the level of the River Meurthe and the Water City below. Seen in plan, the relationship between the city by the river, the city center, and the city of the forest is evident. Visible from the mayor's office on the Place Stanislas, for example, is the massive apartment block on the hill that stretches for almost one kilometer. Despite their distance from and elevation above the old city, the alignment of the housing blocks on the top of the hill was set in parallel to the street pattern of the Stanislas quarter; in some ways the blocks have served as its crown [12-14]. Over the years we have transformed every part of this neighborhood, providing the Forest City with 100 hectares (250 acres) of common, public, and private space; streets; courtyards; and a large central park—as well as a linear park along the highway, and a system of parks and public spaces that links the subdistricts and buildings on the hilltop with the city center below them.

Almost all the trees growing on the site were preserved, with new ones planted to create a dialogue between the older trees and those newly arrived. A kilometer-long wall, constructed of gabions, dampens the intrusion of noise from the adjacent motorway. The dense planting along this linear park is purposeful—both for the functional purpose of sound reduction and for aesthetic reasons as well. For the most part, only forest trees and understory plants were used, intensifying the sense of a natural area along the wall [12-15].

The architect of the housing blocks on Le Haut-du-Lièvre (Hare Heights), Bernard Zehrfuss, christened the buildings using the names of trees: the White Sycamore (Le Blanc Sycomore), the Copper Beech (Le Hêtre Pourpre), the Red Horse Chestnut (le Marronier Rouge), the Silver Linden (Le Tilleul Argenté), and the Blue Cedar (Le Cèdre Bleu). Viewed today, the choice of names seems at best ironic, if not cynical. But the names can also be considered a premonitory sign for the Forest City that arrived a half

**12-13**

Le Jardin de Bièvre.
Gentilly, France,
1992.
Willows
accompany your
walk along the
canalized river.
[Arnauld Duboys
Fresney, 2008]

**12-14**

Alexandre
Chemetoff.
The long linear
Blue Cedar and
Silver Linden
housing blocks
as seen from the
mayor's office on
Place Stanislas: a
crown for the city.
[Alexandre
Chemetoff &
associés]

**12-15**

Le Plateau de Haye, linear park. Maxéville, France, 2013.
For acoustic reasons, the planting is purposefully dense along the length of the park.
[Arnauld Duboys Fresney, 2015]

**12-16**

Alexandre Chemetoff, urban design; Christian Zoméno, architect. Le Plateau de Haye, Le square Laverny.
Nancy, France, 2008.
A courtyard now stands on a former parking lot for the demolished Red Horse Chestnut housing block.
[Arnauld Duboys Fresney, 2015]

century later. To open the view and reconnect the hilltop district with the historical center we decided to chop down the Red Horse Chestnut block, the Copper Beech and White Sycamore blocks, and parts of the Blue Cedar. (Because I studied horticulture and pruning, I know how to deal with those kinds of trees—and have applied that experience to the existing structures).

### *Landscape as Urbanism*

At the start of the project we moved 800,000 cubic meters of earth in order to establish the foundation for the renewed neighborhood. The central park, shaped by the deposition of earth from the grading operations, today occupies the heart of the site. The urban plan itself embodies a dialogue among the site, the new lots, and the streets. The plan also addresses the existing heritage of a prior park, as its vocabulary derives from materials found on the site, like the wood used to protect the new plantings and fences of wattle that shield the pathways. Blocks of new social housing face the park and enjoy direct access to it. The streetscapes were treated as forests—linear forests planted with species that are particularly hearty (*Fagus sylvatica, Sorbus aria*, maples like *Acer platanoides* and *Acer campestre*). No curbs bind the streets; all rainwater flows into the swales and is thereafter collected and distributed.

Around Le Tilleul Argenté, the Silver Linden block, we designed more garden areas, starting with what existed. On the site of the demolished Red Horse Chestnut apartments, a courtyard has replaced a parking lot [12-16]. Some of the existing maples were healthy and were kept; the new hedges are planted with raspberries. At Les Aulnes (Alders), a newly constructed terrace offers splendid views over the Meurthe Valley and the city down below.

### *Houses and Gardens Are for People*

For the block called Le Cèdre Bleu (Blue Cedar) the transformation was more dramatic. Several hundred apartment units were demolished and only the vertical fragment that houses the heating facility and its chimney was kept. The resulting freestanding tower houses facilities for the gardeners and for the bees that occupy hives on the building's third floor. Around the building are 62 vegetable gardens for use by the residents; those who have never gardened can learn from courses given by a former municipal services gardener in the community vegetable garden on-site. [12-17]. The covered open-air kitchen offers the residents facilities for cooking and tables for 300 people who can share a meal beneath the shelter of a common roof [12-18].

## L'Île de Nantes

The Île de Nantes, set almost on the west coast of France, is the first island encountered along the River Loire by anyone coming from New York. The regulating plan for the transformation of the island guided the conversion of buildings and some 350 hectares (865 acres) of land, based on a dialogue between the features of the existing site and the projected development [12-19]. The shipyard that formerly occupied a prominent part of the island had been demolished in the early 1980s, although traces of its structures and processes remained and suggested a direction for designing the new park. Our work involved a search for memory—in some ways an invention of memory—because we found that the past is as uncertain as the future. The park design is thus a reinvented memory of the former industry, created to link the former industrial site and the natural landscape of the riverbank [12-20].

### *As Found*

On the part of the site called l'Île Mabon, our first act was to create a garden. In its design we decided to keep what had been discovered in our explorations and study, and to design a place in accord with the natural processes that currently were shaping the site [12-21]. A concrete slab from the former factory invaded by endemic plants provoked an analysis of industrial waste as some unknown and distant territory. After collecting samples of the existing vegetation, we prepared a herbarium of the species found on the site. Claude Figureau, a biodiversity expert from the botanic garden in Nantes, consulted on the identification of the plants and suggested their possible uses. No new species were introduced; instead, all the plant species growing on the site were retained. The herbarium remains visible onsite through the porcelain-enamel signs that also list the butterflies and birds you may encounter on your visit.

A meteorological station on-site tracks and records the local weather. The plants encountered represent neither "rewilding" nor a true return to nature, but a condition that leads us forward to culture. Given the years of industrial use on-site, a return to nature was impossible; in addition, the variety of species growing there has been very much influenced by people living nearby as well as the industries that had once occupied the land. *Pyracantha coccinea*, for example, does not grow naturally in this area, and yet it thrives. And so the lesson our garden tells brings us forward to culture rather than back to nature. Like a tree, botany is not an isolated subject.

**12-17**

Community gardens, Le Plateau de Haye. Nancy, France, 2015. "Gardens are for people." [Arnauld Duboys Fresney]

**12-18**

Le Plateau de Haye. Residents share a meal beneath the shelter of a common roof. [Frédéric Mercenier, 2017]

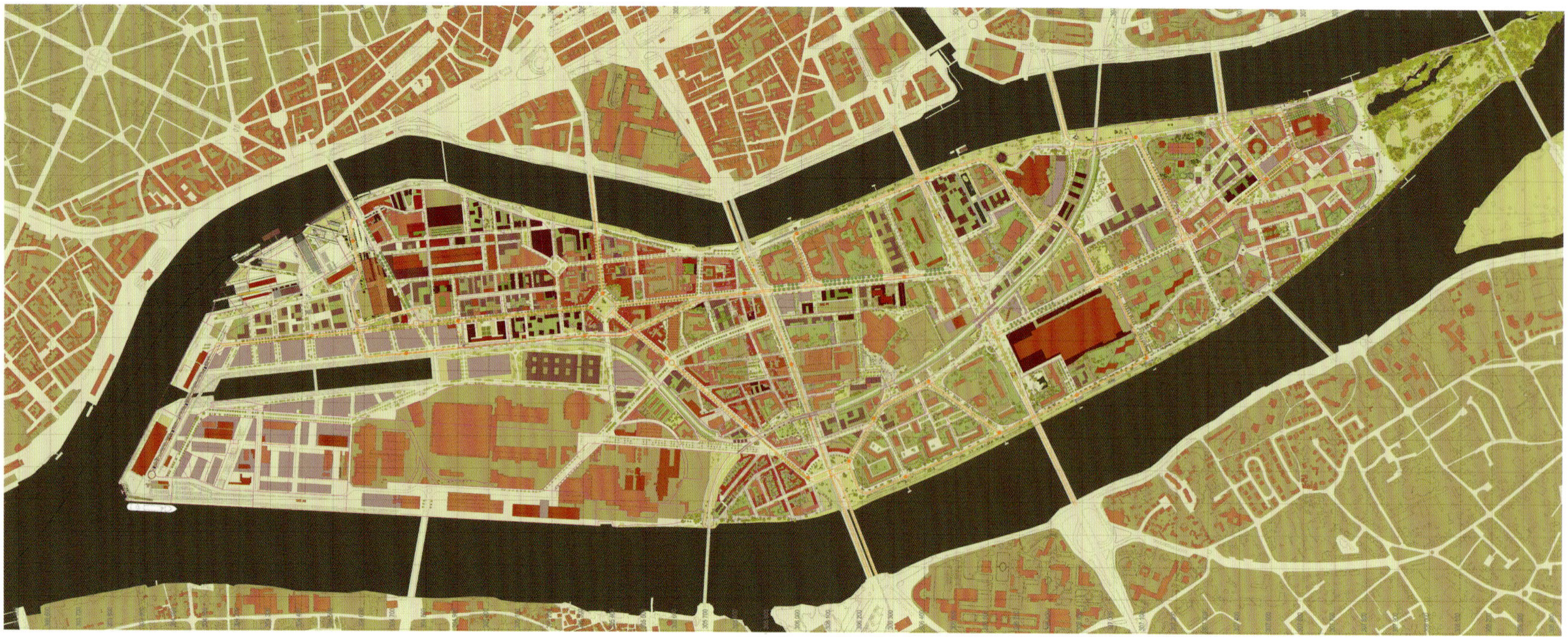

**12-19**

Île de Nantes, Nantes, France, 2008. The site plan for the proposed urban design. [Alexandre Chemetoff & associés]

**12-20**

Parc des Chantiers. Île de Nantes, Nantes, France, 2009. The park reinvents a memory to link the former industrial site and the natural scenery of the riverbank. [Arnauld Duboys Fresney]

*(previous page)*

**12-21**

Square de l'Île Mabon.
Île de Nantes, Nantes, France, 2005.
No planting was added; all species growing on the site were retained.
[Arnauld Duboys Fresney, 2006]

## A Garden Dedicated to Climate Control

The bamboo garden at the Parc de la Villette in Paris addressed the relationship between climate and agriculture. At the time of the competition for the park in the 1980s, the site was barren with no remains revealing its former uses. The idea to make a garden of bamboo was decided early on, but to ensure its longevity we realized that the plants must be protected and that excavating the site was the most practical way of ensuring their longevity. The sunken garden acts as a sun-trap that accumulates heat in summer and collects water when it rains [12-22]. This has been a very successful project, and if any problem plagues the garden it is that the bamboo has grown so well that pruning should be more frequent. As in our other projects, all the species planted in the garden are identified by signage, in this instance, etched into the retaining walls.

## Environmental Architecture

Our primary act in converting a former mail-sorting facility into a digital center in Bègles, near Bordeaux, involved excavating a void through the middle of the building, a swath of space to provide light and ventilation. Because the building was to have no air conditioning, we sought to create a green matrix of which the old building was a part—rather than only landscape as a mere band of trees that wraps the architecture. We relied to a large degree on several species of bamboo, which grow rapidly and do not require large amounts of water once established. Pipes collect rainwater from the roof, which is then stored in tanks and used to irrigate the garden. The planting, in places quite dense, will help cool the building during the hot summer months [12-23]. Here the garden functions as an effective environmental instrument rather than only as an instrument for pleasure. It functions in tandem with the architecture to modulate the climatic effects on the interior spaces of the building.

## Architecture, Landscape Architecture, and Urbanism Are Not Isolated Subjects

If the tree is not an isolated subject, then landscape architecture is not an isolated subject either. Nor are architecture, urban design, and urbanism isolated subjects, as one can see when visiting our office in Gentilly. Although at times also working as an architect, my thinking remains very much rooted in the idea of a total landscape, which is something quite different from the idea of regarding these practices as separate from one another, evident in this last picture of a courtyard in Paris we have been designing as architects as well as landscape architects [12-24]. We treat no element as an isolated subject.

**12-23**

La Cité numérique.
Bègles, Bordeaux,
France, 2019.
The transformation of a former postal sorting facility into a "digital center." The garden functions as an environmental instrument, in tandem with the architecture modulating the climate within the building.
[Arnauld Duboys Fresney]

**12-24**

Bichat–Temple housing.
Paris, France, 2016.
A courtyard for housing, commercial space, and a preschool for which we served as architects as well as landscape architects.
[Arnauld Duboys Fresney]

**12-22** *(opposite)*

Jardin de bambous (Garden of Bamboo).
Parc de la Villette.
Paris, France, 1987.
A garden dedicated to climate control.
[Arnauld Duboys Fresney]

# FINDING OUR WAY THROUGH THE TREES

Peter Walker

13.

**Unless otherwise noted, landscapes illustrated in this chapter have been designed by PWP Landscape Architecture / Peter Walker**

Millennium Park. Sydney, Australia, 2000. Reforestation and ziggurat. [PWP Landscape Architecture]

Instead of discussing my thoughts on a region or ecology in general, I will trace the history of a certain passion of mine that's continued for over 60 years. Professional practice is almost never confined to one type of commission, and over the years I have been involved in a series of projects in many different places. Every site, of course, is different, as are the scale and purpose of every project. However, the track of an artistic idea in one's work over a long time may perhaps be understood as linear. My telling of that track may not be linear, although I hope that a certain order can be discerned that will make the story comprehensible.

I graduated from the University of California, Berkeley, in 1955. Before graduation I had worked for Lawrence Halprin for about six months, and I continued working for him after graduation. At Berkeley, Geraldine Knight Scott taught planting design, and in her teaching, she stressed that it was not the individual plant that mattered but how the plants were used in combination. It was almost an English garden attitude about plants and about their use in gardens. That approach also prevailed in the Halprin office and I assume at the office of Thomas Church as well. Our designs were drawn in pencil on tracing paper and were then given to Jean Walton, who was the "plants person" in the office; she would select the plants for the design of the garden. That is pretty much how those early gardens' plantings were produced in both offices.

**13-1**

André Le Nôtre. Parc de Sceaux. Hauts-de-Seine, France, 1680s. [Marc Treib]

I should note that the teaching of two mentors has had a lasting influence on my thinking and design. During my last semester at Berkeley, Stanley White visited the school and told us not to forget that landscape architecture is a cultural enterprise. I took that to mean that within professional practice there existed a possibility for designing landscapes as art. Practice wasn't just a service; it wasn't just covering the ground with greenery or addressing function—landscape design also offered the possibility of making something artful. As this idea was largely missing in the Berkeley curriculum, it was a new thought to me, and I was taken with it. So, in the spring semester of 1956, I went to Illinois to study landscape architecture with Stanley White. At the end of my first semester, some guy named Dan Kiley came to Urbana to give a talk at the school. At that time, I was barely aware of who he was because he really hadn't been talked about much at Berkeley.

For me, this lecture was my first real introduction to the man and his work. At the end of the lecture, he asked, "Does anyone here have a car?" As it happens, I had driven a Volkswagen Beetle to Illinois, so I raised my hand. He needed to visit a project of his then under construction in Columbus, Indiana; would I take him there? I didn't know where Columbus, Indiana, was, but he seemed like an interesting guy and he also offered to buy me lunch. As we drove, along the way he asked me, "Have you seen Chantilly? Have you been to Sceaux? Have you seen Villandry?" And I said, "No, where are they?" "They're all in France," he told me, "and you'd better get over there as quickly as you can because you're going to want to see those landscapes many, many times in your life. You're going to want to see them in different seasons, in different weather, at different times of the day. You're going to want to go there dozens of times." And Dan was right. Over the years I have seen them many times and they have been very influential on my thinking and design practice.

After I received my degree from Harvard, a fellowship allowed me to travel in Europe. Walking into the Parc de Sceaux was a profound experience [13-1]. Although I don't mean to be overly critical, what we were doing in California were backyards; Sceaux, in contrast, was a grand garden. I remembered that when asked what his ultimate goal might be, Kiley had answered that he wanted to make landscapes possessing the glory of a gothic cathedral. And when I walked through these gardens, with their amazing scale and extent, I understood that landscape architecture could, in fact, be something akin to great architecture. I've never really gotten over that.

Kiley and I drove down to Columbus where he had a garden under construction. He took me around the site and explained how he used the trees, and the importance of the pavement patterns. Of course, it was the Miller garden, which was finished in 1957 [13-2]. It was only years later that it was photographed and published and became the landmark it is for us today. But even then, before it was completed, there was something about the garden that I felt bridged the historic gap between the great French and Italian gardens I had yet to see and the gardens of our time. His idea for garden design and the structure of its spaces, Kiley said, came from early modern architecture, from Mies van der Rohe, Eero Saarinen, Louis Kahn, and so forth. "I think of these trees in the garden as columns," he told me, "and I make space with the columns." It wasn't just French architecture, he believed. It could also be Greek temples; it could be any architecture structured by columns that hit the ground and through their order defined space. Years later he took me to see his landscape for Rockefeller University in New York; it was evident that by then he was really making landscapes using architectural moves with lessons learned from the Bauhaus and American modern architecture.

**13-2**

Dan Kiley.
Miller garden.
Columbus, Indiana,
1957.
[PWP Landscape
Architecture]

At the end of 1960, I returned to California to develop and build the design by Sasaki Walker for Foothill College in Los Altos Hills. At last I had the opportunity to apply some of the lessons I learned from Dan Kiley and to make a space out of "columns" [13-3]. It was harder to do than I had thought, much easier said than done. I found that it would have been a lot easier to approach the design of the landscape and trees in a more romantic way, that making even simple "architecture" using these plants was not so easy. At Foothill we also experimented with other things, for example, the idea of looking up. We arranged a stand of trees in a ring to "draw" a figure in the sky for the students and faculty. What else could we create using trees as the medium for a spatial artwork? The ring of trees in San Francisco's Sidney Walton Park (1975) shares this "form in the sky" technique.

In 1970, for the corporate landscape for Weyerhaeuser headquarters in Tacoma, Washington, I cribbed some of Dan's ideas and used rows of trees as colonnades. As a row they screened the cars from the building, but you could also approach the building and look through them out to the lake to the north or the meadow to the south [13-4]. A bit later on, while I was a resident at the American Academy in Rome, I was introduced to the pinetum at the Villa Doria Pamphilj, where the grid of heroic stone pines (*Pinus pinea*) created a series of articulated spaces in the same way you could make architectural space using a grid of columns [13-5]. Because some trees had fallen down, the intervals between the trees appeared irregular, at least as seen from certain vantage points. This too was a powerful idea for future designs.

About this same time, I started to collect art. I was particularly interested in minimalist works by sculptors such as Donald Judd and Richard Long, but most of all I was interested in Carl Andre [13-6]. Andre was making sculptures by covering areas of a floor with metal plates only about an eighth of an inch thick, defining space essentially in the manner of a great carpet. This really fascinated me and I started thinking that Andre's approach could be applied to making landscapes, although I didn't know quite how to employ this understanding at that time.

On an excursion to France with my Harvard classmate William Johnson and students from Michigan and Harvard, I discovered that another Andre (André Le Nôtre) had solved one of the problems that I hadn't yet figured out [13-7]. After a basically flat plane was established, anything placed upon it—sculpture, plant, or parterre—was read against that plane, especially trees used as architectonic elements.

**13-3**

Sasaki Walker Associates. Foothill College. Los Altos Hills, California, 1957–1960. Bosk. [Peter Walker]

**13-4**

Peter Walker / SWA. Weyerhaeuser headquarters. Tacoma, Washington, 1972. Parking lots and colonnades. [Peter Walker]

**13-5**

Pinetum. Villa Doria Pamphilj. Rome, Italy, 1600s. [Peter Walker]

**13-6**

Carl Andre. *Steel-Aluminum Plain*, 1969. [Peter Walker]

**13-7**

André Le Nôtre. Vaux-le-Vicomte. Maincy, France, 1650s–1660s. [William Johnson]

Applying that idea, we made some experimental gardens using common materials like old tires, Necco wafers, empty flowerpots, and mirrors that took the place of pools. If you could make a flowerpot powerful in a tiny little garden, maybe that idea could be used later in a larger, less experimental landscape.

One of the first opportunities we had to test these ideas was in Saitama Prefecture in Japan. In 1994 we won a competition for a plaza in Ômori, a city north of Tokyo, in which we set a grid of more than 200 nearly identical zelkova trees on an absolutely flat plane [13-8]. The technical solutions needed to support the growth of the trees were complex; irrigation was required as well as a drainage system positioned under two meters of soil, all on top of a building. The plane of the plaza was absolutely flat, surfaced half with stone and half with aluminum panels arranged in stripes. The perforated metal panels allow water to pass to the tree roots and ultimately to the drain. The Saitama project was the first time I really had a chance to apply ideas about flatness and repetition that I'd been thinking about for some time. There are no other living materials except the trees at Saitama. At the presentation of the design, I asked the review board to imagine the zelkovas changing through the seasons, light green in spring, deeper green and full shade in summer, red and yellow in fall, and bare in winter with the sunlight passing through their branches. In Japan, selling the beauty of seasonal change isn't so difficult because an awareness of nature is endemic in the culture.

In 2000, the central Forum of the campus of Novartis Pharmaceuticals in Basel was based on a similar idea: A bosk of trees, in this case, pin oaks (*Quercus pollustrus*) were spaced about 30 feet apart and set in a flat bed of decomposed granite [13-9]. Nearby was the smaller President's Garden, where the main feature—a grove of birches closely clustered and spaced irregularly—produced a completely different kind of space [13-10]. The Forum with its oaks can accommodate everyone in the company—perhaps some 10,000 people. In contrast, the more intimate President's Garden is usually enjoyed by pairs or small groups; it can also hold perhaps a hundred people for small celebrations and commendations. So you can see that while applying the same basic ideas, we designed spaces both large and small, for large groups and for individuals—and that trees were the major players in the character of the design.

When we first received the commission for the Cleveland Clinic in 2005, the president of the clinic said to me, "You know, Pete, when people come into the hospital, they're not

**13-8**

PWP Landscape Architecture with Yoji Sasaki. Sky Forest Plaza, Saitama-Shintoshin Station. Saitama, Japan, 2000. [Yoji Sasaki]

**13-9**

Novartis Forum, Novartis Pharmaceuticals. Basel, Switzerland, 2007. [Peter Walker]

**13-10**

President's Courtyard, Novartis Pharmaceuticals. [Peter Walker]

**13-11**

Cleveland Clinic Heart Center and allée. Cleveland, Ohio, 2008. Entrance to the clinic. [Peter Walker]

**13-12**

Peter Walker / SWA. Tanner Fountain. Cambridge, Massachusetts, 1984. [PWP Landscape Architecture]

in a very good mood; whether it's yourself or a loved one, you're full of anxiety. Can you do anything so that this new landscape will reduce that anxiety? Please make something that will calm our clients." In response we proposed a large, grid of columnar trees and simply let them stand silently beside the new still pool that stretched the two blocks between the city street and the entrance to the clinic's primary building [13-11]. From the big city boulevard, you turn into this quiet area and drive along this long, quiet pool, and then drop people off to enter the clinic. We have been told that their patients and visitors do achieve some calm along the route; that was our way of responding to the president's request, while producing the primary image of the clinic.

In some projects, the trees already existed. The site for the Tanner Fountain at Harvard University in 1984 had neither a Renaissance centering nor any axial relationship to its surroundings. The circle of large, irregular stones animated periodically by mist or steam emitted between the elements is the fountain's primary feature, but the space for the fountain was produced by visually connecting the trees already growing there [13-12]. People sit on the stones next to a tree they find attractive and comfortable. It's that simple.

In the 1991 design for a transit corridor in San Diego designed with Ron Wigginton, we proposed to use plants as objects alternating with lines of trees, the idea being that the "objects," in fact, shaped soil buttons covered with ice plants, would emphasize the vertical nature of the lines of trees. Drawing on the work of Le Nôtre we used these buttons to emphasize the points where the trunks met the ground, reinforcing the dominant order of the trees. Two lines of trees form a central allée and separate the light rail transit corridor from the automobile traffic passing on either side. In the center, a group of larger grass mounds were planted with pine trees in clusters (*Pinus canariensis*) rising from between them. Once again, the verticality of the trees was architectural, providing a center for an otherwise linear landscape while defining the movement of traffic.

In 2002 an existing parking lot destined to be the site of a new cancer research building at Stanford University included about seven or eight mature live oak trees. To transform the parking lot into a sculpture garden, we introduced a series of hedges and then let the existing irregularly spaced trees play against the architectonic order of the new hedge elements, in this fashion playing disorder against the orderly rooms [13-13].

An urban project in downtown Chicago in 1994 presented a far different and more technical challenge. Our site,

**13-13**

Center for Clinical Science Research, Stanford University. Palo Alto, California, 2002. [PWP Landscape Architecture]

**13-14**

One North Wacker Drive.
Chicago, Illinois, 2002.
Section showing planting mounds.
[PWP Landscape Architecture]

**13-15**

PWP with Ballistic Architecture Machine.
*Finite / Infinite.*
Beijing Garden Expo, Beijing, China, 2015
[Ballistic Architecture Machine]

which sat above a huge basement used for deliveries, parking, and other services, was a narrow strip of land that bordered a new high-rise tower. Given the basement below, there was not even room for enough dirt to grow the street trees that are typical of downtown Chicago. To provide sufficient soil, we designed another kind of button. These were made of soil, almost hemispherical in contour [2-14]. The low walls that retained the soil doubled as circular benches containing the roots of the trees.

Of a different order was a small plaza in Beijing, a collaboration with BAM (Ballistic Architecture Machine) completed in 2013. The principal elements of the design are two walls about ten feet high set parallel to one another. The walls are surfaced with mirrors on both sides [12-15]. In plan, the plaza is a circle with the two walls running down its center. Seen from the outside, the mirrors visually complete the semicircular grass parterres and transform them into perfect, if virtual, circles. On the inside, a single row of trees visually continues to infinity. The idea driving the design plays on a certain degree of irony: the most contained space appears without end, while the open and partially formed areas read as geometrically complete.

Millennium Park for the 2000 Olympics in Sydney is the largest project we've ever done, approximately a thousand acres surrounding the Olympic Center designed by Hargreaves Associates. It is the worst site we've ever worked on or ever hope to work on. In the nineteenth century, the land had been the site of a slaughterhouse, followed by a munitions dump developed sometime before the First World War, its use continuing through World War II. The site had become so degraded that by 1975 the government had just given up and had sold parcels of land to factories that dumped chemicals on the ground and into the creek, even though it eventually flowed into the river.

No flora or fauna lived on this highly toxic site except for some frogs that occupied a former brick pit, surviving because it was the one place the chemicals couldn't reach them. To start, Tony McCormick, a landscape architect working in Sydney, asked me to lead a design team of about 16 people. It was the first time I'd worked with such a large team of real experts. This has become more common in our practice today, but in 1999 it was a rare situation. These experts possessed an incredible knowledge of soils, plants, forestry, riparian areas, and fish, and animal habitat—others knew about the history and politics of the area.

Two things had to be done before anything else. Our initial task was to rebuild the land while keeping all the bad soil

**13-16**

Millennium Park.
Sydney, Australia,
2000.
Site plan.
[PWP Landscape
Architecture]

**13-17**

Millennium Park.
Reforestation and
ziggurat.
[PWP Landscape
Architecture]

on-site as required. From that soil we shaped a series of mounds and ziggurats—essentially hill forms made of the toxic dirt [13-16, 13-17; see also chapter opening]. Our soils expert, Simon Leake, manufactured new productive dirt by using other materials from the site that could be remediated. The mounds were capped with the newly made soil. Once the new topography was established and the subsoil controlled, we reforested the entire site and configured it in a series of forms and spaces, suggesting great rooms that shaped the park at large scale. The planting plan by Bruce McKinsey used casuarinas and eucalyptus of various species. In warm weather, in the new wooded areas, young people run around and play soccer and other active sports in the open spaces, while the older folks sit back in the shade along the edges. We called these open spaces "rooms," and the new forests "walls." Spaces resembling corridors run through the forests and connect the open spaces. These forests were planted—typical reforestation projects—with seedlings only about 18 inches tall. After 20 years they're now over 50 feet high.

The project for the Nasher Sculpture Center in 2004 in Dallas presented different problems, with soil again being one of them. When I began the project, Doug Christmas, the owner of the Ace Gallery in Los Angeles, told me, "Pete, if you just put a grid of trees out there all the artists will love you. It'll provide the frame of reference for both organized and disorganized placement of art, either playing against the grid or playing with the grid." We did make a grid, but it was finally more complicated than one marked by consistent intervals [13-18]. A double line of live oaks (*Quercus virginiana*) plays against corresponding geometric groups of deciduous cedar elm trees (*Ulmus crassifolia*) [13-19]. Together they create a series of smaller spaces with a range of possibilities for placing sculptures of varying scale. Stone boundary walls create a box filled with newly manufactured soil six feet deep. Since the compressive strength required for moving large and heavy pieces of sculpture can be extreme, the soil mix is primarily of sand. The site is essentially flat with no catch basins—the water moves down through the flat lawn and then percolates through the sand to be picked up by drainpipes below.

The University of Texas at Dallas had been only a secondary campus in the University of Texas system. The site for this relatively new campus had originally been a cotton field, but when we began our designs in 2006, it looked like an old industrial park with poorly sited buildings. There was little in between the buildings in terms of landscape. Even the playfields looked saggy. The "preindustrial" part of

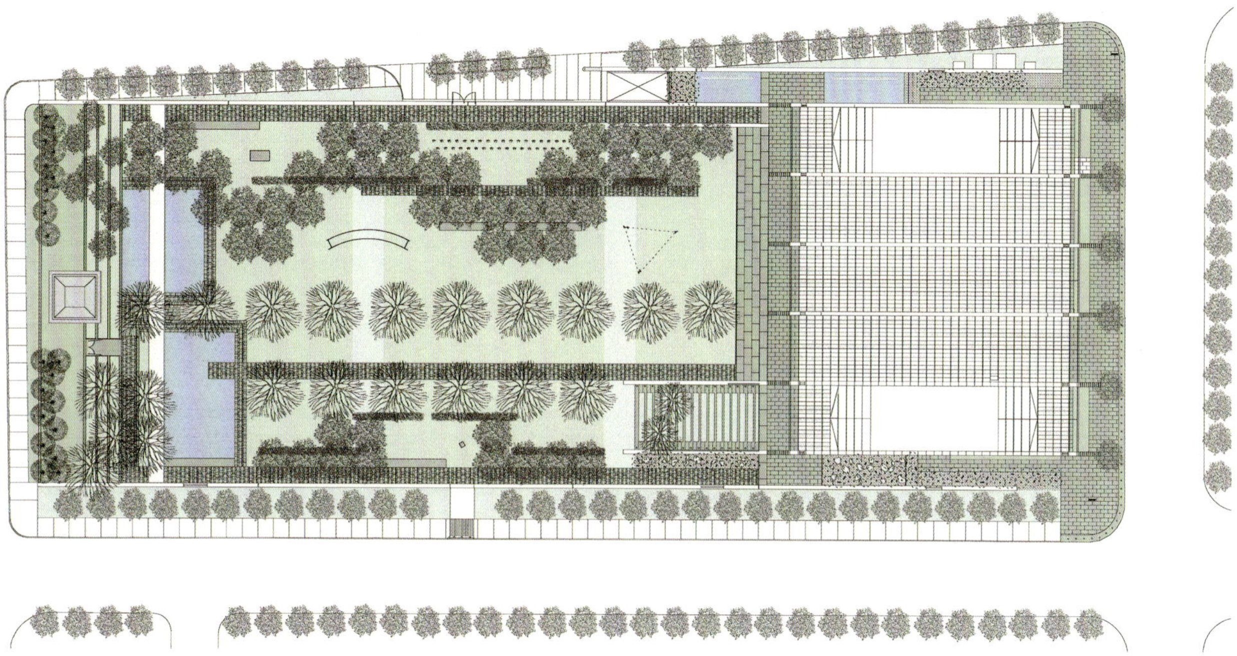

**13-18**

Nasher Sculpture Center.
Dallas, Texas, 2003.
Site plan.
[PWP Landscape Architecture]

**13-19**

Nasher Sculpture Center.
Sculpture Garden.
Trees define the spaces.
[PWP Landscape Architecture]

the site had two creeks, one of them full of beautiful trees. There was also a concrete drainage ditch that ran down the middle of the site with entrance roads that ran on either side.

Two plantings became the first effort to structure the core of the new campus [13-20]. We took our cue from the creeks, striving to make something that all the students would remember and that could become the symbol of the historic past before the existence of the university. The creek planting was refreshed and the drainage ditch similarly planted. Our principal donor was an elderly lady who loved flowers, so we designed a central axis lined with rows of flowering magnolias (*Magnolia* 'Little Gem'). This space has become a linear central park that ends in an arbored square defined by the library and the student center.

Over the period of some 45 or 50 years that our office has been in practice, we've learned an enormous amount from each of the projects we've designed. Each project brought new questions, new challenges, and ultimately new knowledge. In 2000, the architect Michael Arad asked if we would work with his team on the competition to design a memorial for the victims of the World Trade Center disaster. He explained that his primary concept was to excavate voids about 35 feet deep with the same size, shape, and location as the footprints of the buildings that were destroyed on 9/11. We agreed to collaborate on the design. Michael's entry, which was called *Reflecting Absence*, was one of the eight finalists.

To New York's Mayor Bloomberg, the site was too big to be used only for a memorial. He wanted the space to also serve as a public park. Somehow a balance had to be struck between the solemnity due a memorial and the freedom of activity found in a neighborhood park. The site was surrounded by buildings with the highest density in New York, which made the neighborhood among the most densely populated in the world. Those were the constraints facing all the teams.

To me, *Reflecting Absence* recalled sculptures by Michael Heizer, many of which achieve a maximum effect as a void excavated from a level plane, a sculpture made of nothing but negative space. To study the resulting effect of the planting in relation to the voids, we made a large model, 1/8 inch to one foot, to determine what could be seen from beneath the trees as we proposed them. The density of the trees and the purity of the ground plane allowed few additional elements, perhaps only a few benches. The primary question was how to produce scale on an essentially empty site. The ordering of the trees in the wooded part of the memorial design suggests that of an abacus [13-21]. If you enter

**13-20**

University of Texas at Dallas campus. Richardson, Texas, 2011. Central Mall. [PWP Landscape Architecture]

from the north or south, the trees appear as an irregular woods. Seen from the east or west, the woods turn into colonnades. Working together, the placement of the trees and the continuation of the ground plane shape the design.

Very few street trees in New York live more than 10 or 15 years. The average lifespan of a tree in Manhattan is only about 10 years, in fact, but we wanted an 80- to 100-year life span for the trees of the memorial. We knew some technological support would be needed [13-22]. Of the four or five deciduous species that the urban tree experts at Cornell University approved, we selected the swamp white oak (*Quercus bicolor*). When mature, the rows of trees form vaulted spaces that recall the modernized Gothic arches at the base of the destroyed towers. It wasn't easy to acquire the 450 trees needed for the design (plus 50 replacements for any lost in construction). The nurseries in the region couldn't provide the species we wanted in these numbers, so our staff and our forester Paul Cowie went out and explored backyards and fields to find trees to be brought to a nursery in New Jersey near the Hudson River. During the many years of the memorial's construction, the trees were trained to achieve similar forms and branch structures. For the most part, the leaders were straight, the branching was proportionally right, and all were in pretty good condition—although they were of different sizes. Bartlett Tree Experts from Chicago performed operations on the trees similar to intravenous feeding in hospitals. They fed the little ones and starved the big ones, and three years later when we were ready to plant, they were all pretty much the same size and character—perhaps not as well matched as the zelkovas in Japan, but very close.

Of course, there was critical reaction to our design. Manhattan is not Japan, and some people thought that just having a sophisticated forest of one species of tree isn't very interesting or appropriate. The architectural delineator Chris Grubbs made a series of drawings showing how dramatic the changes in color, form, and transparency would be through the year and over time [13-23A,B,C,D]. I tried to get people to look at the trees as trees, not just as ornaments but as living things that changed, not only through the seasons, but also over the years through aging and decline. The positions of the trees may be fixed, but each tree is actually a dynamic form. To sell the idea, I spoke to many groups in New York, using Chris Grubbs's sketches. Within the trees, we created an open glade where each year they read the names of those who lost their lives in the tragedy. The memorial is open day and night, and to accommodate evening visits, lights are mounted inside the tree branches.

Since the entire memorial is planted on-structure, it is essentially a roof garden, like Saitama, and as such requires advanced technology to sustain the trees through the stresses put upon them by urban conditions [see 13-22]. Ditches filled with a special noncompacting soil run across the width of the site. Although these planting rows may appear flat, they actually have a subtle elevation to them. These are paired with a system of drains to collect rainwater and snowmelt that is stored in tanks set seven stories below the plaza level. In July and August, the stored water is pumped up and used for irrigation—although mechanical and constructed, the cistern operates like an aquifer. The soil mixes are perfect for growth, and the trees that were planted first grew half again as large as the trees that had stayed longer in the boxes at the nursery. At the 9/11 Memorial, technology serves the purposes of the design. In the spring and in the autumn, in the night and in the day, the trees give a dimension of life to the memorial. The relationship of the trees to the voids is critical for achieving our goal: to integrate all the elements of the arboreal program and to work with the architect to make a composition both moving and socially useful. The trees are the critical factor.

**13-21**

National 9/11 Memorial. New York, New York, 2011. Model. [PWP Landscape Architecture]

**13-22**

National 9/11 Memorial. Water collection and reuse system. [PWP Landscape Architecture]

**13-23A**
**13-23B**
**13-23C**
**13-23D**

National 9/11 Memorial. New York, New York, 2011. Spring. Summer. Fall. Winter. [Christopher Grubbs]

## Contributors

**Marc Treib**
*Berkeley, California*
Marc Treib is Professor of Architecture Emeritus, University of California, Berkeley, and a historian and critic of landscape and architecture who has published widely on modern and historical subjects in the United States, Japan, and Scandinavia. Recent books include *Pietro Porcinai and the Landscape of Modern Italy* (co-editor, 2016); *Landscapes of Modern Architecture: Wright, Mies, Neutra, Aalto, Barragán* (2017); *The Landscapes of Georges Descombes: Doing Almost Nothing* (2019); and *Thinking a Modern Landscape Architecture, West & East: Christopher Tunnard, Sutemi Horiguchi* (2020).

**Thorbjörn Andersson**
*Stockholm, Sweden*
Thorbjörn Andersson studied landscape architecture in Sweden and the United States and has been in active practice since 1981. He is best known for his designs of urban public spaces, a selection of which were published in *Platser/Places* (2003) and *Nature/Site/Restraint* (2019). Recent projects include the Physic Garden at Novartis, Basel, Switzerland; the Umeå University Campus Park; and the Hyllie Plaza, Malmö. Andersson was also a founding editor of the journal *Utblick Landskap* and has served as professor of landscape architecture at the Swedish University of Agricultural Sciences, Ultuna.

**Cristina Castel-Branco**
*Lisbon, Portugal*
Cristina Castel-Branco received her degree in landscape architecture from the University of Agronomy in Lisbon, a master of landscape architecture from the University of Massachusetts, and thereafter a doctorate focused on garden history. While professor at the University of Lisbon, she has researched subjects in landscape architecture history, restoration, and ecological design. In addition to serving on several boards of cultural and governmental organizations that include the UNESCO-ICOMOS cultural landscape committee, she maintains an active professional practice in Lisbon. Among her awards she has received are the French government's Officier des Arts et des Lettres and the Japanese nations's Praise of Merit.

**Alexandre Chemetoff**
*Paris, France*
Alexandre Chemetoff is a landscape architect, architect, and urban designer whose practice has spanned scales from the garden to the city to the region. Among his many awarded projects are the designs for the redevelopment of the central island in Nantes, the renewal and reformation of neighborhoods and social housing in Nancy, and the celebrated Bamboo Garden at the Parc de la Villette in Paris. For a number of years he also taught at the École nationale supérieure de paysage in Versailles; in 2000, he received the French Grand Prix de l'urbanisme.

**Andrea Cochran**
*San Francisco, California*
Andrea Cochran received her master's in landscape architecture from Harvard University's Graduate School of Design and opened her own landscape architecture practice in 1998. Her work is characterized by a strong sense of logic and appropriateness to site and climate, as well as its sensitive use and mixture of plants. In recognition of its logic, refinement, and appropriate ecology, she has received continuous professional recognition, including numerous awards from the American Society of Landscape Architects.

**Kate Cullity**
*Adelaide, Australia*
Kate Cullity, a founding director of Taylor Cullity Lethlean (TCL), is a landscape architect and artist with a particular interest in the integration of public art with landscape and urban design. Her background in botany and personal interest in horticulture have resulted in the planting design of sites throughout Australia. Projects of note include the Australian Garden, Royal Melbourne Botanical Garden in Cranbourne, and the National Arboretum in Canberra. TCL is recognized as a leading Australian landscape and urban design firm, and has received numerous awards, both in Australia and internationally.

**Erik Dhont**
*Brussels, Belgium*
Erik Dhont has designed a wide variety of projects throughout continental Europe and the United States, for private clients, public bodies, and commercial institutions. His designs, which further the Belgian garden tradition, are characterized by a precision in planning and execution, with shrubs and hedges used as sculptural forms as well as a vehicle for spatial definition. His studies of abstract form test the limits of horticulture and have been exhibited as artworks in and of themselves.

**Richard L. Hindle**

*Berkeley, California*

Richard Hindle, associate professor of landscape archiecture at the University of California, Berkeley, has particular interests in ecological technology, planting design, and site design. His research and practice explore landscape-related technologies across a range of scales, from large-scale mappings of riverine and coastal patents to detailed historical studies on the antecedents of vegetated architectural systems, with a particular interest in patents secured for landscape interventions.

**Laurie Olin**

*Philadelphia, Pennsylvania*

Laurie Olin, Professor of Practice Emeritus at the University of Pennsylvania, is a landscape architect, urban designer, and prolific author, who has practiced for half a century in the United States and abroad. Among his many signature projects, are the redesign of Bryant Park in New York City, the Washington Monument Grounds in Washington, DC, and more recently, the Barnes Foundation in Philadelphia and the new Apple campus in Cupertino. In addition to numerous articles and critical essays, he is also the author of *Across the Open Field: Essays Drawn from English Landscapes* and *Please Be Seated.*

**Tim Richardson**

*London, England*

Tim Richardson is among Britain's most significant garden historians and critics. His books include *Avant Gardeners, Futurescapes*, and *The Arcadian Friends*, a classic study of the English landscape garden. *You Should Have Been Here Last Week*, a collection of his published writings, appeared in 2016. He created the landscape history course offered by Oxford University and currently teaches the subject at London University. Richardson also founded and directs the Chelsea Fringe Festival, an alternative event intended to expand the perception of landscapes internationally.

**Mario Schjetnan**

*Mexico City, Mexico*

Mario Schjetnan—a recipient of the International Federation of Landscape Architects' Sir Geoffrey Jellicoe Medal for lifetime achievement—is an architect and landscape architect who strives to unite social concerns, aesthetics, and ecology, while reinterpreting and celebrating Mexican culture. His interdisciplinary firm Grupo de Diseño Urbano is known for designs in which buildings are equal, or at times even subordinate, to the landscape.

**Christine Ten Eyck**

*Austin, Texas*

Christine Ten Eyck is a landscape architect known for design projects that address and interpret the arid climate of the American Southwest. Her commissions span various scales, from residential gardens to university campuses such as The University of Texas at El Paso Campus Transformation Project. Her work is characterized by a focus on ecology, low water use and restorative urban—yet native—landscapes that encourage social interaction. Committed to advancing landscape architectural practice and education, Ten Eyck has lectured at various conferences nationally and internationally.

**Peter Walker**

*Berkeley, California*

Over six decades of practice Peter Walker has designed hundreds of landscapes, chaired the landscape architecture departments at the University of California, Berkeley, and Harvard University, lectured widely, written, and served as advisor to numerous public agencies. The scope of his concerns ranges from the small garden to the planning of cities—with a particular emphasis on corporate headquarters, plazas, cultural gardens, academic campuses, and urban-regeneration projects. Recepient of the Sir Geoffrey Jellicoe Medal for lifetime achievement in landscape architecture, he initiated the founding of the CEO Roundtable and the journal *LandForum*.

# Index

## End Papers

Front:
Erik Dhont,
La Gara.
Geneva, Switzerland,
2015.
[Georg Aerni]

Rear:
Laurie Olin and
Dennis McGlade.
Getty Center.
Los Angeles, California,
1993.
Cactus garden.
[Marc Treib]